in the field, and in these practically was vested what might be termed the exercise of civil control. Might, in such circumstances, was likely to be held as synonymous with Right. "A people governed after such a manner," says HUME,* "are slaves in the full and proper sense of the word; and it is impossible they can ever aspire to any refinements of taste and reason."

It was practically to put an end to such a system of tyranny, that the Frith-Gilds were called into existence. They were a great improvement on the old state of things. They recognised and enforced the obligations which each of the brethren owed to his neighbour, and to society at large, and brought to punishment the wrong-doer. Though they were a later development of those virtues which led to the establishment of the Religious and Social Gilds, they also served to remind men of their religious duties, by providing for common religious service, and trying to illustrate the humane injunction, "Thou shalt love thy neighbour as thyself." In so far as they became an oppressive and haughty power in the community,—this was but an illustration in the aggregate of poor human nature as we see it illustrated every day. But, as is usual, a corrective was found. Although it was not without much civic turmoil, and even bloodshed and death in some towns, that the Trades or Crafts eventually attained to their just rights, let us, now that these broils are ended, be content to record the sentiment, "All's well that ends well."

The Frith-Gilds of the period were called into existence by the circumstances of the times; they may be said to have been a reflex of the state of society in those days; they were the means of offering a noble resistance to, and eventually of vanquishing, the baronial control; and they were the first organisation which seemed to develop the grand idea of a free popular civic administration.

---

* HUME's *Philosophical Works*, vol. iii.

The Guildry of Edinburgh: Is It an Incorporation? - Primary Source Edition

James Colston

THE GUILDRY OF EDINBURGH:

Is it an Incorporation?

THE GUILDRY OF EDINBURGH:

IS IT AN INCORPORATION?

———◆◆———

THE loss of most of the earlier records of the municipal history of Edinburgh, which the historian Maitland so much deplored, renders it a matter of great difficulty to ascertain the rise and progress of our municipal institutions, as well as the rights and privileges of the various incorporations of Burgess-Guild brethren on the one hand, and Burgess craftsmen on the other.

It appears, however, that there were, in the year 1284, several statutes of the Guildry,* made and constituted by " Robert Bernhame, Mair of Berwick, and Simon Maunsell, and other gude men of the said burgh." These are recorded in the Book of the Majesty (*Regiam Majestatem*), and they seem to have originally contributed most materially to the method of municipal government in the Royal Burghs of Scotland.

At what time Burghs† were first instituted in Scotland cannot

---

* Statuta Gildæ, cap. 1, apud Skene, Veteris Leges Scotiæ, fol. v. 154.

† BURGH, *origin of the term.* This has long been a matter of dispute. George Buchanan says it is of Danish origin. Maitland takes quite another view: p. 291. "The appellation *Burg* or *Burgh* is *Saxon* or *English*, importing a castle. Now, towns being erected in the neighbourhood of castles for their protection, had the name of *Burgh* or *Burgs* given to them ; and as the soldiers who garrisoned the said Burghs, were called Burghers, so the inhabitants of the towns or new Burghs, received likewise the name of Burghers, now corruptly called Burgesses." Buchanan, in his *History of Scotland*, vol. i. book 6, p. 271, referring to a battle engaged in by Malcolm II. (83rd king) against the Danes, wherein the latter were successful, thus writes :—" The king was wounded in the head, and had much ado to be carried off the field into an adjacent wood, where he was put on horseback, and

with certainty be ascertained. It may, however, be taken for granted that their origin and institution, with those peculiar privileges and immunities conferred upon them, were somewhat analogous to those which existed in those days in most of the other countries of Europe.[*]

In primitive times, the inhabitants of villages or hamlets in Scotland were under the protection of some royal or baronial castle. They had no property of their own, and were without rights or privileges, being entirely dependent upon the will or caprice of the lord of the soil. Even industry on their part, and the little traffic in the way of business which they were able to conduct, by barter or otherwise, was subjected to heavy burdens, either on the part of the crown on the one hand, or the over-lord on the other. This state of matters, however, was not destined to endure. The king, and those local magnates began to take a greater interest in the growing prosperity of their vassals, and, strange to say, the school of political economy which seemed to prevail—the rectifier of all their wrongs—was that of exclusive privilege.

Associations of traders, even with the sanction of royal authority,

---

escaped with his life. After this victory, the castle of Nairn was surrendered to the Danes, the garrison being dismayed at the event of the unhappy sight; yet they put them to death after the surrender. They strongly fortified the castle, because it was seated in a convenient pass; and of a peninsula, made it an isle, by cutting through a narrow neck of land, for the sea to surround it; and then they called it by a Danish name, *Burgus.*"

[*] In reference to this subject, we quote the following, from a footnote attached to the late Professor Cosmo Innes's Preface to the volume of the Burgh Records Society, entitled *Ancient Laws and Customs of the Burghs of Scotland*, p. xxxii. He says, "With the twelfth century rose the general desire, through France and over Europe, to shake off the oppression of the feudal lords, and to restore or establish some municipal rights and freedom in towns,—a share at least in the choice of their own magistrates, and in administering their property and affairs. The people of the cities entered vehemently into the struggle for independence; swore mutual support and alliance; and within each town established for their common affairs *guilds, communes, conjurations*, which drew upon them the censure of the early monkish writers, who were mostly good Tories,—*communio, novum ac pessimum nomen*, says Abbot Guibert de Nogent, writing in the twelfth century."

began to be formed, to protect themselves from what was regarded as extraneous injury and oppression, provided that the members of these associations were alone entitled to carry on trade within certain well-defined territorial limits, and under such conditions in the way of customs, rates, or tolls as should be levied upon them.

The more privileged of these associations—which soon began to be known by the names of *hanses* and *gilds*—were no doubt the embryo constitution of those more important organisations which afterwards existed, and were maintained, for so many centuries in the Royal Burghs of Scotland.

To what period in the history of the country the first erection of Royal Burghs can be traced, it is impossible now to prove. Several authorities state that Edinburgh* was raised to the rank of a burgh by David I., who held his court in the Castle of Edinburgh. He also founded the Abbey of Holyrood, and granted, by charter in favour of its canons, "the power to erect the Burgh of Canongate, between the Church and the Toune." William the Lion, the second in succession to David, is said to have given to Edinburgh the dignity of a Royal Burgh, and to have assembled within it the Estates of the realm, and to have converted it into a place of mintage for the king's currency; while Alexander III. constituted Edinburgh as the depository of the insignia of royalty and the records of the kingdom.

Maitland, in his history (p. 7), says that King David I. styles Edinburgh *meo burgo.* He also adds, David "made laws at his town

---

* SIMEON OF DURHAM mentions Edinburgh to have been a town or village in the year 854, its foundation probably being nearly co-eval with its castle (*Dunel. de gest. Reg. Angl. ad an.* 854). Be that as it may, Edinburgh seems to have been of little note, until about the middle of the fourteenth century, at which time it was one of the Four Burghs (*Leg. Burg.* cap. 128) which composed the Chamberlain's *air* or court, held yearly at Haddington, the county town of East Lothian.—*Maitland*, p. 6.

of Newcastle-upon-Tyne, and his charters are still extant in several Scottish burghs; in all probability he erected Edinburgh into a Royal Burgh."

Of such erection, however, there is no direct evidence. On the other hand, if the ancient capitulary styled "*Leges et Consuetudines Burgorum Scotiæ,*" or any considerable portion of it be, as has been supposed, the work of David I., then there must have existed prior to his time Royal Burghs, somewhat similar in constitution and privileges to those which were afterwards established.

The difference between the Burgh pure and simple, and the Royal Burgh, seemed to consist in the latter possessing or occupying property which belonged to the Crown. *Lord Kames** thus describes a Royal Burgh in Scotland :—

"By a Royal Borough is in Scotland understood, an incorporation that hold their lands of the Crown, and are governed by magistrates of their own naming. The administration of the annual revenues of a Royal Burgh, termed the *common good,* is trusted to the magistrates, but not without control. It was originally subjected to the review of the Great Chamberlain, and accordingly the chap. 39, sec. 45, of *Iter Camerarii*† contains the following articles, recommended to the Chamberlain to inquire into—'Giff there be an good assedation and uptaking of the common good of the burgh, and giff faithful compt be made thereof to the community of the burgh; and giff no compt is made, he whom and in quhaes hands it is come, and how it passes by the community.' In pursuance of these instructions, the Chamberlain's

---

* Kames' *Sketches of the History of Man,* vol. iii. p. 464.

† In one of the oldest MSS., compiled in the reign of David II., there is a tract " De articulis inquirendis in Burgo in Itinere Camerarii secundum usum Scotiæ," corresponding in its contents very nearly with a chapter of the " *Iter Camerarii,*" a work supposed to be of the age of James III., but the materials of which may be fairly regarded as, for the most part, of a much earlier period.—*Report of Commissioners on Municipal Corporations,* 1835.

precepts for holding the ayr, or circuit, is directed to the provost and bailies, enjoining them ' to call all those who have received any of the town's revenues, or used any office within the burgh, since the last Chamberlain-ayr, to answer such things as shall be laid to their charge.' "—*Iter Camer.* cap. 1.   And in the third chapter, which contains the forms of the Chamberlain-ayr, the first thing to be done, after fencing the court, is to call the bailies and serjeants to be challenged and accused from the time of the last ayr.*

In the carrying out of this arrangement, individual burgesses obtained a right of property from the crown in their own individual *tofts*, or tenements, as immediate vassals.   They were each bound—along with their personal services, if required—to pay yearly, into the royal treasury, a certain fixed sum.   These rents were collected by the public officials, called *ballivi Regis*, or bailies or stewards of the Crown. But, in addition to those tofts allotted to individuals, there were valuable estates granted for the benefit of the community, under a title which was strictly inalienable, without any payment to the Crown ; the return for which burghal benefaction consisted in the burghers or burgesses, or, as they were afterwards designated, the "honest men of the town," becoming bound under these obligations to the Crown to maintain good order and peace at home, and in times of war to assist in serving their country in the armies of the nation.

Although, as we have previously stated, the first erection of the Royal Burghs cannot be traced, there is no doubt that they existed at a very early period in the history of the Scottish nation, and that their legislative capacity must have been exercised during many centuries.

Dr Gilbert Stuart, a well-known authority on the Public Law and Constitutional History of Scotland, traces the establishment of

---

* For further observations by Lord Kames, *vide* Appendix.

both to a remote antiquity, and as he was himself a friend of liberty and of the people, he has clearly demonstrated that, while the object of the institution of the Royal Burghs was to introduce and to extend commerce and manufactures, their ancient constitutions possessed a very large amount of freedom.

This fact will be made abundantly evident by two quotations:—(1) from the *Leges Burgorum** to which we have already referred; and (2) from the *Statuta Gildæ*, made in 1284 by those "good men" we previously mentioned.

(1.) The former (*Leges Burgorum*), cap. 77, enacts:—

"At the first head court after Michaelmas, the alderman and baillies sould be chosen of faithful men, and of gude fame, be the

---

* THE LAWS AND CUSTOMS OF THE FOUR BURGHS OF SCOTLAND, that is to say, Edinburgh, Roxburgh, Berwick, and Stirling. These are contained in the most ancient MS. now preserved—the Berne MS.—among the public records of Scotland, in Her Majesty's General Register House at Edinburgh. These Four Burghs constituted a court of consultation, in which the Great Chamberlain of the kingdom presided, and where he was assisted in the adjudication of disputes by commissioners from the Four Burghs referred to. To this court appeals were made in difficult questions of law, arising out of the usages of burghs and the rights of burgesses. In 1292, for example, in a Parliament held by Edward I., it was agreed, on the motion of both the contending parties, in a private suit relating to the law and custom of the burghs in Scotland, that the Four Burghs should be consulted:—"*Ideo consulendum est cum quatuor burgis contra proximum Parliamentum hic, Et tunc ad judicium.*" This having been done, judgment was eventually given, "*quia compertum est per recordum et veredictum quatuor burgorum quod lex et consuetudo talis est,*" etc. James II., in 1454, gave to the burgh of Edinburgh the exclusive right to have the Court of the Four Burghs assembled there, by a charter granted on the 5th day of November. On the previous day he had granted the customs of Leith, by Letters Patent under the Great Seal, to the burgesses and merchants of Edinburgh. The duties of the Court of the Four Burghs are thus defined:—"*Ad subeundem ordinandum et finaliter determinandum de et super judiciis burgorum universalium regni* nostri curiis dictis sive contradictis: Ac etiam mensuram ulnæ, firlotæ sive bollæ, largenæ et petræ, more solito leigiis et communibus nostris, dandum liberandum et recipiendum; necnon omnia alia facienda et exercenda quæ in hujusmodi curia Parliamenti secundum leges, statuta et burgorum consuetudines sunt tractanda subeunda et finaliter determinanda." The Court of the Four Burghs came to be finally merged in the Convention of Royal Burghs. . . . The following extract

common consent of the honest men of the burgh" (*communi consilio proborum hominum Villæ*).

(2.) While the latter (*Statuta Gildæ*), cap. 33, provides :—

"We ordain that the common council and the community be governed by twenty-four honest men, of the best, maist discreit, and maist trustworthy of the same within the burgh, chosen for this purpose, together with a president and four overseers. And whensoever the said twenty-four men are called upon to attend on the public business, and do not answer the citation given them, they shall be fined two shillings" (cap. 34). "We appoint that the president and four overseers shall be chosen in presence of the whole community, and with their consent (*per visum et considerationem totius communitatis*). And if any debate shall arise in the election of the president and overseers, the elections shall be made under the oath of the twenty-four men of the said burgh, chosen by the community" (*prædicti burgi electorum per communiam*).

---

tells what became of the duties of the Chamberlain :—"On the suppression of the office of Chamberlain, the power of controuling the magistrates' accounts was vested in the Exchequer; that of reviewing their sentences was left to the ordinary courts of law ; and the power of the Chamberlain himself, in regulating matters concerning the common welfare of the state, was transferred to the Convention of Burghs, a court instituted in the reign of James III., and appointed to be held annually at Inverkeithing. By an Act of James VI., however, it was appointed to meet four times a-year, at any borough they thought proper ; and, to avoid confusion, it was ordained that only one commissioner should appear for every borough, except Edinburgh, which should have two."—*Kincaid's History of Edinburgh*, p. 57, *Edinburgh*, 1787.

* The translation which we have given above is that published by the Royal Parliamentary Commissioners in 1793. It differs from Mr T. Thomson's text, which we have given and translated in the Appendix. But for all practical purposes, the differences do not affect the conclusions at which we have arrived. The text is as follows,—"Statuimus quod commune consilium et communia gubernentur per viginti quatuor probos homines de melioribus, discretioribus, et fidei dignioribus," etc. The other references in this paper relate to the same rendering.

But this state of matters did not always continue. It was very early discovered that communities originally destined for commercial and manufacturing purposes, might be converted into instruments of political power, a fact which soon proved fatal to the freedom of the Burghs. A numerous body of men of probity and honour, in full possession of their rights to exercise the liberty of citizenship, and of those lofty ideas which the very fact of freedom cannot fail at all times to inspire, were not likely implicitly to obey the voice or the fiat of a dictator. A few required to be selected, whom those in power could trust, as the safest mode of carrying out their behests. Hence we find that in 1469 an Act of the Scottish Parliament was passed, during the minority of the then reigning prince, and obtained chiefly at the instance of the nobility, whereby freedom of election on the part of the community was practically set aside; because that statute provided that no officer or council should be continued longer than one year. And it further enacted that the old council should choose the new; and that the new and old council together, with the deacons of crafts, should annually choose all officers pertaining to the town.*

This somewhat arbitrary statute was entirely subversive of the rights of the citizens to elect those who should hold municipal sway

---

* It is thocht expedient, that nain officiares nor counsail be continuit, efter the Kingis Lawis of Burowes, further than ane zeir; And that the chusing of new officiares be in this wise; That is to say, the Auld Counsaill of the Toune sall chuse the New Counsaill in sic number as accordis to the Toune; and the New Counsaill and the Auld, in the zeir foresaid, sall chuse al officiares perteining to the Toune: as Alderman, Baillies, Deane of *Gild*, and vther officiares. And that ilka Craft sall chuse a person of the samin craft, that sall haue voit in the said eelectioune of officiares for the tyme in likewise zeir by zeir.—*Act. Parl. Scot.* 1469, cap. 5, p. 54, of "The Lavvs and Actes of Parliament, maid be King Iames the First and His Svccessovrs Kinges of Scotland." *Imprented at Edinbvrgh, be Robert Walde-graue, prenter to the Kinges Majestie, 15 Martii. Anno Dom. 1597.*

while it placed a comparatively small number of favoured individuals in a position of considerable power, which they could wield to their own advantage, and that of their friends. Besides, by the repeated election of themselves, or their dependants, they received what might almost be called in legal phraseology, an *entail of municipal rule and influence.*

The usurpation of the rights of the citizens, or burgesses, which the Act referred to perpetrated, was made still more harassing by another Act of the Scottish Parliament in the year 1474 (cap. 56), because while by the previous statute the whole Council was to be annually changed, the latter ordained that four persons out of the old should be chosen yearly to serve in the new Council.

It is not our purpose at the present time to enter more fully into the various Acts which were passed at the instance of the nobles, and other interested individuals, as against popular election among the burgesses of those days. What we have sought to prove is, that from a very early period in the history of Scotland, down to 1469, the magistrates and common councils of the Royal Burghs were annually elected by the free suffrage of the burgesses,—otherwise called "the honest men of the town."

In regard to the question of burgess-ship, it may be stated that one of the earliest boons conferred upon the inhabitants of Royal Burghs, was a monopoly in commerce and manufactures within their respective bounds.

These formed the subject of several Acts of the Scottish Parliament ; as, for example, the 152d Act of King James VI. (viz., 1592), his twelfth Parliament ordains that no person exercise the " trafficque "*

---

* That na persone within this Realme, suld exerce the trafficque of merchandice, bot the Burgesses of free Burrowes ; . . . That quha so euer exercisis the said trafficque of merchandise, not being free burgesses ; Their haill gudes and geare salbe cum in escheitte ; The ane

E

of merchandise, but burgesses of free burghs, under pain of " escheat' of their whole goods and gear, the one half to His Majesty and the other half to the burgh apprehender. The same Act likewise gives power to every Burgh by itself, or a collector or commissioner appointed by the Burgh, to search the unfreeman's goods, intromit therewith as escheat, either within the country or any other part, to arrest, call, follow, and pursue, before " unsuspect baillies " to be created by them." *

In the matter of the distinction between foreign or domestic commerce or traffic, and manufacture—or what might perhaps in those days be more popularly called *handicraft*—the more ancient charters from the Crown are not very specific; on two points, however, there seems to be no dubiety, viz., that *freedom* and *residence* are laid down as specially indispensable to the claims of individuals entitled to the privileges. Entry as a burgess was the preliminary and requisite step for anyone being permitted to enjoy commercial or manufacturing privileges.

Although the muniments of the more ancient Burghs of Scotland

---

halfe to our Soveraine Lord, and the vther halfe to the Burgh, quhais Commissioner or Collectour sall first apprehend the same.

    * His Majestie and Estaites foresaidis, gives and grauntis full power and authoritie, to everie ane of the saidis free Burrowes, be themselues or their commissioner or collectour, quhom they sall haue power to depute in that behalfe ; To search and seeke the gudes and geare of the saidis vn-freemen traficquers, to intromet there with as escheit : and to deliver the ane halfe therof, to his hienes Thesaurer, and the vther halfe to the Burgh, quhairof he salbe appoynted commissioner or Collectour, quhidder it be within this realme, or in ony uther part, quhair the same may be challenged. And to arreist the saidis gudes, call, follow and persew therfore, before vnsuspected Baillies or deputs, quhom they sal haue power to creat to that effect, and ordanis the ane halfe of the said escheit, to be intrometted with, be the said Commissioner or Collectour, as said is, be applyed to the common weil of the said Burgh, quha sall first apprehend the saidis escheitte gudes.—*Act. Parl. Scot.*, cap. 152, p. 128. *Vide* Note p. 32, *antea.*

have not been found to afford any example of a direct creation of the whole burgesses of a burgh into the form of a community or corporation, yet there do occur very early instances in royal charters of a licence to establish, and in others to continue and uphold, a Merchant Guild—*Gilda Mercatoria* *— or society of merchants; and although it is doubtful whether this society or corporation was open to all, or only to restricted classes, it is nevertheless matter of history that the practice ultimately prevailed of forming different classes of those engaged in manufacture or handicraft into similar fraternities or corporations. From a very early period, therefore, the distinctive character and rights of burgesses in reference to the two great branches of burghal monopoly already referred to, became as clear and well defined as were the Patricians and Plebeians of Roman origin. The merchant class held that they were superior to the craftsmen,† and had always a larger share in the civic administra-

---

* The Charter of Alexander II. to the burgh of Aberdeen contains the following :— "Concedo etiam eisdem burgensibus meis de Aberden ut habeant gildam suam merchatricem, exceptis fullonibus et telariis."

† Though mechanics were rare in the days of David II., yet, in 1424, we find a statute of James I. empowering handicraftsmen, in their different branches, to elect a preses, who was called a Deacon or Kirk-master, which shows that they must have then been pretty numerous. In 1426, this office was abolished, and the meetings themselves condemned as assemblies of traitors. In 1457, the goldsmiths were allowed to meet, for the purpose of inspecting their work. This soon became general; but, in 1493, their meetings were again checked, for the reasons formerly alleged, and deacons were required to confine themselves entirely to the inspection of work performed by their own crafts. By this time, almost all the trades were incorporated into the societies we meet with in Edinburgh at this day. In 1469, it was enacted that the craftsmen should have a voice in chusing the magistrates; and, in 1475, they began to receive charters of incorporation. The wrights, masons, and weavers received a charter this year, the hammermen in 1483, the butchers in 1488, and the cordiners in 1489. A new art also was introduced in this country, which has contributed more than any other human invention to the advancement of useful knowledge, and the civilisation of mankind. This, though sooner known in other countries, was introduced into Scotland only in 1509, when a breviary was published at Edinburgh, by the Bishop of Aberdeen, for

tion, even although there were included among the craftsmen the wealthy incorporation of the goldsmiths, who, in addition to their avowed occupation, followed the calling of money-lenders to royalty and the nobility of Scotland, notable among whom must ever be remembered *Gingling Geordie,*—our own good George Heriot, founder of the Hospital that used to bear his name.

Under the denominations, therefore, of Burgesses and Guild-brethren or merchant burgesses on the one hand, and trade burgesses or craftsmen on the other, these two classes for many generations continued to maintain their respective rights in the Burghs, not only as against the unfreemen of the Burgh, but also and sometimes very bitterly as against each other.

Many actions at law arose in regard to the relative privileges of the Guildry and the crafts, in the matter of commerce and trade. They came from Aberdeen, Inverness, Perth, and Dunfermline. Nor was Edinburgh an exception.

At so comparatively recent a date as the 2nd of March 1802, a question of this kind was decided. An action was raised by the incorporation of goldsmiths, against certain members of the Guildry, to have it found and declared, that as they were not members of the goldsmiths' incorporation they had no right to sell gold or silver ware within the precincts of the city. It was urged on the part of the defenders, that, as members of the Guildry, they had the privilege of importing and selling goods within the precincts of the city; and

---

the use of his cathedral, printed by Walter Chapman in 1509 and 1510, 12mo. The printers, however, have not been erected into any corporation like the other mechanics, all of whom were successively incorporated, beginning as above mentioned ; the wakers in 1500, surgeons and barbers in 1505, bakers in 1522, and bonnet-makers in 1530.—*Kincaid's History of Edinburgh,* pp. 19-20, *Edinburgh,* 1787.

that from time immemorial, goods of all sorts had been so imported into the city, and sold by members of the Guildry in their shops and warehouses, without the slightest desire to infringe the rights of the craftsmen.

The Court of Session declared that the defenders *were* entitled to *import made articles* of gold and silver work, and to sell and retail the same in the shops kept by them; but they reserved the question as to their right to manufacture the gold and silver work; which seemed to imply that this was a breach of good faith with the craftsmen,—at least, that they had difficulty in deciding against the latter in this department.

While we have thought it right to refer to this case, as illustrative of the manner in which the two great bodies of burgesses sedulously protected their respective rights and privileges as against each other, even down to the beginning of the present century, these differences were more conspicuously as well as frequently apparent, in connection with their struggles for municipal rule.

In regard to the question of the Guildry, we have already referred to the statutes of 1284. The next authority we would desire to quote from, is an Act of the Scottish Parliament of 1593 (cap. 180), which confirms the jurisdiction of Deans of Guild. Their decrees are declared by that statute to have "full strength, force, and effect in all times, according to the loveable form of judgment in all good towns of France and Flanders, where bourses are erected, and constitute, and specially in Paris, Rouen, Bordeaux, Rochelle."

The Dean of Guild and his Court settled all disputes between merchant and mariner, or between merchant and merchant. They likewise had charge of the weights and measures,* and of the stability of the various houses and public buildings in the burgh,—thereby very much resembling the powers exercised by the Ædiles † in Ancient Rome.　It

---

* *Vide* Appendix, p. 183.

† *The Ædiles.*—At the same time as the tribunes were first elected, two *Ædiles* also were appointed, as their assistants, holding towards them somewhat the same relation as the quæstors held towards the consuls.　The persons of the ædiles were similarly inviolable.　The primary duty assigned to them was the charge of the temple where the resolutions of the tribes (and, after B.C. 446, the decrees of the senate) were deposited.　The two *Plebeian Ædiles* were first elected in B.C. 494 as assistants to the tribunes.　They were charged with the special duty of keeping the tablets whereon were inscribed the laws passed by the popular assemblies and (after B.C. 446) the decrees passed by the senate.　In course of time they had new duties laid upon them, and they gradually came to be regarded as independent magistrates.　On the establishment of the prætorship in B.C. 367, the election of two *Curule Ædiles* was agreed upon between the patricians and the plebeians, the chief duty assigned to them being ostensibly the magnificent celebration of the *Ludi Romani*, in commemoration of the union of the two orders. The Curule Ædiles were to be patricians ; next year, however, it was arranged that they should be patrician and plebeian in alternate years, and presently it was agreed that they should be elected from both orders indifferently.　The first Curule Ædiles were elected in B.C. 356. The jurisdiction of the ædiles seems to have been limited.　Their duties are summed up by Cicero in three heads.　First, they were *curatores urbis*, burgh magistrates, and commissioners of police and of public health.　Second, they were *curatores annonæ*, inspectors of the markets, and commissioners for the storing up and distribution of the imports of grain.　In B.C. 45, Julius Cæsar created two additional plebeian ædiles to look after the supply of corn (*Ædiles Cereales*).　Third, the ædiles were *curatores ludorum solennium*, superintendents of the arrangements for the public games.　To the plebeian ædiles also fell the duty of instituting prosecutions against—(1) persons that occupied more than their legal extent of state land (*ager publicus*) ; (2) tenants of state pastures that pastured thereon more than the legal number of flocks and herds ; and (3) money-lenders that exacted an illegal rate of interest—all such persons being regarded as offenders against interests that were peculiarly plebeian.　The ædiles (according to some authorities, only the curule ædiles), on entering office, issued edicts or rules of administration (*jus ædilicium*), and they were empowered to inflict fines,—for example in respect of nuisances, unwholesome provisions, light weights, avaricious hoarding of grain in time of scarcity.　Their judicial powers seem to have been chiefly exercised in reference to sale, and that mostly of grain, slaves, and cattle.　The *jus ædilicium* was reckoned as part of the *jus honorarium.*—*Hunter's Roman Law*, pp. 15, 43-44, *London*, 1885.

is proper to mention, however, that the institution of the Admiralty Court, by the Act 1681 (cap. 16), superseded the Dean of Guild's authority in maritime affairs ; and when the imperial standard measures were introduced, 5 George IV. c. 74 (1824), the Dean's jurisdiction ceased, and contraventions of the statute were afterwards brought under the review of the magistrates of the burgh.

In addition to the Act of Parliament already quoted, the Golden Charter, granted by King James VI. to the City of Edinburgh in 1603, bears that "we are for ever to have, enjoy, and possess, in the aforesaid town and liberties, a Mercantile Gild * (*Gilda Mercatoria*), with its court, councils, members, jurisdictions, liberties, and privileges belonging to the same ; and in all things as freely as is granted by us and our predecessors to the aforesaid town, or to any other royal free burgh within our kingdom." It is right to explain that this Golden Charter confirms twenty-four previous charters.†

Whatever, therefore, may have been the position and privileges of the Guildry of Edinburgh in early times, there is undoubted evidence to show that there was in our ancient metropolis, as in other Royal Burghs, a clear and well-defined distinction between the Merchants or Guildry on the one hand, and the Craftsmen on the other.‡ But

---

* *Sic :*—" Et infra predictum burgum, et bondas ejusdem, pro perpetuo habendi, gaudi-endi, et possidendi, unam mercatoriam gildriam vulgo, cum curiis gilde, consilariis, membris, et jurisdictione ad eandem pertinentibus, libertatibus, et privilegiis ejusdem simile modo et adeo libere in omnibus et per omnia, sicuti per nos nostrosve predecessores predicto burgo, seu cuicunque alio libero burgo regali, infra nostra regnum conceditur."—*Extract from Charter of King James VI., commonly called the " Golden Charter."*

† *Vide* Report of the House of Commons, ordered to be printed 17th June 1793.

‡ In the case of the Guildry of Dunfermline, Lord Kilkerran says :—" There are three sorts of burgesses : burgesses *in sua arte*, who are members of one or other of the corporations ;

there were civic disputes between the two classes of Burgesses; and those quarrels frequently had reference, as in most other Burghs, to their respective rights in municipal matters. The oldest authority for the settlement of these is the decreet-arbitral of James VI. in 1583, which practically put an end to all municipal disputations in Edinburgh at the time; and the government of the Burgh continued less or more upon the lines then laid down by the King, until a sweeping measure of reform was effected by the Burgh Reform Act of 1833— the Act 3 & 4 William IV. cap. 76.

By the decreet-arbitral, it is provided, that " nather the merchants among themselves, nor the crafts, and their deacons and visitors, should hold particular or general ' Conventions,' exceptand always that the Dean of Gild may assemble his brethers and counsel in their Gild Courts, conform to the antient laws of the Gildry and privileges thairof." Further,—" It is agried and concludit that nather the merchands amang themselves, nather the crafts and their deacons or visitors, sall have or make any particular . or general ' Conventions,' as deakens with deakens, deakens with their crafts, or crafts amang themselves, far less to make privat laws or statutes, poind, or dis-

---

burgesses who are guild brothers; and a third sort who are simply burgesses, who are neither guild brothers nor members of any incorporation. Each of these is confined to his proper sphere. A burgess admitted member of a corporation cannot exercise the business of another incorporation; and some carried this so far as to say that a member of a particular corporation had no title to exercise any other sort of business, even such as one simply ' burgess ' might do. But the more general and just opinion was, that this lower sort of burgess-ship was comprehended in that of being burgess in a particular trade; and that, therefore, the membership of a corporation might exercise any business that did not fall within the privileges of any other corporation. A member of the guildry cannot exercise the privileges of any other of the corporations; nor any member of a corporation deal in merchandise, by which was understood dealing in foreign commodities, even in retail." Lord Bankton, a well-known institutional lawyer, entirely concurs in this view.

trenzie (distrain) at their awen hands for transgressions, except by the advice and consent of the provost, baillies, and counsel."

Regarding the holding of "Conventions," Maitland in his *History of Edinburgh* throws considerable light. He says,—"It having till this time been a custom whenever any of the craftsmen of Edinburgh were summoned to appear to answer for an offence committed, he was accompanied by the several corporations of arts to assist him in his defence; which frequently occasioning great commotions, for preventing of which in time coming, it was by the council enacted that no such Conventions shall assemble anytime hereafter, under the penalty of the loss of their freedom, and otherwise to be fined at the discretion of the magistrates."

The ostensible object of the decreet-arbitral of the King, in regard to these Conventions, and to the power of assembling of the Corporations, was to connect the members of the Guildry and the Craftsmen more closely with the Magistrates of the Burgh, or, as we would say in the language of the present day, "to bring them more *in touch* with the Magistracy, and to destroy their powers of acting independently." The expression made use of,—" Conform to the antient laws of the Gildry and privileges thairof," would seem to imply that they had certain powers and privileges well known at that time; and goes a far way by itself to indicate something like incorporation, although at this distant period of time it is impossible to ascertain what these laws, rights, and privileges were.

From many concurrent testimonies, it would appear that the Guildry existed prior to Town Councils; in fact, it was the precursor of the popular system of municipal government which was developed by the election of Town Councils. There is much to favour this statement. It is clearly supported by one act of the Town Council of Edinburgh

F

itself, viz., the well-known case of Provost Dalrymple and the majority of the Town Council against James Stodart and others, in 1778, where the answers on behalf of the Magistrates to a petition for their opponents, commences with these words :—" The Town Council of Edinburgh originally consisted of the Magistrates and Merchants of the Guildry."

In the case of the Burgh of Aberdeen, it may be mentioned that the Common Council appears to have been chosen in the *Curia Gildæ* or *Curia Ballivorum Gildæ*, where all the Guild-brethren were obliged to attend, and where their names, entered in rolls, were regularly called over, and a note taken of those who were absent. In general, the names of the Common Council are entered ; while at other times the election is thus minuted, *Subscripti electi fuerunt in communes Consiliarios*, viz., 1439 and 1474. In the following year, 1475, the record states that they were elected *pro anno sequente.*

While quoting from the Records of Aberdeen, we may state that the earliest notice of a Burgh election which has been preserved is from that city. The record (3rd October 1398) bears that the Alderman and Bailies were elected "with the consent and assent of the whole community of the burgh."

The Burgh of Edinburgh was no exception to this rule. In one of the volumes published by the Scottish Burgh Records Society, which is said to contain "all that is known to exist of what may be termed the Burghal legislation of Edinburgh previous to the 23rd of May 1528, at which date King James V. assumed the reins of government, and which volume is entitled *Extracts from the Records of the Burgh of Edinburgh,* 1403 *to* 1528, there occurs the following entry, an entry which we may say is the first and oldest record of municipal life in our

---

* Constitution of the Royal Burghs of Scotland, from their charters as exhibited in the Report of the Committee of the House of Commons, ordered to be printed 17th June 1793.

ancient city, being five years later than the first extract from Aberdeen already referred to :—

3rd October 1403.

PRIMA GILDA CAPITALIS post festum Beati Michaelis tenta in Pretorio burgi de Edinburgh, convocatis confratribus gilde et comparentibus, 3 Octobris 1403.   Electi sunt officiarij gilde pro ut sequitur :—

[Translated thus :—The first Head Guild, held after the Feast of Saint Michael, in the Tolbuith of the Burgh of Edinburgh, the brethren of the Guild being called, and compearing, 3rd October 1403.   The officers of the Guild were elected as follows :—]

[*Prepositus* *—ALEXANDER NAPIER.

---

* *Prepositus,* or *Provost.*—Maitland says,—"Although the Aldermen and Provosts be the first officers we read of to have presided in *Edinburgh*, yet I cannot learn whether their Offices, or that of Bailiff, be here the most antiquated.   Now as both those Officers are of a *French* origin, and that the latter was Collector of the Prince's Revenues, I think it is more probable that the Office of Bailiff was exercised in this City before that of Provost; for this being a Royal Burgh of great antiquity, the King must have had a Bailiff, or Rent-gatherer, residing within the same, for Receipt of the Royal Revenues, who was likewise constituted a Magistrate to administer Justice to the people : Be these things as they will, the Bailiffs at present seem only to be Assistants to the Provost, by their being conjointly and severally his Deputy-Sheriff, Coroner, and Admiral, within the City and Liberties of Edinburgh" (pp. 227-8).
. . . "The chief magistrate of *Edinburgh*, who is dignified with the title of *Lord Provost*, is an officer of great Authority, being Lord Lieutenant, High Sheriff, Coroner, Colonel of the City's Regiment of Trained Bands, Captain of the Town's Company of Fusiliers, Admiral, President of the Common Council, Justice of the Peace in the county of *Edinburgh*, or shire of *Midlothian*, and before the Union of the Kingdoms of *Scotland* and *England*, was usually a member of the Privy Council, and one of the City's Representatives in Parliament, and always a Member of the Convention of Royal Burghs" (p. 225). . . . "*Philip*, King of *France*, in the year 1190, appointed in the City of *Paris*, an Officer, called the *Provost of Merchants*, who is the chief magistrate of that City, as our Provost is of *Edinburgh*.   Be that as it will, it is by all agreed to be derived from the *Latin, Praepositus,* a Governor, Warder, or Guardian, Magistrate, or any chief in office or place" (*Ibid*).   "Mayor" seems, according to the *Statuta*

Decanus gilde et custoditor operis Ecclesie—Symon de Schele.

Balliuus de Leyth—Joannes Robertsoun.

Thesaurarius—Joannes Lamb.

Seriandi gilde—Willelmus Talzefer, Willelmus Dauidson. ·

Appreciatores carnium—Willelmus Rynweh, Hugo Tod, Math3eus Cloig.

Appreciatores vinj.—Willelmus Layng, Jacobus Robertsoun.

Duodene burgi—William of Cranstoun, William of Libertoun, George of Fallow , etc. etc.

Regarding the creation of the Burgh Magistracy, we consider that it may be safely assumed, from what we have already stated as to the *ballivi* (bailies) of the Royal Burghs, whose duty it was, as Stewards of the Crown, to collect the Crown rents, that they would be nominees

---

Gilda, to have been the title of the first chief magistrates. "Alderman" followed, and is so noted in Maitland, down to 1425, when the term "Provost" is used. Among the Edinburgh Records is a "Letter from the Alderman, Bailies, and Council of the Burgh of Edinburgh to King James I., 20th September," year supposed to be 1423.

   * The following are the names of the *Duodene burgi :*—William of Cranstoun, William of Libertoun, George of Fawlow, William Cameroun, Adame Cant, William Bully, Th. of Prestoun, Sanders of Stanely, Adam of Carkettill, James of Boncle, Jh. of Cairnis, °Thom Johnestoun, °Jh. Lamb, Rychert of Fairnly, °Laurence of Elphinstoun, °Watt Young, James of Lawder, Henry Diksoun, Nicol Spathy, °Thom. Symth, °Jh. Wade, °Robyn Michelsoun, °Malcome Boyde, °James of Touris, °Androw Crawfurd, °David Lanerok, °William Rynd, °James of Schele, °Robyn of Prestoun, Jh. of Harlaw, °Will Skynner, Sanders of Wod, °Jh. Howden, Will. of Sydeserfe, Th. Williamsoun, Jh. Hayne, James of Fyndguid, °Th. Quhyteloke, °Will. of Lawder, Jh. of Farnly of Irwyn, °Rot⸱ Merchell, °Robyn Blak, °Robyn of Wintoun, °James of Fowlfurde, °Will. of Carkettill. 45.

   (This amang the lowse leiffes of gild courtes, and this leiff merket with (3). I think thir (°) stands for thame that comperit and wes sworne.

   Nota 1458. I find siclyke on the leiff merket with this nummer (4) amangs the lowse lieffes of gild courts, bot duodene are bot 38.—*Transcriber.*—*Extracts from the Records of the Burgh of Edinburgh,* 1403-1528, *printed for the Scottish Burgh Records Society,* 1869.

of the Sovereign. It would further appear that, along with the office of Steward, was associated the duty of trying offenders for what might be regarded as petty crimes, before any adequate system of police was established, in those days when it was the province of the burgesses of the town " to watch and waird."

The *Statuta Gildæ* already referred to, seem to have been the first indication of a body of Burghers or Burgesses elected to take charge of the Burgh affairs, viz., that besides the mayor and four bailies, there shall be twenty-four men thus described :—" Probi homines de melioribus et discretioribus et fide dignioribus ejusdem burgi ad hoc electi." • Upon this body (cap. 34) was devolved the power of declaring who should be magistrates, if there should be much controversy in public regarding the nomination.

The Act of Parliament 1469, to which we have already referred, put an end to the meetings of the Burghers for the election of Magistrates, and inaugurated that system of close and secret administration of our Burgh affairs which was so long a blot upon the municipal history of Scotland. We need not be surprised that, under such a system of affairs, high-handed tyranny and every kind of corruption should occur. In place of the Provost and Magistrates and Common Council of the Burgh being elected at the *Prima Gilda Capitalis* in Edinburgh, or the *Curia Ballivorum Gildæ* in Aberdeen, the whole mode of election was under such a system entirely changed ; and the self-elected civic rulers began to assume the duty of electing the Dean of Guild and his Court.

This practice seems to have had its origin in a resolution of the Town Council at the beginning of the year 1584. The Constitution and Bye-Laws of the Dean of Guild Court, which are still in existence, date back to the 3rd day of March of that year, and begin with this somewhat peculiar statement :—" I. That the Dean of Guild's Council,

---

• *Statuta Gildæ* (cap. 33) apud Skene, fol. 159.

now chosen by the bailies in council, and deacons, conform to the act of their election, made the aucht of January last, to continue till fifteen days after the election of the Magistracy at Michaelmas next."

This practice was ratified, and became Statute Law by an Act of the Scottish Parliament, 13 James VI., passed on the 21st day of July 1593, in reference to the Confirmation of the Dean of Guild's jurisdiction. It is in the following terms :—

"(180). FORASMEIKLE as our Soveraine Lord, and Estaites of this present Parliament, having considered how necessarie and expedient it is, that the power and jurisdiction of the Deane of *Gild* and their Councell within Burgh, be approoved and allowed, as it is now vsed in the toun of Edinburgh ; quhilk is to the great furtherace of justice to our Soveraine Lord's Lieges, in al actions & maters concerning merchands ; betwixt merchand and merchand, & betwixt merchand & mariner ; quhilk actions aught not, nor suld not byde delay : Bot be exped & decerned be the Deane of *Gild* and his Councell summarlie ; as men chosen and appoynted zeirlie, be the councel of the Burgh ; maist apt and able to judge and decerne, in all actiones concerning merchandes, as said is : Quhairfore OVR said SOVERAINE LORDE, with advise of the Estaites, in this present Parliament, ratifies and confirmis, the judgment of the said Deane of Gild and his Councell, in all actiones concerning Merchandes ; as the same is set downe be the Provest, Baillies, Councell, and Deacones of the Burgh of *Edinburgh*."

Whatever the orignal connection between the Town Council and the Guildry was originally, it appears that in most Burghs, the Town Council for many years got possessed of the Guildry funds, and elected the Dean of Guild from their own Magistrates. During the beginning of the present century, however, several Guildries succeeded in wresting from their Burgh Councils the right of controlling their Funds and electing their Dean. Edinburgh did not succeed in this, although in the Sett of the Burgh (art. 10) it is enacted, "The dene of gild and his counsall haif power to raise taxatiouns upoun the gild-brether for the weilfare and mayntenance of their estaitt, and the help of their failzeit brether, thair wyffes, children, and servandes." * How this money was applied, we shall have occasion afterwards to tell.

Nor are we without some evidence, from passages in the Records of the Town Council themselves, which seem virtually to recognise the *Gilda Mercatoria*, or Guildry, as a Corporation. Thus, on the 8th February 1686, the minute bears that the Town Council "appoint each incorporation within the Burgh to call the Masters of each family belonging to the said incorporation before them, and cause them to sign the obligation already drawn, and only to the deacon of every incorporation, obliging them to be answerable to His Majesty," etc. And again, on 17th February, the Dean of Guild produced the bond, subscribed by the merchants, brewers, and vintners of the city, and as also produced a bond subscribed by several of the stablers, and the deacons each produced his own craft's bond.

In olden times, every Guild-brother on entry had to take the following oath :—

"I shall give the best councill I can, and conceal the councill shewen to me. I shall not consent to dispone the comon good but for ane comon caus, and for ane comon profit; I shall make concord where discord is, to the outtermost of my power. I shall give my leiall and true judgment in all lineations and neighbourheads, without price, preyer, or reward.—Soe help me God, and by God himself."

This oath continued to be administered until the beginning of the present century, when it fell into desuetude.

There is only one other matter which it may be advisable to

---

* In those days apprentices lived in family with their masters.

mention here, in passing. The meetings of the Guildry had for many years been given up. But there was a notable exception to this, viz., on 25th August 1740, and which is mentioned in the *Scots Magazine* of the period. The advertisement, which appeared in the *Caledonian Mercury* of the 21st and 25th August, had reference to the various complications arising out of what was well known at the time as the *Porteous Mob,*[*] and was as follows :—

---

[*] The most remarkable transaction relating to Edinburgh, during this, or perhaps any other period, was the hanging of Captain John Porteous in 1736. At this time, though the Magistrates professed the utmost loyalty to Government, and took every opportunity of presenting the most servile addresses to the throne, yet, with the bulk of the people, it was far otherways. They had not yet forgot their discontents on the score of the Union. The malt-tax had excited many tumults in different parts of the kingdom ; and though the City of Edinburgh had been so quiet as even to be taken notice of by Government on that account, it was still very far from being acceptable to the people. They imagined also, that they had reason to consider Government as very severe, and inclined to punish with death, on very slight occasions, those whom the ministers were pleased to account their enemies ; while, on the other hand, the friends of ministerial tyranny might commit murder even, with impunity. Their fury broke out this year, when Captain John Porteous, above-mentioned, Commander of the Town-Guard, having occasion to quell some disturbances at the execution of one Wilson a smuggler, rashly ordered his soldiers to fire among the crowd, by which six were killed and eleven dangerously wounded. Porteous was tried for murder and condemned, but reprieved by Queen Caroline, Regent, in the absence of her husband George II., who was, at that time, in Hanover. It was determined, however, by the people in general, that he should not escape ; and their enterprise was conducted in such a manner as showed that more than the mere rabble were concerned. On the evening before the day appointed for his execution, a number of people assembled from different quarters of the country, and having disguised themselves in various ways, they surprised the Town-Guard, disarmed them, forced open the prison-doors, and having dragged from thence the unhappy object of their vengeance, after many reproaches, hanged him on a dyer's post at the south-west corner of the Corn-market, near the spot where the people had been killed by the fire of him and his men. During this tumult, the Magistrates used every method they could think of to disperse or appease the people ; but they were themselves threatened with death, and obliged to desist ; and though the Command-ing Officer of the Castle was waited upon by Mr Lyndsay, Member of Parliament for the City, he refused to send any body of troops into the town, because he had no written order from the

"Whereas there have been applications made to the Dean of Guild of Edinburgh, and his council, by several members of the Guildry, desiring a meeting of their brethren to concert some matters of a general concern ; these are, therefore, to intimate that the Dean of Guild and his council will attend at the Merchants' Hall in the Parliament close, on Monday next, at three o'clock afternoon, to meet with such members of the Guildry as are pleased to come there for the purpose above mentioned.   GEO. HALIBURTON, *Dean of Guild.*"

The object of the meeting was to present an address to His Grace the Duke of Argyle, in name of "the Guildry of the City of Edinburgh," to return His Grace their hearty thanks for many favours—especially for the protection which in Parliament he gave to this city and its Magistrates, when "her privileges and even her well-being as a corporate body, were in the utmost danger."

The Duke in reply expressed the "high regard which he had for a

---

Magistrates. When news of this transaction were received at Court, it was determined to execute the most severe vengeance upon the Magistrates of Edinburgh. The Lord Provost was imprisoned, and not admitted to bail for three weeks. He was then commanded to attend the House of Lords at London, along with four Bailies, and three Lords of the Justiciary. An attempt was made to invalidate the sentence of Captain Porteous, but in vain. A bill was then brought in for disabling Provost Wilson from holding his present, or any other magisterial office, in Great Britain, confining him in prison a full year; demolishing the Nether-bow-port, and taking down the City-Guard. This bill passed in the House of Lords, but was altered in the House of Commons. Instead of the clauses for imprisoning the Provost, abolishing the City-Guard, and taking down the Nether-bow-port, a fine of £2000 was imposed on the City, to be paid to the Captain's widow ; however, in consideration of the favours shown her by the Town Council, she accepted of £1500 in full. To prevent such disasters in time to come, it was enacted by the Town Council, that, on the first appearance of an insurrection, the principal officers in the different Corporations should, without loss of time, repair to the Council, to receive and execute the orders of the Council and Magistrates, under a penalty of £8, 6s. 8d. sterling.—*Kincaid's History of Edinburgh*, pp. 85-88.

G

body of men so valuable to society; which could never be rightly supported without a proper regard to the cause of liberty."

We now begin to enter upon a more interesting period of history, viz., that during the later years of the past century, and the first thirty-three of the present.

The municipal unrest which prevailed during the period between 1785 and 1800, as well as subsequently, was, as might be expected, very closely mixed up with the politics of the day. Parliamentary reform and Burgh reform were being loudly called for. Parliament did not quite lend a deaf ear to the latter. A Committee was appointed to " examine the several Petitions presented to the House in this Session of Parliament, from the Royal Burghs of Scotland, together with the several Accounts and Papers relating to the internal government of the said Royal Burghs, which were presented to this House in the last Parliament;" and which Report was ordered to be printed on the 17th June 1793.

That Report, which is chiefly statistical, deals largely with the case of Aberdeen, and also at some length with Glasgow. In regard to Edinburgh, there seemed to be little information furnished by the Town Clerk of the time; because the Report states—(1) "Although many of the Burghs appear to have been possessed of a great number of Charters, yet in general only one or two Charters have been produced to the House of Commons. Thus Edinburgh has produced only one charter, but that charter confirms twenty-four other charters which are not produced."

While we have thought fit to refer to the Report of this Parliamentary Committee in passing, yet as it did not contribute much light on the question under discussion, we proceed to state that the difficulties which caused the matter of Burgh reform to remain for

THE GUILDRY OF EDINBURGH:

Is it an Incorporation?

With INTRODUCTORY REMARKS concerning "GILDS," And an APPENDIX.

BY JAMES COLSTON.

Edinburgh: Richard Cameron, and other Booksellers.

OPINIONS OF THE PRESS.

From the "SCOTSMAN."

THIS handsomely appointed volume contains an interesting contribution to that department of literature, the creation of quite modern times, which is made up of works investigating the origin and history of municipal institutions. Only in comparatively recent years has the development of the institutions of free government, apart from the general progress of the State, become a subject of study for others than antiquarians. Perhaps to Dr Brentano, the learned historian of Guilds and Trade Unions, is due the acknowledgment, now general, that light can be shed upon the principles of self-government, and a valuable aid derived in their application to the practical problems of municipal economy from the study of past organisations of craftsmen possessing corporate privileges and peculiar rights as compared with the community at large. Be that as it it may, this field of history has of late been extensively and profitably cultivated, and there can be little doubt that such publications as those of the Scottish Burgh Records Society provide material for setting the history of municipal institutions upon a broader basis of fact than that upon which it has hitherto rested. Councillor Colston's work, though similar in subject, and drawing largely upon such sources of information, is of a different kind. It is rather an argument on a set thesis than a historical essay. But the proofs adduced in the course of his discussion, and more particularly the documents printed in his copious Appendix, have a direct bearing upon the municipal history of Edinburgh, and for this reason the book will be set upon the shelf alongside of the works belonging to the class referred to.

The author explains the nature of the work in describing the circumstances which led to its production. He says :—"The farce annually acted by the Town-Clerk of recording in the minutes of the Town Council that 'there was no incorporation of the Guildry' seemed to be so unnecessary, and so unlikely to lead to any good result, that I thought it might be interesting to the Members of the Council, and the public generally, to have placed before them information on the subject in a handy form." He accordingly addresses himself to the discussion of the question stated on his title page. But before doing so, he sketches in an introductory chapter the history of Guilds upon the Continent, and in this country, from their origin as family guilds down to the form of municipalities, which they have assumed in modern times.

These preliminary observations review in broad and general terms the progress of the principles of free, popular, civic administration from the infancy of society to the present day. The work then proceeds to deal with the municipal history of this city. After discussing the evidence as to the original incorporation of the burgh, and explaining its early constitution, it goes on to consider its special subject, the position of the Guildry as a body independent of the municipality and possessing a separate identity. It is shown that the Guildry of Edinburgh originally possessed privileges and exercised functions which are usually characteristic of a corporation. The precise nature of the Guildry after the sixteenth century, however, seems to be lost in obscurity. When in the early part of this present century the question of its constitution and privileges became matter of legal judgment and inquiry by a Select Committee of Parliament, the Court decided against its right to the enjoyment of the privileges it claimed, while the Committee reported in terms inconclusive of the issue raised in these pages. Councillor Colston interprets the Committee's report as favouring the claims of the Guildry, and goes on to say :—

"We need not say that with so divergent opinions as were at that time propounded in Parliament on the one hand, and the Outer House of the Court of Session in Scotland on the other, it becomes us at once to pause and say—

Look here upon this picture and on this.

We have no hesitation whatever in accepting the former, and rejecting the latter. The former was based on a full inquiry, not only in reference to the affairs of Edinburgh and its Guildry, but also after a minute investigation into those of Aberdeen, Dundee, and Dunfermline. The latter can only be described as a hash of special historic or legal extracts, culled at random, 'fearfully and wonderfully' intermixed with a large amount of judicial imagination. It reminds us very much of the statement of the Irishman, who undertook to prove from the New Testament that suicide got encouragement from the sacred canon. When called upon for his proof, it was as follows :—(1) Have you not seen in one place that 'Judas went and hanged himself ?' and (2) Have you not seen in another place—'Go, thou, and do likewise ?' Subsequent investigation into the Burgh Records has only tended to strengthen the soundness of the judgment of Committee, while the decision of Lord Cringletie has been found to be inaccurate in history, in antiquarian research, as well as in good logic and in good law. Lord Cringletie may have been an excellent man, with the very best intentions, but the traditions of his occupancy of the judicial bench, which have come down to us, do not point him out as a most erudite lawyer. Indeed, the following epigram, written during his day, and attributed to that celebrated wit of the time, John Clerk, Lord Eldin, very plainly states the case :—

> Necessitie and Cringletie
> Tally to a tittle ;
> Necessitie has nae law,
> And Cringletie as little."

Therefore—'*Requiescat in pacem.*'"

Accordingly, Councillor Colston does not hesitate to give an affirmative answer to the question propounded by him at the outset of the discussion. Doubts will still exist, however, as to whether he has proved his case. But he has supported it by an argument forcibly stated and based upon a study of recondite authorities. Apart from his considerations on the main question, his pages contain many interesting passages of comment on the state of the Town Council at various periods of its history. In the large Appendix at the end of the work are printed the Laws of the Guild of Berwick, with a translation into English ; selections from the Guildry Records of Aberdeen ; and a long series of extracts from the accounts of the Dean of Guild of Edinburgh. These documents increase the value of the work, and will commend it to the attention of all students of municipal economy.

From the "SCOTTISH LEADER."

IN the preface to this volume, Mr Colston explains that he was induced to undertake the investigations of which it embodies the result, by what he rather sharply stigmatises as "the farce annually acted by the Town-Clerk" of Edinburgh in protesting, when the Lord Dean of Guild takes his seat in the Town Council, on the ground that "there is no incorporation of the Guildry," and making a record to that effect in the minutes of the Council. In one sense, no doubt, the protest is a farce, because the Lord Dean of Guild is never deterred by it from exercising all the privileges and powers of a member of the Council. But though the action of the Town-Clerk thus has no practical effect, we are not sure that there is any particular reason for desiring that it should be discontinued. It is a kind of annual memento of a municipal dispute, which is of some importance in the local annals of Edinburgh. That it is not wholly unproductive of results, Mr Colston's volume is itself a tangible proof, because without the Town-Clerk's protest we should not have had the book. Furthermore, while we think Mr Colston has at all events succeeded in amassing a strong body of testimony in support of his contention that the Guildry is not only a corporation, but was incorporated long before the Town Council itself, he also shows that there has been a difference of legal opinion on the subject, and that there is actually a judicial decision—probably not worth much, but never actually reversed—on the other side; and since this is the case, the Town-Clerk has some show of reason for the contention that his annual protest is a matter of simple official duty.

The real question at issue, as our readers will probably be aware, is not whether the Lord Dean of Guild has a right to a seat in the Council—this he enjoys by prescription—but whether or not he has a right to take that seat without going through the form of election by the Council. In this is, of course, involved the question whether there exists an incorporation of the Guildry—a body which legally, as well as by sufferance or usage, can give to its elected head, the Lord Dean of Guild, the official status he actually enjoys? In the researches he has made for the settlement of this point, Mr Colston has been led into a line of general inquiry as to the history and position of Guilds throughout Great Britain and Europe, of which he sums up the fruits in some "Introductory Remarks concerning Guilds." The subject is one that has engaged the attention of antiquarians and archæologists for a long time, and it cannot be affirmed that our author throws any new light upon it; but he brings together within small compass a great number of facts collected from divers sources not ordinarily accessible, and traces very clearly the circumstances of origin of the Mercantile Guilds, the manner in which they assumed the responsibilities of municipal government, and the rise of the Crafts' Guilds in opposition to their exclusive pretensions. He observes that "the Berwick Gild Statutes are, by common consent, admitted to be the foundation on which civic government in the Royal Burghs of Scotland mainly rested." Coming to the special subject of his work, he cites documents to show that prior to 1469 the Magistracy and Common Council of Edinburgh were practically identical with the governing body of the Gild as defined by the Berwick Statutes. In the year mentioned, however, the Scottish Parliament, "at the instance of the nobility," passed an Act practically destroying freedom of election on the part of the community, for it "provided that no officer or Council should continue longer than one year, and it further enacted that the old Council should choose the new; and that the new and old Council together, together with the deacons of crafts, should annually choose all officers pertaining to the town." Meantime, those engaged in the various branches of commerce and crafts in Edinburgh were incorporated by different charters, and an Act of the Scottish Parliament of 1593 confirmed the jurisdiction of the Dean of Guild; while the Golden Charter, granted by King James VI. to the City of Edinburgh in 1603, sets forth that "we are for ever to have, enjoy, and possess, in the aforesaid town and liberties, a Mercantile Gild, with its court, council, members, jurisdictions, liberties, and privileges belonging to the same; and in all things as freely as is granted by us and our predecessors to the aforesaid town, or to any other royal free burgh within our kingdom." This

Golden Charter, as Mr Colston mentions, confirms twenty-four previous charters. Here, surely, there is a distinct incorporation of the Guildry ; and that it preceded the Town Council as the municipal authority, was formally acknowledged by that body itself in 1778, for, in an "answer" given in the course of an action in the Court of Session, it was explicitly stated that "the Town Council of Edinburgh originally consisted of the Magistrates and Merchants of the Guildry." In 1584, however, the Town Council asserted the right of electing the Dean of Guild and his court, and this was ratified by an Act of the Scottish Parliament in 1593; while the Council also acquired the control of the Guildry funds. For more than two hundred years everything like free municipal institutions remained extinct in Scotland, and in Edinburgh, as elsewhere, the Town Council was a self-elected close corporation. In 1817, however, the question as to whether there was not an independent incorporation of the Guildry began to be strongly agitated among the more liberal-minded of the merchant guild brethren of the city. Mr Alexander Henderson, at that time Lord Dean of Guild, made common cause with the Town Council against the agitators. Lord Archibald Hamilton's Committee of the House of Commons reported in 1819, after careful inquiry, that there was "abundant evidence of the original existence of the Guildry of Edinburgh as a corporation," and that it still possessed powers which the committee could not suppose to exist save in a corporation. But an action was raised in the Court of Session to determine the relative position of the Guildry and the corporation, and a decision was given in favour of the latter by the Lord Ordinary (Cringletie), while the case was unfortunately never carried to the Inner House. Mr Colston is very severe on Lord Cringletie's judgment, and on his general judicial capacity, quoting Lord Eldin's epigram :—

> Necessitie and Cringletie
> Tally to a tittle :
> Necessitie has nae law,
> And Cringletie as little.

Whether Lord Cringletie's decision was right or wrong, however, the fact remains that there is a judicial award in support of the attitude now taken by our Town-Clerk, and none on the other side. But the Municipal Reform Act of 1833 gave back to the members of the Guildry the right to elect their own Dean—a claim of which they had been deprived since 1584 ; and thereby it practically admitted their right to be regarded as an incorporation. Mr Colston's contention is that "the Common Council and its popularly elective constitution flowed out of the *Statuta Gildæ*. For the Town Council, therefore, to deny the Guildry as having a corporate existence, is like the son lawfully begotten to deny his own paternity ;" and, on the whole, he seems to have fairly proved his case.

More than half of this volume is occupied by an Appendix which presents a series of very interesting and valuable documents bearing on the subjects discussed. There are the Berwick Gild Statutes in their original Latin, with an English translation ; the Constitution and Bye-Laws of the Guild Court of Edinburgh, as ratified by the Scottish Parliament in 1593 ; numerous extracts from the Deans of Guild's Accounts, from 1554 to 1744 ; a list of the gentlemen who have filled the office of the Dean of Guild in Edinburgh from 1583 to the present time, and a list of members of the Dean of Guild Court from 1833 till 1886.

many years in abeyance, were largely owing to the state of the country in regard to the complications of continental affairs, and the strong feelings engendered at the time in the question of state politics. The late Lord Cockburn* graphically describes the situation. He says :—

"Government was the master of nearly every individual in Scotland, but especially in Edinburgh, which was the chief seat of its influence. . . . The pulpit, the bench, the bar, the college, the local institutions, were so completely at the service of the party in power, that the idea of independence, besides being monstrous and absurd, was suppressed by a feeling of conscious ingratitude. . . .

"The true state of things, and its effects, may be better seen in a few specific facts, than in any general description.

"As to our *Institutions*—there was no popular representation; all town councils elected themselves; the Established Church had no visible rival; persons were sent to the Criminal Courts as jurymen very nearly according to the Sheriff of the county; and after they got there, those who were to try the prosecution were picked for that duty by the presiding judge, unchecked by any peremptory challenge. In other words, we had no free political institutions whatever. . . .

"There was no free, and consequently no discussing press. . . . Nor was the absence of a free public press compensated by any freedom of public speech. Public *political* meetings could not arise, for the elements did not exist. . . . No one could have taken a part in the business, without making up his mind to be a doomed man. No prudence could protect against the falsehood or inaccuracy of spies; and a first conviction of sedition by a judge-picked jury was followed by

---

* *Memorials of His Time*, by Henry Cockburn. Edin. 1856, pp. 86-96, 263, 280, 319-321.

fourteen years' transportation. *As a body to be deferred to, no public
existed.* . . .

"The Council Chamber was a low-roofed room, very dark, and very
dirty, with some small dens off it for clerks.

"Within this Pandemonium sat the Town Council—omnipotent,
corrupt, impenetrable. Nothing was beyond its grasp: no variety of
opinion disturbed its unanimity. . . . Reporters, the fruit of free discussion, did not exist; and, though they had existed, would not have
dared to disclose the proceedings. Silent, powerful, submissive, mys-
terious, and irresponsible, they might have been sitting in Venice.
About the year 1799, a solitary schism amazed the public, by disclosing
the incredible fact that the Town Council might contain a member who
had an opinion of his own. A councillor, named Smith,* electrified the
city by a pamphlet showing that the burgh was bankrupt. Time has
put it beyond all doubt that he was right; and fortunate would it have
been for the city and its creditors if this had been acknowledged at the
time, instead of being aggravated by years of subsequent extravagance
and concealment. But his rebellion drove Mr Smith out of his place. . . .

"The class called *citizens*—that is, the tradesmen, shopkeepers, and
Merchants, even in Edinburgh did not exist politically. They were
ripening, for they soon produced fruit. . . . To be sure, there were no
political movements to excite them. Every public concern was superseded by volunteering and the war. But this was because the people
were not capable of being moved. If any of the measures which
twenty years afterwards agitated every political nerve in the kingdom,
had been propounded, however actively, they would have fallen to the

---

* Address to the Town Council of Edinburgh, by Thomas Smith, Esq., one of the present
old Bailies, delivered in his place at the Council Table, on Friday, September 27, 1799, at
choosing the leets for new magistrates; containing some account of the City's Affairs—its Debt,
Revenue, Expenditure, etc. Edin. 1799.

ground cold. The total absence of public meetings exposes our whole condition. . . .

"The return of peace" (in 1815) " was distinguished by nothing peculiar to Edinburgh. We got new things to speak about; and the entire disappearance of drums, uniforms, and parades, changed our habits and appearance.

" It was matter of course, that as soon as the country began to awaken, the great question of Burgh Reform should be revived. Those who were bent on this object, had the advantage of having to deal with a single and clear evil, capable of being removed only in one way. By the constitution of all the Royal Burghs in Scotland (above 60 in number) each Town Council elected its own successor; which in practice meant that they all elected themselves. The system of self-election was universal, and very jealously adhered to. The effect of this system in depressing the civic communities, and encouraging muncipal abuse, could not be exaggarated. Hence it was one of the earliest of the constitutional vices which public-spirited men saw the necessity of attacking when the era of political reform began to dawn. The subject had been keenly agitated, but with little hope of success and no general support, so far back as 1785. But as the Town Councils were the only electors of our city representation in Parliament, and these bodies were easily kept in ministerial order, by simple, direct, and scarcely concealed bribery, their unchanged continuance was defended as obstinately as the drawbridge of the castle. . . .

"The election of the magistracy of Montrose became void from a failure to comply with the *Sett*, or Constitution, of the Burgh. On this, the Crown revived the magistracy by a *Poll Warrant*—that is, a warrant to elect—addressed to the burgesses at large. The effect of this was the creation of a Town Council with a taste for some independence. Other burghs instantly saw that this was a precedent which might be followed, wherever legal ingenuity could detect a flaw. . . .

"Government soon, however, repudiated the example which it had been misled to rear up, and would grant no more poll warrants. . . .

"In order to try whether the Crown would persist in always restoring the old magistracies, several complaints of undue election were brought into the Court of Session. One of these, directed against the Town Council of Edinburgh, made a great noise. Only two of them—from Aberdeen and Inverness—succeeded, and in both cases the Crown adhered to its principle. This raised a crop of new legal proceedings; first, by burgesses, who challenged the Crown's right to grant any other than poll warrants, and then by the Officers of State, who challenged its right to grant these. . . .

"While these matters were agitating the courts, Lord Archibald Hamilton, one of the very few active and independent Scotch members, succeeded (by a miracle) in obtaining a Committee on our burgh system. Loud were the rejoicings on the one side, and sad the dismay on the other, when the tidings of this scarcely credible vote reached Scotland. Edinburgh seemed to have wakened into a new existence, when its civic functionaries were obliged to repair to London, and to open the windows of the Council Chamber, and let in the light."

That this was very much required, particularly in regard to the affairs of the Guildry, will be made evident by a movement which was inaugurated a short time before this. The question as to Whether there was a legal Incorporation of the Guildry? began to be strongly agitated, chiefly among the merchants of the High Street, and North and South Bridges. On the 4th day of December 1817, the Lord Dean of Guild had the following requisition addressed to him :—

" MY LORD,—We, the undersigned Guild-brethren, request your Lordship to convene the Guildry on as early a day as possible next week, to take into consideration their rights and privileges as a Corporation, the state of their funds, and also the propriety of an alteration of the Town Polity."—(*Signed by* 31 *Guild-brethren.*)*

To this communication the Lord Dean of Guild returned the following reply :—

"CITY CHAMBERS, EDINBURGH, *Dec.* 8, 1817.

" GENTLEMEN,—I had the honour, late on the evening of the 5th current, to receive yours of the 4th, requesting me 'to convene the Guildry on as early a day as possible next week, to take into consideration their rights and privileges as a Corporation, the state of their funds, and also the propriety of an alteration of Town polity.' As I do not feel it to be my duty to assemble the Guildry for the purposes mentioned in your letter, I must beg leave, with all due

---

* The signatories are as follows :—

ALEX. CRAIG.	PETER BROWN.	JOHN WRIGHT.
PETER FORBES.	CHAS. BAXTER.	RICHARD PATERSON.
ALEX. ROSS.	ARCH. ANDERSON.	JOHN RUSSELL.
JAMES ROMANES.	WM. MACINTOSH.	JOHN THOMSON.
JAMES THOMSON.	ADAM BLACK.	JOHN LEWIS.
ANDREW SCOTT.	JOHN BRADFUTE.	D. BRIDGES, Jun.
JAMES INGLIS.	ABRM. THOMSON.	THOS. HERIOT.
JOHN ALEXANDER.	ARCH. GLEN.	JOHN REDPATH.
WILLIAM CREASE.	LAMONT SCOTT.	GEO. ANDERSON.
JOHN SKEADE.	DANIEL MACINTOSH.	ROBERT GRAY.
JAMES LEECHMAN.		

respect for yourselves as individuals, as well as for the Guildry-brethren generally, to decline calling any meeting.

(*Signed*)   "ALEX. HENDERSON,
Dean of Guild, Edinburgh."

On the 13th day of the month, a protest was lodged by Mr Phin, against the Lord Dean of Guild's conduct, and an advertisement was published, convening a meeting of the Guildry, to be held within the Freemasons' Hall, Niddry Street, on Tuesday, the 16th instant. To this Henderson replied that, "as Dean, and acknowledged Head of the Guildry, he conceives he has the sole and only right to convene the Brethren," and that every "meeting not called by his authority, must be considered to be irregular and unauthorised, and all matters transacted thereat null and void."

Nevertheless, the meeting was held. There was a good attendance. On the motion of Mr (afterwards Lord Provost Sir James) Spittal, Mr William Phin was called on to preside, and Mr William Bell, W.S., was appointed clerk to the meeting. The following resolutions were moved by Mr Andrew Scott, seconded by Mr John Milne, and supported by Mr Inglis and Mr James Gibson :—

RESOLUTIONS :—

I.—That it is not consistent with expediency, and is peculiarly repugnant to the principles of the British Constitution, that any great and recognised public body should be without a voice in the nomination of its own officers, and without any direct control in the management of its own funds.

II.—That the Guildry of Edinburgh is the first and most ancient incorporation of this city; that although the invaluable practice of holding meetings for the discussing of its interests and its rights has unfortunately been discontinued for a long period, there is no reason to conclude that its privileges as a Corporation have been lost; yet that these privileges have of late been so little exercised, that they are in danger of becoming a mere name.

III.—That for the sake of averting so great an evil, and of either replacing the Guildry on the high station it once occupied, or of *now* securing the rights which are due to it as a public body, every lawful and temperate exertion ought to be made, by investigating the mode in which its funds are administered, and the legal character of the existing establishment, and by trying to introduce, before it be too late, the best system for the protection of both.

IV.—That while reflecting on the peculiar state of their own institution, the Guildry cannot avoid sympathising with the calm but unanimous struggle which is now making by the other great public bodies, for improving the government of this Burgh, by the introduction of such changes in the constitution as shall give to the constituent bodies that influence in the appointment of their own representatives, and the management of their own affairs, to which they are entitled—changes which are loudly called for by the radical defects of the existing system, and clearly suggested by the analogy of everything that is characteristic of the admirable constitution under which we live.

V.—That the Guildry laments that the Dean has been able

H

to reconcile it with his duty to decline calling, or presiding at, this meeting; especially when he was requested to do so by so many members; when the prospect of once more seeing his brethren publicly assembled ought to have reminded the highest officer of the establishment of *their* history and *his own* dignity; and when he might have foreseen that his absence exposed him (however unjustly) to the imputation of indifference towards the character and the rights of the body to whose name he owes his rank in the burgh.

VI.—That in order to carry the preceding resolutions into effect, a committee be appointed;* that this committee

---

* The following citizens were appointed a Committee, viz. :—

JOHN SINCLAIR, West Bow.
CHARLES PHIN, South Bridge.
JAMES STEWART, Crichton Street.
JOHN THOMSON, Insurance Broker, South Bridge.
JOHN BAXTER, South Bridge.
CHARLES BAXTER, Potterrow.
JOHN CLAPPERTON, High Street.
JOHN MILNE, High Street.
THOMAS EDMONDSTON, Grassmarket.
WILLIAM INGLIS, Queen Street.
ALEX. CRAIG, South Bridge.
JAMES KILGOUR, Baker.
JAMES GIBSON, York Place.
JOHN ROBERTSON, Park Street.
JAMES MILNE, Founder, High Street.
ANDREW SIEVWRIGHT, South Bridge.
JOHN WRIGHT, Princes Street.
JAMES THOMSON, South Bridge.
JOHN BALFOUR, Broughton Place.

JAMES BRUCE, Blair Street.
ALEXANDER LAWRIE, George Square.
JAMES ROMANES, South Bridge.
ANDREW SCOTT, South Bridge.
D. BRIDGES, jun., Lawnmarket.
ALEXANDER ADIE, Nicolson Street.
ALEXANDER ROSS, South Bridge.
PETER BROWN, South Bridge.
JOHN RAMSAY, South Bridge.
JOHN ALEXANDER, Surgeon, Grassmarket.
ROBERT GRAY, Argyle Square.
ADAM BLACK, South Bridge.
THOMAS IRELAND, South Bridge.
JOHN CRAIG, Leith.
ALEX. JAMIESON, Grassmarket.
JAMES CHADWICK, South Bridge.
THOMAS DICK, Patrick Square; and
Mr ANDREW SCOTT, *Convener.*

have power to name a sub-committee ; that the Dean, or Convener, be empowered to call and report to another meeting of the Guildry ; that the committee shall manage the business committed to their charge, according to the best of their judgment, but that they are hereby specially instructed to request the aid, in the first instance, of the Lord Provost and the Lord Dean of Guild, and their respective Councils, towards the furtherance of the objects of this meeting ; that they also co-operate with the other public bodies, or their committee, in the joint adoption of such measures of the same tendency as they may deem expedient ; and that they shall superintend a subscription by the brethren, which, it is hereby declared shall be opened for assisting in carrying these resolutions into effect.

VII.—That these resolutions shall be inserted once in all the newspapers printed in Edinburgh.

The above resolutions were carried *nemine dissente*. Nevertheless, the Dean of Guild, the Lord Provost, Magistrates, and Town Council remained in a condition of as deadly opposition as they had formerly shown to the requests of the assembled Guildry-brethren.

But Lord Archibald Hamilton's Committee shed a flood of light upon the municipal affairs of Edinburgh. The circumstances under which this Select Committee was appointed were as follows :—

The City of *Edinburgh*, besides being the capital of the country, had the election of its Magistrates and Council set aside by a decision of the Court of Session, which was then under review ; by which, if adhered to, the city would have been left without executive officers or municipal government. The election of the Council and Magistrates of Aberdeen had also been set aside by an action in the Law Courts, and the municipal affairs of the burgh were confided to the care of interim managers, in 1817. Dundee likewise had its difficulties between the magistrates and burgesses in regard to a more liberal Sett or Constitution of the burgh. In these circumstances, the Imperial Parliament appointed this Committee to report upon the complaints of the burghs as to—

> *1st.* The mode of election of the Magistrates and Town Council common to all the Burghs of Scotland, under the Act of the Scots Parliament 1469, cap. 30, by which the old Council elects the new, and the new and old Councils together choose the Magistrates. By such mode of election, the persons once obtaining a majority in the Council had it in their power to re-elect themselves, or to elect others in their interest, and thus to continue the control and management of the affairs of the burgh in their own hands, and in those of their adherents in perpetual succession.

> *2nd.* The want of a due representation of the several Corporations of the burghs, namely, the Guildry and Trades (where such corporations exist) in the Council, arising from the mode in which the Dean of Guild, Merchant Councillors, Trades Councillors, and Deacons of Crafts, the nominal representatives of those Corporations, are elected into that body.

> *3rd.* A want of control in the Burgesses, and in the Corpora-

tions, over the expenditure of the revenues of the burgh, over the sale of the common good or property of the burgh, and over the contracting of debts, for which the community is rendered liable.

The Select Committee, of which Lord Archibald Hamilton was appointed chairman, spent twenty-four days between May 31st and July 8th, in investigating the civic affairs of Edinburgh. It is not our intention to refer to the voluminous and important evidence adduced regarding the city's affairs, other than as bearing upon the subject now under discussion. One fact, however, may be mentioned in passing, viz., that according to the then constitution of the Town Council, those who once obtained a majority of the Corporation, had the means in their power of securing the re-election of themselves and their friends *in perpetuo;* and it was brought out in the evidence that this had occurred ever since the various witnesses had held a place in the municipal administration. Mr Cuningham, the Town Clerk, being asked, "Whether, if a majority is once established in the Town Council, is it not a very easy matter to keep it up?" Answers, "I should think it a very easy matter for a majority of the Town Council, or any other body who have the choice of their own successors, to maintain themselves." In such a state of affairs, the Dean of Guild was compelled to be submissive to the fiat of the majority, or be turned down stairs, as Bailie Smith was, for having the courage of his opinions, and for being too conscientious in his discharge of public duty. The Dean of Guild of the day was, therefore, the creature of the majority, without one spark of independence.

On the question of the incorporation of the Guildry and as bearing on what is to follow, it may be well here to quote part of the evidence given by Mr Cuningham, Town Clerk, viz. :—

Do you know of whom the Guildry and corporation of the Guildry is composed ? *Answer.* There is no such incorporation in Edinburgh.

Upon what grounds do you state that there is no such corporation in Edinburgh ? I do not know of the existence of any such body collectively.

Was there ever any such corporation ? . . . If ever there was, its existence is lost in antiquity; as far as I ever could discover, there are no distinct traces of their having ever been associated together as a corporate body.

Do you know of any corporate act of the Guildry at any time ? I do not.

What do you understand by the office of Dean of Guild ? The Dean of Guild is one of the Town Council; the office would certainly indicate that he presided over some body; but I know of no such body as the Guildry incorporation having ever existed in Edinburgh.

There is a fund called the Dean of Guild and Guild-brother's fund,—of what does it consist ? It consists of the sums received for the entry of burgesses and Guild-brethren, of the sums taken for the booking of apprentices who serve for the freedom of the town : I think that is all.

What do you understand by the entry of Guild-brethren ? I understand it as an entry of the same kind as that of a burgess.

What privileges are conferred by entering as a Guild-brother ? A Guild-brother has the privilege of paying less shore dues for goods imported to Leith ; he has also the privilege of certain charities for the education of his children : I am not aware of any other privileges attached to being a Guild-brother.

Has he any privileges in respect of the trade he may carry on in the city ? None whatever as being a Guild-brother; a burgess is entitled to carry on trade without being a Guild-brother.

Then there is a distinction between a burgess and a Guild-brother ? It would seem so.

.   .   .   .

Have they any common funds ? I never heard of any.

In other burghs in Scotland, does it consist with your knowledge that there *are* corporations of guildries ? I understand there are.

There is no such thing as a corporation of burgesses ? I never heard of any.

Interrogated in regard to the admission of Guild-brethren, Mr Cuningham says :—

No oath is required on admission, either for burgesses or Guild-brethren; the form of the burgess ticket contains the oath, but they are never asked to swear it. Upon recollection, I rather think this form is now omitted altogether in the burgess and Guild ticket. I never knew of any person being asked to swear an oath on admission.

Was it formerly the practice ? I believe it was.

Do you know what led to the alteration ? I cannot say.

Or when it took place ? Neither can I say when it took place.

As supporting the independence of the Guildry, the two first witnesses called were Mr Spittal and Mr Adam Black. The former gave important testimony in regard to the privileges of the Guild-brethren, as contrasted with the Town Clerk's statement. He told the Committee that none but the members of the Guildry could deal in articles of merchandise such as cloth, etc.,—what is called in Edinburgh "*elling* and *telling;*" also that when merchants deal in articles of the description of *ell* and *tell*,* they are compelled by the Guild Court to enter of the Guild; but in other descriptions they deal by sufferance." Mr Adam Black brought forward the very lax state of matters as to the affairs of the Guildry, and among others he adduced the following :— " When I called myself at the Guild office, in order that I might be admitted a Guild-brother, and receive my ticket, I claimed to enter as the apprentice of a Guild-brother, John Fairbairn, who was a Guild-brother in Edinburgh. In turning up the books, they did not readily find his name. I put them in mind that he was a merchant councillor, and had held another office in the Town Council ;

---

* *Ell* and *Tell*; apparently what may be measured and numbered.

and as soon as they were satisfied of that, they looked no longer after the name, but considered that a sufficient proof that he must have been a Guild-brother, and of course I was admitted at the lower rate." Mr Black also reported to the Committee his vain attempts along with Mr Spittal to get a statement of the funds in the Book of the Dean of Guild revenue, and of the Dean's refusal to give any help to decayed members of the Guildry. He also strongly advocated the right of popular election of the Dean by the Guildry.

Mr James Ivory, advocate (afterwards Lord Ivory), and Mr William Bell, W.S., who had been employed respectively as counsel and agent in several cases regarding the constitution of several of the Scottish Royal Burghs, and the corporations thereof, tendered most important evidence. Mr Ivory brought out the fact that in most of the Royal Burghs of Scotland there was a trace of the existence of a corporate body under the denomination of the Guildry or Guild-brethren. He gave it as his opinion as a lawyer, that a Guildry could not to any extent exist, unless it be a corporation ; and that Guildries existed long before crafts or trades corporations. While in their constitution the Guildries of the burghs were similar, yet in the extent of privileges they differed.* He referred to the town of Dundee, where for a considerable time back the property and privileges of the Guildry had been usurped by the Magistrates, and where the Guildry had during the previous year recovered possession, by an action at law, of their property, amounting to £2000. By this step the Guildry of Dundee regained the full exercise of their privileges,

---

* At Inverness, and I believe at other towns in Scotland, is an officer called " Dean of Guild," who, assisted by a council, superintends the markets, regulates the price of provisions ; and if any house falls down, and the owner lets it lie in ruins for three years, the Dean can absolutely dispose of the ground to the highest bidder.—*Pennant's Tour in Scotland,* 1769, p. 138.

viz., to elect their own Dean, who was *ex officio* a member of the Town
Council, and to control their own funds, by receiving the dues of entrance,
and applying the funds to the purposes of their corporation. When
dealing with the question of Edinburgh, he dwelt strongly upon the
great defect of records; and then quoted extracts from the "Sett
of the Burgh," from Maitland's History, from the charter of King
James VI. in 1603, and of Charles I. in 1636. He brought under the
attention of the Committee the assembling of the Guildry to present an
address to the Duke of Argyle, to which we have already referred, and
attributed the loss of many of the privileges of the Guildry to the fact of
their not electing their own Dean. Mr Bell gave concurring evidence,
and produced copies of the various documents referred to by Mr Ivory.

Other witnesses were called, to whose evidence we need not here
refer, but shall now quote the terms of the Select Committee's Report
on the question. It is as follows :—

"The members of the Guildry of Edinburgh, petitioners to the
House, complain not only that they have not the election of any persons
to represent them in the Town Council (the Dean of Guild and the Merchant-Councillors being according to the Sett chosen by the Council
itself out of the merchants), but that the existence of their corporation
is denied, as a body having distinct corporate privileges, interests, or
funds ; and that an action of declarator having been brought in the
Court of Session, by certain members of the Guildry, to have it found
and declared that they are an existing body corporate, with all the
rights and privileges annexed to a body corporate by the laws of the
kingdom, in this action the Dean or Deacon of the Guild himself, along
with the Magistrates and Council, has appeared as a defender, and
pleaded that the Guildry of Edinburgh are not a corporation.

"This question being now under discussion in the competent

I

court, your Committee would refrain from giving any opinion on its merits, and will content themselves with shortly stating the result of the evidence regarding the nature of the complaint of this class of the petitioners.

"Your Committee are of opinion that THERE IS ABUNDANT EVIDENCE OF THE ORIGINAL EXISTENCE OF THE GUILDRY OF EDINBURGH AS A COR-PORATION ; that persons admitted Guild-brethren, in terms of the Sett of the Burgh, still possess certain privileges ; and that the power exists of continuing the body, by means of the admission of members to parti-cipate in these privileges, in perpetual succession, by the Dean of Guild and his Council, members of the body—a power which it does not appear to your Committee can be supposed to exist in any but a corpora-tion. Whether they have lost the right of administering their funds, or of assembling for the regulation of their affairs, is a question which your Committee does not think it necessary to decide. That the funds originally destined to the support of their decayed members, among others, have been long diverted from that purpose, and that rights and privileges they once possessed have been allowed to fall so much into disuse as now to be questioned in a Court of Law, your Committee con-sider to be just subject of complaint, and to have arisen from the cause to which the petitioners ascribe it, namely, to the want of any vote or voice in the Council."

This then was the deliberate judgment formed by a Select Parliamentary Committee, after hearing both sides of the case. Before proceeding further in our investigation, it may be proper at this stage that we should produce the evidence of Mr Bruce, the City Accountant, in reference to the disposal of the Guildry funds. This seems the more requisite, inasmuch as the Report of the Committee, which was ordered by the House of Commons to be printed 12th July 1819, states that

" the funds originally destined to the support of the decayed members, among others, have been long diverted from this purpose." The evidence is as follows :—

Mr Bruce examined :—

Will you state from this book the Dean of Guild Revenue from Michaelmas 1816 to 1817 ;—what was the amount received for entry of Burgesses and Guild-brethren ? To this he replied, £587, 18s.

He then informed the Committee of the House that the dues were as follows :—

Entering Burgess or Guild-brother in right of father or wife, . £4 10 0
    „   Burgess or Guild-brother in right of master, .   .   6 5 0
    „   Burgess or Guild-brother, by purchase, .   .   12 10 0
    „   Burgess and Guild-brother, in right of father or wife, .   9 0 0
    „   Burgess and Guild-brother, in right of master, .   .   12 12 0
    „   Burgess and Guild-brother, by purchase,   .   25 0 0

Mr Bruce then explained that the total sum received in the Dean of Guild Revenue for the year was £747, but nothing had gone to support decayed burgesses or guild-brethren. The revenues of the fund were chiefly devoted to the repair of churches, and the account shows under that head the sum of £2909, 8s. 6d.

When requested to state whether the Committee are to understand that the account under the head Dean of Guild Revenue is kept without any part of the expenditure being appropriated for any purposes connected with the Guild, agreeably to the Sett of the Burgh, Mr Bruce thus replies :—

All payments entered in that account ought properly to be made by the Dean of Guild ; the Guildry funds have been kept separate from the proper revenue, and levied by the Dean of Guild, who has under his direction the holding conferences with the ministers, providing the sacramental elements, and all repairs necessary to the churches, as stated in that account.

It would be interesting to know when and by what act of Council this ecclesiastical connection began. Our English friends know of the Dean as a church dignitary, but we understand the term Dean in a quite different relation, in fact as a Deacon, or chief of the Incorporation. Mr Bruce then proceeds to say :—

Formerly the Guildry funds were given in charity, * as appears by the Council Records, and acted upon by the quarterly statements until the year 1742, when the Poorshouse † was established, and the quarterly sum of £50 appropriated to it, out of the city's revenue; besides which there are charities

---

* *Vide* Appendix, page 95.

† The Edinburgh Charity Workhouse is situated 200 feet south-west of the place where Bristo port stood, and 350 south-east of Heriot's Hospital, on a part of the ground formerly denominated the High Riggs, bounded on the north by the cemetery ground belonging to the Grayfriars church, on the south, by the city wall, on the west, by the ground known by the name of the New Burying ground, also a part of the High Riggs. It was erected in 1743, and the expence defrayed by voluntary contributions made by the inhabitants. At midsummer (that year) the house was opened for the reception of the poor. Here they are employed according to their ability, and are allowed twopence out of every shilling they earn. The annual expence of maintaining each person, amounts to about £4, 10s. It was defrayed by a tax of two *per cent.* on the valued rents of the city, half the profits of the ladies' assembly room, the collections at church-doors, and other voluntary contributions ; and by what is got for the labour of the poor people in the house. All these resources, however, have been found deficient, and the house has often been so much indebted, that large contributions have been applied for and obtained. It has therefore been in contemplation to establish a permanent fund by way of Poor's Rate, instead of those above mentioned. It was, however, urged by the Gentlemen of the Law, that they were not liable to any burden of this kind, and therefore refused to be assessed along with the rest of the inhabitants. On their refusal, the Lord Provost and Magistrates determined, that it would be altogether improper to burden one part of the inhabitants of the city, and free such a large body, whose circumstances were well known to be at least as affluent as the generality of others ; but as these gentlemen continued obstinate, an action was commenced, in name of the town of Edinburgh, before the Court of Session, which is still depending.—*Kincaid's History of Edinburgh*, pp. 140-142. The City Poor House was removed in 1870 to Craiglockhart, near Edinburgh, and for many years the Assessments for the poor have been laid on all citizens—proprietors and tenants.

paid by the order of the Magistrates, and claimed weekly, also forming a head in the proper revenue account.

It is right to observe that Mr Bruce, by way of apology or defence for the use of the funds to ecclesiastical purposes, put in the following extract :—

In the sixt parliament of King James the Fourth, halden at Edinburgh the elleventh daye of March, the zeir of God one thousand five hundred and three zeirs, caput 86, it is statute and ordained, That in time to cum, na provest, baillie, nor alderman of ony townes mak burgesses nor guild-brother without the consent of the great councell of the town, and that the profitt that is tane for the makin of ilk burgesse or gilde be put to the common gud, and wared on the common warkes.

As against this Act of King James IV., which applied to "ony townes," therefore to all burghs, must be cited the case of Dundee already referred to, where, until 1818, the whole property and privileges of the Guildry had for a very considerable period previously been usurped by the Magistrates of the town, the Guildry recovered from the Magistrates their property, and began to resume the full exercise of their privileges and control of their own funds. The same remark applies equally to other Royal Burghs.

We now proceed to the next phase in this battle of the Guildry *versus* the Town Council.

We have quoted the proceedings of the meeting in the Free-masons' Hall, which was referred to by several witnesses examined before the Parliamentary Committee. The decision of that meeting was to have the question tried in the Law Courts as to the relative positions of the Guildry and the Town Council, and their respective rights. The action raised by these brethren of the Guildry is, as we have seen, referred to in the Report afterwards issued by Lord Archibald Hamilton's Select Committee. But the case does not, so far as we have been able to trace, appear in the Decisions of the Court of Session, for the reason that it was carried no further than the Outer House, where there was a judgment given in favour of the Town Council, and against the Pursuers, by Lord (Ordinary) Cringletie. For a statement of this process we are, therefore, compelled, in the absence of all other documents, to fall back upon the Town Council records of the period. These are as follow :—

Excerpts from the Council Records of the City of Edinburgh, *20th May 1818.*

On the Council taking up the consideration of a summons served upon them at the instance of certain persons styling themselves Members of the Incorporation of Guildry, concluding that it ought and should be found and declared that the Guildry of Edinburgh is an existing body corporate, with all the rights and privileges annexed to a body corporate by the laws of the Kingdom, and the complainers and the whole remanent members thereof entitled in particular to exercise and enjoy the whole privileges and immunities conferred upon them by being entered therewith according as the same have been enjoyed heretofore, or as they may establish their right thereto to the satisfaction of our said Lords ; And the said Lord Provost, Magistrates, and Council of the City of Edinburgh ought and should be decerned and ordained, by decree foresaid, to admit and receive the said Incorporation and its members into a full and free participation of all the rights and privileges which, as a corporation, or individual members thereof, they are entitled to exercise and enjoy in common with the other societies and corporations of the said burgh ; and also to communicate and preserve to them the whole of the exclusive rights and privileges to which, as members of the Guildry, they are or shall be found entitled to lay claim ; And it ought and should be also found and declared, by authority foresaid, that the members of the said Corporation, or any ten of them in number, have an undoubted right to call upon the Dean, by requisition, to convene them, and if he shall refuse to comply with the terms of such requisition, that the members shall then be entitled to assemble, after advertisement or otherwise, as may be consistent with law ; That the various meetings above referred to, called after requisitions to the Dean of Guild, have been regularly and legally summoned, the proceedings thereat valid and effectual ; And the said whole defenders ought and should be also decerned and ordained to cease and desist from interfering with the affairs of the Company in any manner of way in all time hereafter ; and also to make payment to the Complainers of the sum of £100 sterling, or such other sum as our said Lords shall modify as the expences of the process to follow hereon, over and above the expence of extracting the decree to be pronounced therein, conform to the rights and privileges of the said Corporation, and in its members and laws, and daily practice of Scotland used and observed in the like cases, in all points, as is alleged. And the Council remitted the same to the City's Agent to attend to the interest of the community, against which remit Deacons Anderson and Lawrie protested in their own names, and in the names of such as might adhere to them, for reasons afterwards to be given in, and took Instruments in the Clerk's hands.

12th January 1820.

Read a letter from the Agents, transmitting a copy of the Interlocutor of the Lord Ordinary in the Guildry case, which Interlocutor the Council directed to be recorded, and it is of the following tenor :—

COPY NOTE and INTERLOCUTOR, by Lord Cringletie, *in causa*
The Guildry against the Magistrates.

The Lord Ordinary has attentively considered this case, and thus communicates to the parties what has occurred to him.

Originally the word "Gild" seems to have applied to a society of merchants only, see statutes of the Gild in 1283 ; and by the statutes of William, c. 35, the whole merchants of the realm *are declared to enjoy and possess their Merchant Gild*, with liberty to buy and sell in all places within the *bound of the liberties of the burghs*, so that according to this, if the Guildry were an Incorporation, it comprehends all the merchants of Scotland, all of whom were equally free to buy and sell within the city of Edinburgh, as those individuals who lived in the city.

Nothing therefore can be derived from the mere name of *Gild*, to shew that the merchants of Edinburgh in particular ever were an Incorporation, because they were part of a Guildry belonging to all Scotland. As, however, merchants were a more respectable class of the community than tradesmen, it is easy to suppose that the government of Burghs would in early times have been committed to their exclusive management, who again would naturally secure to themselves certain privileges, and it seems equally clear that they created dissensions and dissatisfaction in the city of Edinburgh, as much as the privileges of the Senators did in Ancient Rome, and made way for the admission of the trades to participate in the government and privileges of the city; but the government of the town having been committed to the Guildry or Merchants, and their having obtained privileges, by no means prove that they were an Incorporation, the more particularly, Firstly, As the right to buy and sell was granted to them by statute, and *was not exclusive in Edinburgh to them alone*, the same right being competent to the whole merchants of the realm; and Secondly, That out of this same Guildry arose all the different Corporations of Craftsmen. For, if the Lord Ordinary mistake not, the craftsmen of Edinburgh are many of them brethren of the Guild. At least if they be not, certain it is that by the Decreet-Arbitral of King James the Sixth, in 1583, they all may be so, as is there decreed. "*Item*, toward the long controversies for the Guildry, it is finally with common consent appointit, agreeit, and concludit, that *as weill Craftsmen as Merchants* shall be receivit and admittit Gild Brether, and the ane not to be refusit nor secludit therefra mair nor the uther, they being Burgesses of the Burgh, alsmeit qualified therefor, and that Gild Brether to have liberty to use merchandize;" and by the same Decree, it is ordered that no person shall act *as a merchant*, or as a craftsman, *unless he be a burgess* and freeman of the burgh. This decree was ratified in Parliament, and therefore after this period the general right of the original Guildry, or Society of Merchants of the realm, was abridged so far that they could not trade in Edinburgh, unless they were admitted as burgesses; but on the other hand there was no incorporation of the merchants and craftsmen of Edinburgh into one corporation. In short, it appears to the Lord Ordinary, that originally the term "Guildry," applied to a description of persons, viz., merchants, as much as the terms Clergy, Navy, or Army characterise particular descriptions of subjects having each particular privileges, but by no means can entitle these or either of them to be considered as corporations, in the proper legal sense of that word.

Accordingly the Guildry of Edinburgh never chose their own Dean, neither do they chuse his Council, nor any of the officers of his Court. Secondly, They do not even admit their own members, who by said Decreet-Arbitral are admitted by the Provost, Magistrates, and Council, Dean of Guild and his Council. Thirdly, They have no funds peculiar to themselves, all fees arising from their own admissions, or on account of their apprentices being at the disposal of the Magistrates and Council. Of course they have no box-master, all of which are decided evidence of their not being an incorporation.

In these answers, it is said that since 1487 downwards, there is no evidence of the Guild-brethren having ever held courts or meetings, for the purpose of conducting business of any kind, and opposite to this passage, on the margin of the page, are written with pencil these words, " Disproved by the recently discovered entries in the Guildry Records, *circa* 1500." For sake of argument the Lord Ordinary will admit this note to be correct. But what follows? Just this, that after the crafts were to be admitted as well as the merchants into the Guildry, such meetings were considered to be highly exceptionable, as leading to turbulence, since by the said Decree all meetings were prohibited, and since that date it is not even alleged that there have been meetings of the Guildry, till those giving rise to the present action; and indeed there could not properly be meetings of the Guildry, since that word, instead of applying as originally to merchants only, now comprehends not only them, but all the craftsmen of Edinburgh, and as all of these are incorporated into separate corporations, having each separate officers, there cannot exist any common interest in the Guildry (*i.e.*, the whole) other than what is common to all inhabitants of the city, who may as well claim to be a corporation as the collective body of merchants and tradesmen. Accordingly the very purpose for which some of the members of the Guildry lately called on the Dean of Guild to assemble the whole, was avowedly one in which every inhabitant of the city was as much interested as the Guildry. It was one which, prior to 1583, disturbed the tranquillity of the city, and of

K

course was chiefly in the view of the King and Arbiters, when they prohibited all conventions.

The Lord Ordinary is therefore of opinion that the term Guildry applied originally to the merchants of the whole kingdom, and that those of Edinburgh never were embodied into a corporation; consequently, that they are not now a corporation, and in a particular manner that they have no right to call on the Dean of Guild to call meetings of the Guildry, or failing of his doing so, for any number of the members of it to call meetings.

As to the title to pursue, the Lord Ordinary of course thinks that as a body the Guildry has none, and particularly without concurrence of the Dean and his Council, who have disclaimed this action; but he thinks it was competent for individuals to pursue, for the purpose of having it found that they are members of an incorporation, as much as they can sue for any privilege, honour, or emolument.

INTERLOCUTOR.

11th January 1820.—The Lord Ordinary having advised the summons, defences, the condescendence for the pursuers, these answers, productions for both parties, and the whole process, for the reasons explained in the foregoing Note,—Sustains the title of the Pursuers, as individuals, to carry on the action, but assoilzies the Defenders therefrom and decerns: Finds the Pursuers liable for expenses, to be taxed by the Auditor of Court, to whom remits the account when the same shall be given in. (Signed) J. WOLFE MURRAY.

Here, therefore, we have arrived at a remarkable municipal fix. A Select Committee of Parliament, after twenty-four days' earnest inquiry,*

---

* The Committee consisted of Lord Archibald Hamilton, *Chairman ;* Sir James Mackintosh, *Lord Advocate,* Mr Abercromby, Sir James Montgomery, Mr J. P. Grant, Mr Mackenzie, Mr Kennedy, Mr J. Hunter Blair, Sir R. C. Ferguson, Mr Sinclair, Mr James Macdonald, Mr K. Finlay, Mr Maxwell, Mr Hume, Mr Wm. Douglas, Mr Macleod, Mr Robt. Grant, Mr Fred. Douglas, Mr Wilberforce, Mr Frankland Lewis, the Rt. Hon. W. Dundas, and Sir George Warrender.

The Report of the Committee was published *verbatim et literatim* in the *Scotsman* (Nos. 140-1) Sept. 25, and Oct. 2, 1819.

reports that " there is abundant evidence of the original existence of the Guildry of Edinburgh as a Corporation; that persons admitted Guild-brethren, in terms of the Sett of the burgh, still possess certain privileges; and that the power exists of continuing the body, by means of the admission of members to participate in these privileges, in perpetual succession, by the Dean of Guild and his Council, members of the body—a power which it does not appear to your Committee can be supposed to exist in any but a Corporation." This, then, is the essence of parliamentary wisdom. But, *audi alteram partem.*

Lord (Ordinary) Cringletie is of opinion that " the term Guildry applied originally to the merchants of the whole kingdom, and that those of Edinburgh never were embodied into a Corporation. Consequently that they are not now a Corporation, and in a particular manner that they have no right to call on the Dean of Guild to call meetings of the Guildry, or failing of his doing so, for any number of the members of it to call meetings."

We need not say that with so divergent opinions as were at that time propounded in Parliament on the one hand, and the Outer House of the Court of Session in Scotland on the other, it becomes us at once to pause, and say,—

" Look here upon this picture, and on this."

We have no hesitation whatever in accepting the former, and rejecting the latter. The former was based on a full inquiry, not only in reference to the affairs of Edinburgh and its Guildry, but also after a minute investigation into those of Aberdeen, Dundee, and Dunfermline. The latter can only be described as a hash of special historic or legal extracts, culled at random, "fearfully and wonderfully" intermixed with a large amount of judicial imagination. It reminds us very much of the statement of the Irishman who undertook to prove

from the New Testament that suicide got encouragement from the sacred canon. When called upon for his proof, it was as follows :—
(1) Have you not seen in one place that "Judas went and hanged himself"? and (2) Have you not seen in another place,—"Go thou and do likewise"? Subsequent investigation into the Burgh Records has only tended to strengthen the soundness of the judgment of the Committee, while the decision of Lord Cringletie has been found to be inaccurate in history, in antiquarian research, as well as in good logic, and in good law. Lord Cringletie may have been an excellent man, with the very best intentions, but the traditions of his occupancy of the judicial bench which have come down to us, do not point him out a most erudite lawyer. Indeed, the following epigram written during his day, and attributed to that celebrated wit of the time, John Clerk, Lord Eldin, very plainly states the case :—

> " Necessitie and Cringletie,
>   Tally to a tittle ;
>   Necessitie has nae law,
>   And Cringletie as little."

Therefore—*requiescat in pacem.*

In the circumstances, it is much to be wondered at, as well as regretted, that this decision was not appealed against, by presenting a Reclaiming Note to the Inner House. Possibly the members of the Guildry trusted to a higher power restoring to them their ancient rights and privileges, when the mode of election for Members of Parliament, as well as for Members of the Town Council, should be entirely changed, and made to depend on the voice of the community at large. An example had been already set in popular election by the Police Act of 1812, by which most of the Police Commissioners obtained their place at the Board by an electoral poll.

The Reform Bill of 1832, and the Municipal Reform Act of the following year, placed matters on a much better footing. Two Members of Parliament were by the former Act given to Edinburgh, and their election depended upon the majority of the suffrages of the ratepayers who paid £10 and upwards of yearly rental, and whose names were placed upon the electoral roll by the Town Clerk, who charged a fee of half-a-crown for each entry. The roll of parliamentary voters was declared to be the same for municipal representation, in so far as the ancient and then extended royalty of the city was concerned, and the royalty was divided into five wards, returning thirty-one members of the Town Council. Of these wards, the Fourth Ward, which is now called St Andrew's Ward, and embraces chiefly the same territory, used to be designated " The Golden Ward," inasmuch as, while the other four districts each contributed six members to the Corporation, the Fourth Ward contributed seven. These thirty-one members, along with the Dean of Guild and the Convener of Trades, composed the Council of thirty-three members, until the year 1856, when the functions of the Police Commissioners were devolved on the Town Council, and the separate Burghs of Canongate and Portsburgh were anni- hilated, and the Commissioners for the Southern Districts ceased to exercise their authority—the Parliamentary and Municipal area being then made the same,—the number of the Town Councillors increased to forty-one, and the wards to thirteen, as they are at present.

The chief matter to be noted here, however, is, that the Municipal Reform Act gave back to the members of the Guildry the right to elect their own Dean, a right of which they had been deprived by the Act of the Town Council on the 8th day of January 1584, ratified by an Act of the Scottish Parliament of 21st July 1593.

This recognition of the Guildry by the Legislature seemed again to raise the *quæstio vexata*, which came under the review of the "Commissioners appointed to enquire into the state of Municipal Corporations in Scotland," and whose Report was presented to both Houses of Parliament in 1835. From that Report it appears (p. 54) that the Dean of Guild at one time possessed powers which have now fallen into desuetude. For example, by the Act 1593, cap. 184, it was declared that "his jurisdiction shall embrace all actions and matters concerning merchants, betwixt merchant and merchant, and betwixt merchant and mariner, in the manner already used in the town of Edinburgh, and in all good towns of France and Flanders, where bourses are erected and constituted." His duties now consist in taking care that buildings within the burgh do not encroach on private property, nor on the public streets ; and that houses in danger of falling be taken down. In his own judicial department he possesses powers to the exclusion of the ordinary Magistrates. His decisions are subject to review only in the Court of Session."

Sections 21, 22, and 23 of the Municipal Reform Act appeared to the members of the Guildry to recognise their character and privileges as an Incorporation ; and representations were therefore made to the Royal Commissioners to decide the question. This, however, they seemed not inclined to do. On the other hand (p. 94), they state in reference to the offices of both the Dean of Guild and the Convener of Trades :—"We have been unable to discover why these particular Corporations should be endowed with that extraordinary privilege. In the towns where this anomaly exists, even more generally than in those of an inferior class, the members of these Corporations are also, with perhaps a few exceptions, qualified electors under the statute ; and the practical result must be, to bestow upon them a double share of representation in the general council of the burgh." Holding these views, it was not to be expected that the Commissioners

were likely to take much trouble in solving the matter, although they
express the opinion that it is " very desirable that those differences
should be adjusted on fair and reasonable terms."

It cannot fail here to be noted that all the privileges of freemen,
either merchants or craftsmen, have under a more enlightened and
civilised economy been freely and ungrudgingly surrendered. Incorporations of the craftsmen now exist chiefly for the purpose of manag-
ing the funds which, in some cases for generations, have been
accumulating for the benefit of those who are privileged to be or
become members of the body, as well as to elect Deacons of Incorporations from among whom, and by whom, the Convener of Trades is
elected a constituent member of the Town Council. The merchant
class, in so far as any monetary incorporation benefits are concerned,
must look to the Incorporation of the Merchant Company, which,
being directly connected with the Guildry, has no doubt arisen out
of the treatment which the Guild-brethren received from the Town
Council in the dark days of municipal abuse. The Merchant Company
was incorporated by Royal Charter, of date the 19th October 1681.
This Charter, which was ratified by Parliament in 1693, erected " the
then haill present merchants, burgesses, and gild-brethren of the burgh
of Edinburgh, who were importers or sellers of cloaths, stuffs, or other
merchandise, for the apparell or wear of the bodies of men or women,
for themselves and successors in their said trade in all time comeing,
in a society or company to be designed the Company of Merchants of
the City of Edinburgh." A subsequent Charter and two Acts of
of Parliament—one of which was dated 28th May 1827, regulated the
dues of entry, and gave authority to the Company to admit a wider
range of applicants, viz.,—all persons " being merchants, burgesses,
and guild-brethren, or entitled to be chosen merchant-councillors or

magistrates of the city of Edinburgh." Since that date, other statu-
tory powers have been obtained by the Merchant Company, and the
basis of admission has been very much widened. Indeed, several who
are not merchants, and never have been, such as professional men
(architects, artists, and chartered accountants, for example), have been
admitted. While the Merchant Company has thus opened its doors
wide for admission to its number—although, as has been stated, it was
always looked upon as the Patrician class of freemen—the craftsmen
have most sedulously closed their doors against any entrants without
the very special qualification required,—the ancient Plebeians thus
showing themselves the more conservative of the two. It may be
proper to state, as a notable outcome of the change of the times, that
many of the members of the Craftsmen Incorporations have, in virtue
of the wider gates of entrance to the Merchant Company, got themselves enrolled in the latter Company also ; so that their widows
receive a double pecuniary benefit.

But the "Merchant Company of Edinburgh," as it is now popularly
designated, though in its funds, and through its benefits, it may be
regarded as the chief association of merchants, nevertheless falls short
of the *Gilda Mercatoria*, whose traditions and history descend to the
Guildry. The Merchant Company has important and noble functions
to fulfil. The educational and charitable endowments which are en-
trusted chiefly to its care are very great responsibilities. But it does
not elect, and has no right to elect, a member to the Town Council.
This was fully stated by Mr Adam Black in his evidence in 1817.

The right of election of a member to the Town Council vests in
the Guildry, and it is but fair to state that whereas at one time, when
the privileges of trade and commerce, to which reference has been made,

prevailed, the body consisted of at least one thousand members, at another time this number was reduced to between three hundred and four hundred. In fact, few or none became members of the Guildry, unless with a view to entering the Merchant Company. It was, and still is, a *sine qua non* that each entrant of the Merchant Company should produce his qualification as a Burgess and Guild-brother of the city.

In recent years, however, the Town Council, which has from time immemorial assumed the right to fix the entrance fees of Burgesses and Guild-brethren, reduced the same to a single payment of one guinea; and the result of this well-timed measure has been greatly to popularise the Guildry, and increase its numbers.

There is now presented, in these pages, a brief narrative of the History of the Guildry question down to the present time, in so far as we have been able to obtain the same from the most reliable sources.

That the Guildry is an Incorporation, cannot be proved by a direct charter. Its charter of incorporation has not been found. The muniments of the Guildry, if such existed, are not the only "writings" or "parchments" which have been lost for ever to the city of Edinburgh. The Town Council seems to have had in ancient days gradually acquired far too much influence over the *Gilda Mercatoria*, and its revenues; and the bitterness of feeling with which the old Town Council—prior to the Reform Bill—treated the question of the Guildry as a separate and independent corporation—as well as their high-handed conduct towards the Guildry-men—was very apt to engender the feeling that there were special reasons on the part of the Corporation of those days for such conduct being manifested.

It is right, however, here to state that the claim of the Guildry to

L

be an Incorporation has a much wider and broader as well as older significance than the various Incorporations of Trades or Craftsmen. Their origin and constitution is what is called a "Seal of Cause," granted to them by the Lord Provost, Magistrates, and Town Council. For example, the seal of cause to the Hatmakers was granted by the Council, 18th February 1473, that to the Skinners, 2d December 1474, that to the Wrights and Masons, 15th October 1475, while that to the Wobstaris (or Weavers) was 31st January 1475-6. These bodies, there-fore, as well as the various other incorporations of trades, "lived, and moved, and had their being" in consequence of their having been created or erected into such by the Town Council of Edinburgh.

It is otherwise, however, with the Guildry. It had a municipal existence as an authority in the burghs before we have any record of Town Councils at all. In fact, so far as history can prove, it is by the fiat of the *Statuta Gildæ* that the Town Council is called into existence (cap. 33), *sic*,—"We ordain * that the common council and community be governed by twenty-four honest men, of the best, maist discreit, and maist trustworthy of the same within the burgh, chosen for this purpose, together with a president and four overseers." The *Leges Quatuor Burgorum*, which were passed about the same period, are not inconsistent in their provisions with the *Statuta Gildæ*. On the contrary they corro-borate the same ; but they make no provision for the Common Council. They simply enact that "the alderman and baillies sould be chosen of

---

* Some of the statutes of the Guildry refer to lepers coming into the burgh, how, if they get admitted, they should be thrust out by the serjeants of our burgh (cap. 18). They also refer to keeping the burgh clean,—"We ordain that no one presume or dare to place fulzie, or any dust or cinders on the common way, or in the market place," etc. (cap. 19). They also refer to the grinding of wheat, the buying and selling of fish, corn, and other edibles, also to the buying and tanning of hides, to the sale of cloths, wines, etc., and that no one should have more than one mill to grind with.— *Vide* Appendix, p. 91.

faithful men, and of gude fame, be the common consent of the honest men of the burgh."

The extracts we have given from the Guildry records of Aberdeen * and Edinburgh, unmistakably prove that up to the end of the fourteenth, and for more than half of the fifteenth century, the Chief Magistrate, the Dean of Guild, and the civic rulers generally were elected at a meeting of the Guildry—called the first " Head Court after the feast of St Michael." It is well for history that this the earliest municipal record regarding Edinburgh has been discovered recently among the "lowse leiffs" in the Advocates' Library ; for it corroborates the minutes of Aberdeen, and serves to show the original practice in municipal affairs.

The latest entry of the kind, and which is still more corroborative, and which also is to be found in the *" lowse leiffs,"* is as follows :—

" In the Heid Court after Michaelmas 1463, is electit *ane* provest, dene of gild, and thesaurer, *ane* watter baillie, *twa* gild seriands, *twa* appreciatores vini, and duodena burgi or *thirty-two* in nummer, quhairof euerie ane stylit be his craft." The minute of the previous year is practically in the same terms.

It will thus be evident that the Common Council and its popularly elected constitution flowed out of the *Statuta Gildæ.* For the Town Council, therefore, to deny the Guildry as having a corporate existence, is like the son lawfully begotten to deny his own paternity.

That the Town Council eventually got control of the Guildry, and of its revenues, is without doubt. How this was effected it will not be

---

* For several other extracts from Aberdeen, *vide* Appendix, p. 184.

difficult to explain. That most damning Act of the Scottish Parliament, passed six years after the Minute of the "Heid Court" of the Guildry above referred to, viz., in 1469, at the instance of the Nobles and for political purposes, whereby popular election was set aside, and the one Town Council elected its successor, gave to those in power an absolute control. In course of time they were not slack in throwing off all outside municipal influences, and becoming still more an *imperium in imperio.* Hence we find that they passed an Act of Council on the 8th of January 1584, wherein they wrested from the Guildry their right to elect the Dean and his Council, and secured the nomination to themselves. This practice they got the Scottish Parliament to ratify, by the Act for this purpose passed on the 21st day of July 1593.

It is *after* this Act that the Guildry funds become diverted, and in place of being devoted, in terms of the Sett of the Burgh, to the "support and relief of the failzit and decayit burgesses, merchands," etc., were given over for ecclesiastical purposes. It is *after* this Act that meetings of the Guildry are never held except once, and on that solitary occasion for the purpose of thanking the Duke of Argyle for having practically spared the Lord Provost and Corporation from everlasting municipal disgrace. It is *after* this Act that the headquarters of the Guildry are centred in the Council Chamber of Edinburgh, and its affairs become a sealed book to the members, while the Dean of Guild gets transformed into a mere creature of the municipal powers that existed at the time.

It ought not to be lost sight of, however, that whatever the Town Council did with the Guildry or its funds,—it never usurped, or attempted to usurp, the Guildry's judicial functions, which were greater during the thirteenth, fourteenth, and fifteenth centuries, than they are at present. The decisions of the Dean of Guild's Court were, and still are, amenable to no civic tribunal or inferior court of the country. They can only be reduced or altered on appeal to the Court of Session of Scotland. A Court, therefore, charged with such high and important functions, and dealing, as at one time it did, between burgher merchants on the one hand, and foreign subjects on the other—between merchant and mariner—must have possessed some good and legal authority for its existence. All judicial authority must flow from either of two sources — from the Crown, or from the people. That the Guildry of Edinburgh had its Charter originally from the Crown we are prepared to allege, although its existence has not been directly proved. But we shall go further and say that, if it owed its primitive existence to the people, as a public body, its corporate capacity has been recognised by Royal Charter.

The Charter of King James VI., granted to the city of Edinburgh in 1603, commonly called the Golden Charter, is very specific on the point :—" We are forever to have, enjoy, and possess, in the aforesaid town and liberties, a Mercantile Gild (*Gilda Mercatoria*), with its court, councils, members, jurisdictions, liberties, and privileges belonging to the same, and in all things, as freely as is granted by us and our predecessors to the aforesaid town, or *to any other royal free burgh within our Kingdom.*" Here, then, is a most ample privilege conferred upon the Guildry of Edinburgh, by royal charter from the King. And this charter was confirmed by Charles the First in 1636.

It is right, however, to observe in passing, that this Charter was not produced by the Magistrates and Town Council in the process before Lord Cringletie, when he gave his decision in reference to the rights of the Guildry. Referring to this matter, Lord Archibald

Hamilton, in the Report of his Select Committee, put to the late Lord Ivory the following two questions, viz. :—

Question. Have you in evidence referred to the charters of King James VI. and King Charles I. expressly recognising the Guildry as a corporate body : were those charters not produced in that action on the part of the Guildry ?

Answer. Those charters are in favour of the Provost, Bailies, Council, and community of the town, and were in possession of the Magistrates ; and the Guildry, of course, had them not to produce ; they have, however, founded upon translations of the passages as they find them stated in Maitland.

Question. Has the Dean of Guild, as a member of the Town Council, and *ex officio*, not access to the charters in the hands of the Magistrates and Council ?

Answer. I dare say the Dean of Guild has ; but the Dean of Guild, in that action, instead of supporting the rights of his Corporation, and the privileges of his brethren, enrolled himself as one of the defenders in the action along with the other Magistrates, and was a party to the plea that the Corporation of which he had the year before called himself the acknowledged head, was not in existence.

In reference to the duration of the privileges conferred or continued by the royal charters alluded to above, Blackstone says :—" When artificial persons are thus constituted, they maintain a perpetual sucession, and ' enjoy a legal immortality.' * Nay it is held that if the King grants to a set of men to have *gildam mercatoriam,* a mercantile meeting or assembly, this is alone sufficient to incorporate and establish them for ever." † Other institutional writers hold the same views.

But we must again return to the terms of the Golden Charter. All " jurisdictions, liberties, and privileges " belonging to the Guildry

---

* Blackstone, p. 265.   † *Ibid.* p. 467.

of Edinburgh, in respect to "its court, councils, members," *et cetera*, are to be enjoyed as freely not only as these had formerly been, but as they were enjoyed "by any other royal free burgh within our Kingdom." We cannot fail at this stage to interpose the case of Aberdeen, which has a direct Royal Charter from Alexander II., the terms of which are :—

"Concedo etiam eisdem burgensibus meis de Aberden, ut habeant gildam suam merchatricem, exceptis fullonibus et tellariis."

TRANSLATION.—I grant also to my same Burgesses of Aberdeen, that they possess their Merchant Guild *(Gilda Mercatoria)*, the fullers and weavers being excepted.

Here we have in Aberdeen a Royal Charter granted in favour of the Guildry of Aberdeen. If the Golden Charter of King James was designed, on the one hand, only to continue and recognise the Guildry—the latter clause of the same which enjoined that the privileges of the Guildry of Edinburgh should be enjoyed as "freely as any other royal free burgh within our Kingdom, was *ipso facto* a charter of incorporation, if none other had previously existed.

We have not taken the trouble of searching for the Royal Charters of other burghs. For our present purpose, it is sufficient to say *ex uno est veritas*. Nevertheless we may explain that not only the Guildry of Aberdeen, but that of Stirling, Dundee, and Montrose were all successful either in retaining, or by a process at law in regaining, their right to elect their own Dean, and manage their own financial affairs.

We cannot, therefore, fail to come to the conclusion that Lord Archibald Hamilton's Select Committee was right when it reported to Parliament that " there is abundant evidence of the original existence of the Guildry of Edinburgh as a Corporation ; that persons admitted

Guild-brethren, in terms of the Sett of the Burgh, still possess certain privileges ; and that the power still exists of continuing the body by means of the admission of members to participate in these privileges in perpetual succession, by the Dean of Guild and his Council, members of the body—a power which it does not appear to your Committee can be supposed to exist in any but a Corporation.

The Question we proposed at the outset to discuss, was :—

THE GUILDRY OF EDINBURGH : IS IT AN INCORPORATION ?

We unhesitatingly answer in the AFFIRMATIVE.

APPENDIX.

APPENDIX.

I.—STATUTA GILDÆ.

Hic incipiunt statuta Gilde apud Berwicum facta.

IN nomine Domini Dei et indiuidue Trinitatis et beate Marie Virginis et omnium sanctorum Hec sunt Gilde burgensium statuta per dispositionem domini Roberti de Bernhame militis tunc maioris de Berwico, Symonis Maunsel et aliorum predicti Burgi proborum virorum primo et principaliter constituta, Vt per multa corpora in vno loco congregata sequatur et vnica voluntas et vna eorumdem in relacione vnius ad alterum firma et sincera dilectio ne particulariter aliqui Burgensium nostrorum congregati aliquo [loco] generalis Gilde libertatem uel statuta possint elidere aut noua consilia contra Gildam hanc possint concipere in futurum.

LAWS OF THE GILD.

Here begin the Statutes (Laws) of the Gild made at Berwick.

IN the name of the Lord God, and the undivided Trinity, and the blessed Virgin Mary, and All Saints,—Here are the Statutes of the Gild of Burgesses, by the disposition of Robert Bernhame, Knight, at that time mayor of Berwick, and Simon Maunsell, and of other good men of the said Burgh, at first and specially constituted; so that very many persons being gathered together in one place, there may follow unanimity and concord in the relations of one to the other, as well as firm and sincere love; so that no congregation of our Burgesses in any place shall be able to suppress the freedom or statutes of the general Gild, or be able to initiate in future new designs against the Gild.

I.

Prohibicio ne aliqua alia Gilda procuretur.

STATUIMUS ut omnes particulares Gilde hactenus in Burgo nostro habite abrogentur et catalla eis rationabiliter et de jure debita huic Gilde exhibeantur. Et nullus amodo aliquam aliam ab ista in Burgo nostro presumat procurare. Set habito omnium membrorum ad vnum capud vno respectu vnum inde in bonis actibus proueniat consilium, vna societas firma et amicitia verissima.

A Prohibition against other Gilds prevailing.

WE statute that all particular Gilds hitherto in use in our burgh, shall be dispersed (or repealed), and the chattels, reasonably and by law owing to this Gild, shall be given up by them. And, no one in any other manner or way shall presume to govern in this our Burgh. But by the demeanour of all the members towards one head, one counsel shall hereafter prevail in respect of good deeds, one strong fellowship and a most truthful friendship.

II.

De forisfactis spectantibus ad Gildam.

STATUIMUS quod omnia forisfacta excedentia octo solidos nisi fuerint de tollonio Regis, juri uel libertati communi prepositorum spectantia, huic Gilde exhibeantur.

Concerning Extraordinary Forfeits to the Gild.

WE statute that all forfeits exceeding eight shillings, except those that be of the King's toll, or those that belong to the right and the freedom of the Bailies, shall be given to this Gild.

III.

Quod fratres Gilde legent aliquid ad Gildam.

STATUIMUS etiam ut fratres huius Gilde in dispositione testamentorum tertio loco secundum quod eis libuerit de parte eos tangente huic Gilde delegent nisi ex necgligencia fuerit omissum ita quod aliquid legent.

That the Brethren of the Gild assign something to the Gild.

WE statute also that the brethren of this Gild, in the disposition of testaments, in the third place, shall assign, after what is distributed to them of the part belonging to the Gild, lest through negligence it be omitted to do what is required.

IV.

De illo qui non est confrater Gilde.

ITEM si quis non fuerit confrater huius Gilde et in extremis suis aliquid de bonis suis eidem Gilde delegauerit recipimus eum in confraternitatem nostram et ad debita sua perquirenda et in aliis necessitatibus suis ac si esset confrater predicte Gilde eidem concilium nostrum et auxilium concedimus.

Concerning him who is not a Brother of the Gild.

ALSO, if any person, who is not a brother of this Gild, and in his old age shall have left any of his goods to the Gild, we receive him into our brotherhood until his property be realised; and in other necessities we grant him our counsel and help, as if he were a brother of the foresaid Gild.

V.

De delicto confratris Gilde contra confratrem.

ITEM Statuimus insuper quod si quis confratrum nostrorum verbotenus deliquerit, ad Gildam nostram adeundo uel morando ibidem seu inde redeundo, erga confratrem suum, primo, secundo, et tercio emendacionem faciat Gilde in xl. denarijs.

Concerning the Dereliction (or Trespass) of a Brother of the Gild against another Brother.

ALSO we statute, that if any of our brethren be a delinquent (trespasser) more than he should (statute) in any words he utters, regarding those dwelling among the Gild, or going from the Gild,—such brother shall therefor make amends to the Gild in forty *denarii* (pennies) the first, second and third times.

VI.

Ordinacio qualiter transgressor puniatur.

ITEM si quarto deliquerit verbo uel facto, condempnetur et puniatur secundum arbitrium Aldirmanni, Ferthingmannorum, Decani et aliorum confratrum Gilde et secundum decretum eorumdem satisfaciat leso.

An Ordinance after what manner a Transgressor shall be punished.

ALSO, if he shall a fourth time trespass, by word or deed, he shall be condemned and punished according to the sentence of the Alderman, the Fetheringmen,* the Dean, and the other brethren of the Gild, and he shall give satisfaction of this second sentence.

VII.

Alia ordinacio de transgressoribus.

ITEM si quis confratrum nostrorum pungno alium percusserit emendet Gilde in dimidia marca et secundum arbitrium Aldirmanni [Decani et] aliorum confratrum satisfaciat leso. Et si quis confratrum ab alio sanguinem extraxerit violenter emendet Gilde in xx. solidis, et secundum arbitrium Aldirmanni [Decani et] et ceterorum confratrum leso satisfaciat secundum delicti quantitatcm . nec debet aliquid de emendis istis prece alicui relaxari.

Another Ordinance concerning Transgressors.

ALSO, if any one of our brethren shall strike another (brother) with his fist, he shall make amends to the Gild in one half merk; and shall according to the decree (or judgment) of the Alderman [and Dean] and the other brethren give the utmost satisfaction. Also, if any one of the brethren by violence draws blood of another (brother), he shall make amends to the Gild in xx. *solidis* (shillings), and he shall give compensation in proportion to the severity of the blow, according to the judgment of the Alderman [and the Dean] and the other brethren: and he ought not to get release from these by prayer or in any other way.

VIII.

Inhibicio contra contumeliosum.

STATUIMUS insuper quod nullus contumeliosus audeat uel presumat infra lumina Gilde nostre cultellum cum puncto portare quod si fecerit emendit Gilde in xij. denariis.

---

* Fetheringmen—literally, Farthingmen, or Governors of one-fourth of a whole—*sic*, the four Bailies of the Burgh. This is what is to be understood by the expression.

A Prohibition against a Violent Person.

WE statute likewise that no contumelious (wrangling) person shall within the bounds of the Gild dare or presume to carry a knife with a point, which if he does he shall be fined in the sum of twelve *denarii* (pennies).

IX.

De sanguine extracto.

ITEM si quis baculo aut armo ferreo ab alio sanguinem violenter extraxerit aut aliquod membrum mutilauerit secundum arbitrium Aldirmanni condempnetur.

Concerning the drawing of Blood.

ALSO, if any person by violence draws blood from another with a staff, or with an iron weapon, or if he mutilates any limb, he shall be punished according to the judgment of the Alderman.

X.

De forisfacto pertinente ad lumen Gilde.

ITEM si quis minxerit super calciamenta sua in vili modo aut super parietes domus Gilde nostre durante Gilda nostra emendet in quatuor denariis ad lumen Gilde.

Concerning Forfeits pertaining to the Gild Light.

ALSO, if any one commit nuisance at the gate of the Gild or on the walls of the Gild, he shall make amends in a fine of four *denarii* (pennies) to the Gild light.

XI.

Ordinacio confratris Gilde.

STATUIMUS etiam ut nemo recipiatur in confraternitatem nostram huius Gilde nostre minus quam xl. solidis exceptis vero filiis et filiabus burgensium et confratrum Gilde nostre.

An Ordinance as to a Brother of the Gild.

WE statute also that no person shall be admitted into our brotherhood of this Gild, unless he pay forty *solidis* (shillings), except in truth they be sons and daughters of burgesses, and of the brethren of our Gild.

XII.

De confratre in decrepita etate vel morbo.

ITEM si quis confratrum nostrorum Gilde nostre in decrepitam etatem uel paupertatem aut morbum incurabilem inciderit et de proprio non habuerit vnde possit sustineri secundum disposicionem Aldirmanni et aliorum confratrum releuetur secundum facultates Gilde nostre.

Concerning a Brother in decrepit old age or disease.

ALSO, if any of our brethren of our Gild fall into decrepit old age, or into poverty, or into incurable disease, and does not possess any means of his own, nor be able to acquire any whereby he may be supported, he shall receive relief according to the capacity of our Gild, by the disposition of the Alderman and the other brethren.

XIII.

De filia confratris Gilde.

ITEM si quis confratrum nostrorum Gilde post obitum suum relinquat filiam suam ex eius vxore coniugata que sit laudabilis conuersationis et bone fame et non habens de proprio vnde sibi prouideri poterit de viro vel de domo Religionis si caste viuere voluerit secundum dispositionem Aldirmanni et aliorum proborum secundum facultates Gilde de viro vel de domo Religionis sibi prouideatur.

Concerning the Daughter of a Gild Brother.

ALSO, if any of the brethren of our Gild, after death, leaves his own daughter, born of his married wife, and if she be of lovable conversation, and of good repute, and if she does not possess any property of her own from which she can be provided for of a man (or of a religious house, if she desire to live chaste) after the disposition of the Alderman and the other good men, according to the capabilities of the Gild, such shall be provided to her of a husband, or of a religious house.

XIV.

Ordinacio super exequias fratris Gilde in paupertate.

ITEM si confrater Gilde nostre moriatur et non habuerit de proprio unde exequias suas poterit celebrare confratres Gilde nostre de facultatibus eiusdem Gilde corpus defuncti honorabiliter faciant humari. Et si qui de confratribus Gilde in villa existentes ad humacionem confratris sui non venient sint in forisfacto vnius bolle ordeacei brasei.

An Ordinance regarding the Burial of a Gild Brother who is in Poverty.

ALSO, if any brother of our Gild die, and has not any property wherewith he is able to pay for his funeral, the brethren of our Gild, according to the capability of the same Gild, shall place the body honourably under the ground. And if any of the Gild brethren being in town shall not come with the brethren to the funeral of such brother, they shall each forfeit one boll of barley malt.

XV.
De confratre calumpniato quomodo vicini cum eo laborabunt.

ITEM si quis confratrum nostrorum aut plures extra burgum de vita et membris fuerint calumpniati uel vexati probi viri duo vel tres de Gilda laborabunt cum eo duas dietas recedendo super expensas Gilde si vero vltra duas dietas cum ipso laborauerint reus tunc propriis expensis suis eos cum ipso adducet et reducet. Similiter si necesse fuerit vlterius super expensis rei cum eo laborabunt. Si per aliquem super aliquo facto iniuste vexatus fuerit. Si vero iuste vexatus reus adducet super propriis expensis confratres et secundum arbitrium Aldirmanni etc. condempnabitur.

Concerning a Brother calumniated—the Mode in which his Neighbours shall travel with him.

ALSO, if any one or more of our brethren be calumniated or accused outside the Burgh, regarding life or limb, two or three honest men of the Gild shall travel with him two days on the outward journey, at the expense of the Gild; if indeed they shall travel for more than two days, then the accused shall take them with him, and bring them back at his own expense. Likewise, if there is need, they shall travel with him still further at the expense of the accused, if he has been unjustly accused by any one regarding some deed. But if he shall have been justly accused, he shall pay all the expenses of the journey, and in addition shall be punished according to the sentence of the Alderman, etc.

N

XVI.

De vicino nolente laborare cum vicino.

ITEM statuimus quod siquis confratrum nostrorum hanc confraternitatem nostram contumaciter neglexerit nullus de confratribus nostris ei consilium uel auxilium verbo vel facto infra Burgum uel extra ministrabit. Et si etiam super vita et membris placitatus fuerit uel in aliquo honorem terrenum tangente vexatus fuerit non ei succurremus.

Concerning a Neighbour who is not neighbourly.

ALSO, we have ordained that if anyone of our brethren contumaciously neglect his duty to the Gild, none of the brethren shall give him counsel or help, by word or deed, within or without the Burgh. And likewise, if he should be placed in a position of danger either of life or limb, or vexed in anything concerning his reputation, he shall receive no succour from us.

XVII.

Ordinacio qualiter vicini aggregari debent.

STATUIMUS etiam ut quocienscumque Aldirmannus et Ferthingmanni et ceteri probi congregare voluerint confratres ad negocia Gilde tractanda omnes confratres Gilde conveniant indilate audita campana super forisfactum xij. denariorum.

An Ordinance whereby the Brethren ought to be gathered together.

WE statute also that whenever the Alderman, and the Fetheringmen, and other honest men have a desire to gather together the brethren of the Gild for the transaction of business, all the Gild brethren shall assemble when they hear the tolling of the bell, under a forfeiture of twelve *denarii* (pennies).

XVIII.

Constitucio de leprosis.

STATUIMUS ut nullus leprosus ingrediatur limina portarum Burgi nostri et si quis casualiter ingressus fuerit per seruientes Burgi nostri statim eiciatur. Et si contra hanc prohibicionem nostram aliquis leprosus portas Burgi nostri consuetudinarie ingredi presumpserit indumenta sua quibus indutus est capiantur et comburantur et nuduo ciciatur quia de communi consilio prouisum ut eis colligantur elemosine ad eorum sustentacionem in loco competenti extra Burgum nostrum et hoc dico de leprosis alienigenis.

An Ordinance concerning Lepers.

WE statute that no leper shall come within the thresholds of the gates of our Burgh, and if casually one shall be permitted to enter, he shall forthwith be ejected by the serjeants of our Burgh. And if contrary to this prohibition of ours, any leper shall have the presumption to make a habit of coming within the gates of our Burgh, the clothes in which he is clad shall be taken hold of and burnt, and himself ejected naked, because it is provided by common consent, that eleemosynary aid shall be collected for the sustaining of lepers in a competent place beyond our Burgh. And this I say regarding alien lepers.

XIX.

Ordinacio ne fimum ponatur in foro nec in communi via.

STATUIMUS ut nullus presumat uel audeat apponere fimum uel aliquod puluerulentum uel cineres in via communi uel in foro uel super ripam de Twede in dampnum et lesionem circumtransientium. Et si quis hoc fecerit condampnetur in octo solidis ad forisfactum.

An Ordinance, that no one place Fulzie in the Forum (Market-Place) or on the highway.

WE statute that no one presume or dare to place fulzie, or any dust, or cinders on the highway or in the market-place, or on the banks of the Tweed, to the hurt and annoyance of travellers passing. And if any one do this, he shall make amends in eight *solidis* (shillings), by way of forfeit.

XX.

Ordinacio loquendi in curia.

STATUIMUS quod in placitis nostris nullus loqui audeat de hoc quod tangat causam nisi tantummodo actor et reus aut eorum aduocati. Et tantummodo

Balliui qui tenent curiam, et hoc ad inquisitionem cause vtriusque partis. Set tam actor quam reus ad consilium suum vnumquemque indifferenter poterit euocare. Et si quis contra hanc prohibicionem nostram venire presumpserit condempnetur in octo solidis.

An Ordinance concerning speaking in Court.

WE statute that in our Courts no one shall dare to speak on that which relates to a cause, unless he be the pursuer, or the defender, or the advocates of either, and except also the Bailies who hold the Court, and that for trying the case of each party. But the pursuer, and the defender also, may call upon any man to give counsel. And if any one presume to contravene this prohibition of ours, he shall make amends in eight *solidis* (shillings).

XXI.

De Burgensi carente equo.

STATUIMUS insuper ut quicumque Burgensis habuerit in catalla x. libras habeat in stabulo suo equum decentem ad minus de valore xl. solidorum. Et si quis ab equo suo aliquo casu priuatus fuerit, morte, vendicione donacione, uel quocunque alio modo equum perquirat infra xl. dies, sinautem condempnetur in octo solidis ad Gildam.

Concerning a Burgess who has not a Horse.

WE statute, moreover, that any burgess who has effects equal to ten pounds, shall have in his stable a proper (decent) horse at least worth forty shillings. And if he should be deprived of his horse by any casuality, by death, sale, donation, or in any other manner or way, he shall provide another horse within forty days. Failing which, he shall make amends of eight *solidis* (shillings) to the Gild.

XXII.

Ordinacio de molis manualibus.

STATUIMUS quod nullus frumentum, mastilionem uel ciliginem ad molas manuales molere presumat nisi magna tempestate cogente uel penuria molendinorum hoc faciente, et si quis in tali casu moluerit ad molas manuales dabit pro multura, xiij. vas. Et si quis hanc prohibicionem nostram contraire presumpserit a molis

LAWS OF THE GILD.

LAWS OF THE GILD.

manualibus priuetur imperpetuum, et braseum suum molet ad molendina ad xx. iiij. vas.

An Ordinance concerning Handmills.

WE statute that no one shall presume to grind wheat, mixed grain or rye, at handmills unless on account of a great tempest compelling them, or a scarcity of mills; and if any one, in such case, shall grind at handmills, he shall give for multure the thirteenth measure. And if any one shall presume to act contrary to this prohibition of ours, he shall be deprived in perpetuity of his handmills, and shall grind his malt at mills for the twenty-fourth measure.

XXIII.

De libertate confratris Gilde.

STATUIMUS ut nullus emat coria lanam aut pelles lanutas ad reuendendum aut pannos scindat nisi fuerit confrater Gilde nostre uel extraneus mercator ad sustentacionem officij sui et non habebit Loth neque Cauel cum confratre nostro.

Concerning the liberty of a Brother of the Gild.

WE statute that no one shall buy hides, wool or woolskins to sell over again, or shall cut cloth, unless he be a brother of our Gild, or a stranger merchant, for the sustaining of his office, and he shall not have lot (*loth*) nor cavil (*cauel*) with our brother.

XXIV.

Ordinacio de sutore tannatore.

STATUIMUS ut nullus sutor debet tannare aliqua coria nisi quorum cornua et aures fuerint eiusdem longitudinis equalis. Et nullus tannator debet salsare aliqua coria.

An Ordinance concerning a Shoemaker Tanner.

WE statute that no shoemaker ought to tan any hides, unless they be those, the horns and the ears of which are of the same equal length. And no tanner ought to salt any hides.

XXV.

De aliena pecunia non mercanda.

STATUIMUS ut si quis confrater noster accipiat denarios alicuius mercatoris alienigene ad negociandum et de hiis super forum certum lucrum capiat de sacco lane uel lasta coriorum aut de pellibus uel aliis mercimoniis, condempnetur primo et secundo in xl. solidis. Et si tercio super hoc conuictus fuerit amittet Gildam in perpetuum. Nisi Aldirmannus et confratres Gilde sibi gratiam concedere voluerint.

Concerning an Alien's Money—not to be traded with.

WE statute that if any of our Brethren accept of any money of any merchant-alien for negotiating the same, and if he take from it a certain profit above the market, of a sack of wool or a last of hides, or for skins or other merchandise, he shall be fined for the first and second (time) in forty shillings. And if a third time he shall be convicted of this, he shall lose (his rights of) Gild in perpetuity, unless the Alderman and the brethren of the Gild be pleased to grant him pardon.

XXVI.

Ordinacio super empcione allecium et piscium.

ITEM statuimus quod nullus emat allec [nec] pisces aliquos qui per nauim deferuntur ad villam antequam nauis iaceat super siccam terram et remus foris mittatur. Nec aliqua alia mercimonia scilicet de blado, fabis, pisis, uel sale. Et si quis conuictus fuerit super hoc dabit vnum dolium vini ad Gildam pro forisfacto aut per vnum annum et diem a villa euacuetur.

An Ordinance as to the Purchase of Herrings and Fishes.

ALSO, we statute that no one shall purchase herrings [nor] other fish which are by ship brought to the town until the ship shall lie along the dry shore, and the oars be sent from it. Nor any other merchandise, such as corn, beans, peas, or salt. And if any one shall be convicted regarding this, he shall give one cask of wine to the Gild by way of forfeit, or be expelled from the town for one year and day.

XXVII.

Ordinacio quod nullus neget vicino suo partem de hiis subscriptis.

ITEM si quis emerit allec, sal, bladum, fabas, aut pisas ad naues uel aliquod de consimilibus mercimoniis non negabit vicino suo partem quantum voluerit emere ad cibum suum ad sustentacionem domus sue pro foro quod ille emerit. Sin autem condempnabitur in suo plenario forisfacto vnius dolii vini ad Gildam. Et similiter qui emerit plus quam ad cibum suum et vendiderit eadem pena puniatur quia dixit se tantum ad cibum suum emere et super hoc partem petierit et optinuerit. Et quod quarta pars tocius rei empte semper remaneat emptori. Et quod soluat infra bordam cum optinuerit rem emptam.

An Ordinance that no one deny to his Neighbour a share of the things underwritten.

ALSO, if any one have purchased herrings, salt, corn, beans, or peas at ships, or other of such like merchandise, he shall not deny to his neighbour as much as he may desire to purchase for food to sustain his household, at such price as he himself paid. Otherwise, he shall be condemned in his full forfeit of one cask of wine to the Gild. And in a similar manner, he who shall purchase more than for his food, and shall sell the same, he shall be punished with the like punishment, because he said that he bought so much for his own food only, and on that ground asked for a part and obtained it. And that the fourth part of the whole thing which is bought should remain always to the purchaser. And that he pay on board ship, whenever he has obtained the article purchased.

XXVIII.

Constitucio de arris datis mercatori.

ITEM si quis emerit allec uel alia predicta mercimonia et dederit denarium dei uel aliquod argentum in arris, gacabit mercatori a quo predicta emerat secundum forum prius factum sine felling uel herlebreking et si non fecerit et in hoc conuictus fuerit dabit vnum dolium vini ad Gildam aut a villa per annum et diem euacuetur.

A Statute concerning Arles given to Merchants.

ALSO, if any one buy herrings, or other aforesaid merchandise, and give God's *denarium* (penny) or any silver in arles, he shall pay to the merchant from whom he purchased the said merchandise according to the price before agreed upon, without felling or herlebreaking (a breaking of contract). And if he does not, and is convicted of this, he shall give one cask of wine to the Gild, or be expelled from the town for a year and a day.

XXIX.

Constitucio de mercatura bona super et deteriore subquam.

ITEM statutum est si contigerit quod emptor alicuius rei viderit aliquod merci-monium quod bonum sit supra et deterius subquam emendare debeat venditor rei per visum et consideracionem proborum hominum ad hoc assignatorum.

Statute concerning Merchandise, good above and worse below.

ALSO, it is made statute, that if it should occur that the buyer of anything shall see that any merchandise which is good above and deteriorated below, the seller of the thing is bound to amend it, at the sight and consideration of the honest men assigned to see this done.

XXX.

Constitucio de Carnificibus.

ITEM statutum est quod nullus carnifex donec voluerit officium exercere emat lanam aut coria nisi velit abiurare suam securim et quod manum suam bestiis non apponat.

Statute concerning Butchers.

ALSO, it is made statute that no butcher, so long as he chooses to exercise his calling, shall buy wool or hides, unless he desires to abjure his axe; and, as to his hand, shall not place it on the beasts.

XXXI.

Quomodo Broccarij eligi debent.

STATUIMUS quod Broccarii sint electi per visum communitatis ville Berwici qui dabunt singulis annis vnum dolium vini communitati ville predicte ad festum sancti Michaelis sine vlteriori dilacione. Et nomina eorum per commune cousilium inbreuientur.

In what manner Brokers ought to be chosen.

WE statute that brokers are to be elected at the sight of the community of the town of Berwick, who shall give one cask of wine each year to the community of the said town at the Feast of St Michael, without further delay. And the names of those (so doing) shall be minuted by the general consent.

XXXII.

Constitucio de regratariis quod non emant ante certam horam.

STATUIMUS etiam quod nullus regratarius emat pisces, fenum, auenas, caseum uel aliquod aliud quod ad Burgum differatur vendendum ante pulsacionem campane in berfredo. Et si quis vero contra hanc prohibicionem nostram venire presumpserit, res empta capiatur et secundum considerationem Balliuorum nostrorum pauperibus ville erogetur.

A Statute concerning Regraters (Retailers) that they do not buy
before a certain hour.

WE statute also that no regrater (retailer) buy fish, hay, oats, cheese, or any other thing whatever which is carried to the Burgh to be sold, before the tolling of the bell in the belfry. And truly if any person presume to go contrary to this our prohibition, the thing purchased shall be seized, and in the discretion of our Bailies, shall be distributed among the poor of the town.

XXXIII.

Constitucio de mercimoniis emendis.

STATUIMUS insuper quod nullus emat aliqua mercimonia que ad Burgum differantur ad vendendum super pontem de Twede neque in Briggate neque extra portas ville antequam ad forum Burgi perueniat. Et si quis super hoc conuictus fuerit rem emptam amittet et commodum illius ad Gildam nostram vertatur.

A Statute concerning the Purchase of Goods.

WE statute, moreover, that no one shall purchase any goods which are carried to the Burgh to be sold, on the Bridge of Tweed, nor in the Briggate, nor

O

beyond the gates of the town, before it has arrived at the market-place of the Burgh. And if any one be convicted on this point, he shall forfeit the thing purchased, and his profit shall be given to our Gild.

XXXIV.

Constitucio facta de lana et de corio venientibus ad villam.

ITEM statuimus quod nulla mulier virum habens emat lanam in vico nec aliquis burgensis habeat tantummodo vnum garcionem ad lanam uel coria emenda. Et si quis irrationabiliter emat lanam uel coria vltra statutum mercatorium in deteriorationem communitatis ville dicta lana vel coria capiantur et ad commodum Gilde vertantur et dictus homo uel garcio sit in forisfacto viij. solidorum.

A Statute concerning Wool and Hides brought to Town.

ALSO, we statute that no woman having a husband (*virum*) shall purchase wool in the streets, nor shall any burgess have more than one servant to purchase wool or hides. And if any one shall, in an irrational way, purchase wool or hides beyond the ordained market-place, to the hurt of the community of the town, the said wool or hides shall be seized, and charged to the common good of the Gild, and the said man or servant (*garcio*) shall be fined eight shillings.

XXXV.

Constitucio quod nullus procuret forinsecum pro eo placitare contra vicinum suum.

ITEM ordinamus et stricte precipimus quod nullus comburgensis noster procuret aliquem forinsecum extra libertatem nostram manentem ad placitandum pro ipso contra aliquem vicinum suum super plenariam forisfacturam vnius dolii vini sine fauore vel prece leuandi.

An Ordinance that no one procure a Friend from without (the Burgh) to plead for him against his Neighbour.

ALSO, we ordain and strictly charge that no fellow burgess of ours shall procure any one from without, dwelling beyond our liberty, to plead for him against any neighbour of his, under the full forfeiture of one cask of wine, levied without favour or prayer.

XXXVI.

Constitucio facta de conspiratoribus.

ITEM statuimus si aliquis faciat conspirationem aliquam retro communitatem ad eam separandam vel spergendam et super hoc conuictus fuerit dabit vnum dolium vini ad forisfactum.

An Ordinance made concerning Conspirators.

ALSO, we statute that if any one shall make any conspiracy against the community, to separate it, or to scatter (it), and be convicted of this, he shall give one cask of wine as forfeiture.

XXXVII.

Constitucio facta de gubernacione communitatis Berwici.

STATUIMUS insuper per commune consilium quod communia de Berwico gubernentur per xx. iiij. probos homines de melioribus et discretioribus ac fidedignioribus eiusdem Burgi ad hoc electos vna cum maiori et quatuor prepositis. Et quandocunque predicti xx. iiij. homines fuerint citati ad commune negocium tangendum, qui non venerit ad citacionem sibi factam ultra noctem dabit duos solidos ad Gildam.

An Ordinance made concerning the Government of the Community of Berwick.

WE statute, moreover, by common consent, that the community of Berwick shall be governed by twenty-four good men, from among the better, more discreet, and more faithful within the Burgh, together with the Mayor and four Bailies, chosen to that effect. And whensoever the said twenty-four men shall be called upon to treat or advise, on any common turn or affairs (of Gild), if any one of them, having been summoned on the previous day, does not compear, he shall make amends of two shillings to the Gild.

XXXVIII.

Constitucio de electione maioris et prepositorum.

ITEM statuimus quod maior et prepositi eligentur per visum et consideracionem tocius communitatis. Et si aliqua controuersia fuerit in electione maioris uel prepositorum fiat tunc electio eorum per sacramenta xx. iiij. proborum hominum predicti Burgi electorum ad eligendum vnam personam ad dictam communitatem regendam.

An Ordinance concerning the Election of the Mayor and Bailies.

ALSO, we statute that the Mayor and Bailies shall be chosen by the sight and consideration of the whole community. And if any controversy shall happen anent their election, in that case the election shall be made by the oaths (*sacramenta*) of the twenty-four honest men of the Burgh elected to choose one person to rule the community.

XXXIX.

De consilio ostenso contra sacramentum.

STATUIMUS insuper si aliquis Burgensis contra sacramentum suum prestitum consilium uel secreta Gilde nostre ostendere presumpseitt prima vice secundum considerationem Aldirmanni et aliorum fidedignorum Gilde nostre puniatur. Si vero secunda vice in tali casu deliquerit libertatem Burgi nostri per annum et diem amittet. Et si tercia vice super talia conuictus fuerit libertatem Burgi amittet pro termino vite sue. Et sciendum est vltra quod infra illud Burgum nec in aliquo alio infra regnum amplius libertatem gaudere de iure non poterit, quia infamis reputatur.

Concerning the publishing of counsel contrary to Oath.

WE statute, moreover, that if any burgess, contrary to his oath, shall presume to publish the counsel or reveal the secrets of our Gild, for the first time he shall be punished according to the consideration of the Alderman and other most faithful men of our Gild. But if he offend a second time, in a like cause, he shall lose the liberty of our Burgh for a year and a day. And if he be convicted a third time of such an offence, he shall lose the liberty of the Burgh, to the termination of his life. And let it be further known that he shall not within that Burgh, nor in any other Burgh within the kingdom, be able any more to enjoy (rejoice in) freedom of his own right (*de jure*), because he is reputed to be infamous.

XL.

· Constitucio facta de cyrotecariis et pellipariis de pellibus lanutis.

ITEM statuimus quod nullus pelliparius aut cyrotecarius aut aliquis alius Burgensis faciat lanam de aliquibus pellibus a festo Pentecostis vsque ad festum Sancti Michaelis set vendat pelles quales fuerint secundum quod melius poterit.

Et si aliquis pelliparius uel cyrotecarius super contrarium conuictus fuerit ab officio suo per vnum annum et diem depriuetur. Et si aliquis Burgensis contrarium fecerit et super hoc conuictus fuerit quociens esset dabit vnum dolium vini ad Gildam.

An Ordinance made concerning Glovers and Skinners, regarding the Woolskins.

ALSO, we statute that no skinner or glover, or any other burgess, make wool of any skins, from the Pentecostal (Whitsunday) Feast even unto the Feast of St Michael, but he shall sell the skins as they are and as he best can. And if any skinner or glover is convicted of breaking this ordinance, he shall be deprived of his craft (office) for one year and day. And if any burgess shall act in a contrary way, and be convicted of this, he shall, for each offence, give a cask of wine to the Gild.

XLI.

Constitucio facta de allecibus et de modo empcionis eorumdem.

ITEM statuimus ut quicunque Burgensis emerit allec omnes vicini sui quicunque presentes fuerint ad empcionem dictorum allecium habebunt pro eodem precio quo ipse emit sine aliqua fraude. Et si quis voluerit partem habere qui ad empcionem dictorum allecium presens non fuerat dabit emptori ad lucrum xij. denarios. Et si quis conuictus fuerit de contrario dabit vnum dolium vini ad Gildam. Et si quis non satisfecerit venditori dictorum allecium de solucione pecunie sibi debite et super hoc conuictus fuerit similiter ipse dabit vnum dolium vini ad Gildam. Et hoc intelligendum est de confratribus Gilde et non de aliis.

An Ordinance made concerning Herrings, and concerning the mode of purchase of them.

ALSO, we statute that whatever burgess shall purchase herrings, all his neighbours who were present at the purchase of the said herrings shall get them for the same price he himself bought at, without any fraud. And if any desire to possess part, who was not present at the purchase of the said herrings, he shall give to the purchaser by way of profit twelve *denarii* (pennies). And if any one shall be convicted of acting in a contrary way, he shall give one cask of wine to the Gild. And if any one shall fail to give satisfaction to the seller of said herrings, concerning the money due to him as payment, and shall be convicted of this, he himself shall likewise give one cask of wine to the Gild. And this is made an intimation concerning the brethren of the Gild, and concerning none else.

XLII.

A.D. MCC.LXXXI.

Constitucio facta de tractagio vini.

ITEM statutum fuit die Mercurii proxima ante festum sancti Marci Anno domini m° cc° iiij^{xx} primo, quod quilibet Burgensis dabit plenum tractagium pro quolibet bolio vini quod ponit in tabernam et quod ponit in nauem et extra. Pro dolio remouendo de vno sellario ad alterum dabit duos denarios et obolum, videlicet vnum denarium ville et denarium et obolum pro Beriuagio. Et pro uno dolio ad potum suum dabit denarium pro Beriuagio.

An Ordinance made concerning the Drawage of Wine.

ALSO, it was made statute, on the nearest Wednesday before the Feast of St Mark, in the year of our Lord 1281, that every burgess shall give full drawage for every cask of wine which he places in his tavern, and what he places in ship, or out of it. For removing a cask from one cellar to another, he shall give two *denarii* (pennies) and an *obolum* (halfpenny), viz., a penny to the town, and a penny and a halfpenny for beer-money. And for one cask for his own drinking he shall give a penny for beer-money.

XLIII.

De auenis venientibus burgo vendendis.

ITEM statutum fuit in Ecclesia sancti Nicholai in crastino sancti Cuthberti proximo sequente anno superdicto quod nulla mulier emat in foro auenas ad faciendum braseum ad vendendum plusquam vnam celdram. Et si plus emerit amittet quantum emerit. Et sciendum est quod tercia pars remanere debet Balliuis Burgi et residuum ad Gildam.

Concerning Oats brought into the Burgh for sale.

ALSO, it was made statute, in the Church of St Nicholas, on the morrow of St Cuthbert, next following, in the year above mentioned, that no woman purchase oats in the market-place for the making malt for sale more than one chalder. And if she purchases more, she shall forfeit so much as she purchases. And let it be known, that the third part shall be owing to the Bailies of the Burgh, and the residue to the Gild.

XLIV.

A.D. MCC.LXXXIII.

Constitucio facta de carnificibus animalia ementibus.

ITEM statutum fuit die Mercurij in vigilia apostolorum Symonis et Jude Anno M.CC.LXXXIII. quod nullus carnifex a festo sancti Martini vsque ad Natale debet ire extra villam ad obuiandum bestiis venientibus ad villam vendendis nec aliquo die infra dictum tempus bestias emere in foro ante prandium nec in fraude procurabit sibi bestias vsque post prandium teneri. Et si quis vero contrarium fecerit ab officio suo per annun et diem exponatur.

An Ordinance concerning Butchers buying Animals.

ALSO, it was made statute, on the Wednesday in the Vigil of the Apostles Simon and Jude, in the year 1283, that no butcher, from the Feast of St Martin until Christmas, ought to journey beyond the town for the obtaining of beasts journeying to town for the purpose of being sold; nor on any day within the said time, to buy beasts in the market-place before dinner; nor shall he procure, through fraud, beasts to be kept for himself until after dinner. And if any one shall act to the contrary, he shall be expelled from his calling (office) for a year and a day.

XLV.

Constitucio de corio tannato.

ITEM statuimus quod nullus extraneus ferens coria tannata ad vendendum vendat ea infra domum set in foro communi et hoc tantum per diem fori statutum. Et licet coria fuerint cesa in frusta dabit tolloneum.

An Ordinance concerning Tanned Hides.

ALSO, we statute that no strange person carrying tanned hides for being sold, shall sell these within a house, but in the common market-place, and this only upon the ordained day of the market. And he shall pay toll (custom) although the hides shall have been cut in pieces.

XLVI.
Constitucio de molis manualibus.

ITEM nullus habeat nisi duo paria molarum et qui plura habuerint a molis suis per vnum annum et diem priuentur.

An Ordinance concerning Handmills.

ALSO, no one shall possess unless two pairs of mills, and those who possess more shall be deprived of their mills for one year and day.

XLVII.
A.D. MCC.LXXXIV.
Constitucio de congregacione communitatis pro communi negocio.

ITEM ordinatum fuit die Sabbati proximo post festum sancte Trinitatis anno Domini mᵒ· ccᵒ· octogesimo quarto quod quandocunque Aldirmannus et Ferthingmanni propter commune negocium tractandum voluerint confratres Gilde congregari campana per vices pulsata in berfredo scilicet primo, secundo, et tercio, debet per interualla pulsari. Et quicunque confrater Gilde hoc audierit et ad locum congregationis possit accedere et noluerit venire antequam a pulsacione cessatur sit in misericordia xij. denariorum.

An Ordinance concerning assembling the community for common business.

ALSO, it was ordained, on the day nearest to the Sabbath (Saturday) after the Feast of the Holy Trinity, in the year of our Lord 1284, that whensoever the Alderman and the Ferthingmen wish the brethren of the Gild to assemble for treatment of the common business, the bell placed in the belfry shall be tolled by turns, viz., once, twice, and thrice, and it ought to be tolled at intervals. And whatever brother of the Gild shall hear it, and shall be able to come, but shall not come to the place of assembling, before the bell has ceased tolling, shall be fined twelve *denarii* (pennies).

XLVIII.
Constitucio de Loth et Cauyl.

ITEM die Jouis proximo ante festum beati Mathei apostoli Anno domini mᵒ· ccᵒ· iiijˣˣ· iiijᵗᵒ· ordinatum fuit quod nullus confrater Gilde nostre debet habere lotte neque cauyl cum alio in minori quam dimidio quarterio pellium et dimidia dacra coriorum et in duabus petris lane.

Ordinance concerning Lot and Cavil.

ALSO, on the Thursday (*die Jovis*) next before the Feast of St Matthew the Apostle, in the year of our Lord 1284, it was ordained that no brother of our Gild ought to have lot neither cavil with another in less than a half-quarter of skins, and half a dacre of hides (one-sixth), or in two stones of wool.

XLIX.

A.D. MCC.XCIV.

De empcione fabarum et pisarum vel similium ad naues.

PRIMA curia tenta die Jouis ante festum Penthecostes anno Domini m⁰ cc⁰ nonogesimo quarto in aula fratrum ordinis sancte Trinitatis statutum et ordinatum per vnanimem concensum et assensum expressum et voluntarium omnium fratrum Gilde quod nullus emat aliquod genus bladi, fabarum, pisarum, salis, carbonum, seu cetera venalia apud Berwicum venientia per mare nisi sit ante bordam nauis videlicet *at the Rade bra*, nec portet dicta bona empta de naue ante ortum solis set ab ortu vsque ad declinacionem solis fiat portagium sine requie. Et si quis huius rei contrarium fecerit et super hoc conuictus fuerit dabit vnum dolium vini fratribus Gilde.

Concerning the Purchase of Beans and Peas or similar Commodities at Ships.

AT the first court held on Thursday before the Pentecostal Feast (Whitsunday), in the year of our Lord 1294, in the hall of the brethren of the order of the Holy Trinity, it was statute and ordained, by the unanimous consent and assent expressed and voluntarily of all the brethren of the Gild, that no one shall purchase any kind of grain, beans, peas, salt, coal, or other merchandise coming to Berwick, by the sea, unless it be at the side of the ship, viz., at the Rade bra, nor carry the said goods bought from the ship before the rising of the sun, the carrying shall be done from the rising even unto the setting (declining) of the sun, without rest. And if any one acts in a contrary way to this, and shall be thereupon convicted, he shall give one cask of wine to the brethren of the Gild.

L.

De amerciamentis leuandis confratribus Gilde.

ITEM ordinatum fuit eodem die per assensum et consensum omnium fratrum

P

Gilde in aula predicta in crastino sancti Mathei anno supradicto, Quod omnia merciamenta capta ab extraneis mercatoribus pertinere debent fratribus Gilde et Burgensibus ville exceptis illis que pertinent ad dominum Regem que sibi de iure sunt reseruata.

Concerning the exacting of Fines from the Brethren of the Gild.

ALSO, it was ordained, on the same day, by the assent and consent of all the brethren of the Gild, in the aforesaid hall, on the to-morrow of St Matthew, in the year mentioned above,—that all amercements taken from extraneous (stranger) merchants ought to pertain to the brethren of the Gild, and to the burgesses of the town, except those which pertain to our lord the King, which are reserved to him (*jure*) by law.

LI.

Constitucio facta de Burgense forishabitante.

ITEM eodem die ordinatum est ex assensu et consensu predictorum confratrum Gilde quod nullus Burgensis vel confrater Gilde nostre forishabitans audeat nec presumat aliqua mercimonia ad Gildam nostram pertinentia infra Burgum nostrum emere vel vendere nisi tantum in die fori. Et quod nullus forishabitans emat aliqua victualia ad Burgum nostrum per naues venientia ad tabernanda nisi tantum ad sustentacionem domus sue. Et si quis contrarium fecerit et super hoc conuictus fuerit dabit vnum dolium vini ad Gildam nostram.

An Ordinance made concerning Burgesses dwelling beyond the Liberties.

ALSO, on the same day, it is ordained, with the assent and consent of the before-mentioned brethren of the Gild, that no burgess or brother of our Gild, dwelling beyond the liberties, shall dare nor presume to purchase or sell within our burgh any merchandise pertaining to our Gild, unless only on the day of the market. And that no one dwelling beyond the liberties shall purchase any victuals, coming to our burgh through means of ships, to be sold in shop (or warehouse), unless only for the sustaining of his household. And if any one shall act in a contrary way to this, and be thereupon convicted, he shall give one cask of wine to our Gild.

II.—CONSTITUTIONS and BYE-LAWS of the GUILD COURT of EDINBURGH, ratified by Act 184, Parl. 1593.

Edinburgh, 3d March 1584.

I. That the dean of guild's council, now chosen by the bailies in council, and deacons, conform to the act of their Election made the aucht of January last, to continue till fifteen days after the election of the Magistracy at Michaelmas next. And the said dean of guild and his council, upon the Friday next preceding the said fifteen days, to come in before the provost, bailies, and council, and remember them upon the day of the election of the said dean of guild's council; quhilk provost, bailies, council, and deacons of crafts, with the dean of guild and his council, in the year preceding, shall, at the same day yearly, elect and chuse the new council to the dean of guild, quha shall be men of good fame, known experience, care, and zeal, towards the common-weal, and quha are guild-brether, and has been three years upon the great council of the town of before. And that the said new council may be the better informed of the things done by their predecessors, the old dean of guild be one of the said new council for that year to come.

II. *Item,* The said dean of guild and his council shall conveen every Tuesday at two hours of the afternoon, and oftener, as the necessity of the common affairs under authority committed to their charge shall require, being warned thereto be the dean of guild, or his officers, to be given to him, and elected be him and his council, when they think good; and the person absent the said day and hour owlklie but farther warning, and at other times being lawfully warned, quha are nocht sick, or six miles furth of the town, shall pay an unlaw of six shillings eight pennies, swa oft as they fail; but give they be absent twa days together, to pay the second day thirteen shillings four pennies, and the absence three days together, to pay the third day twenty shillings ilk person; the dean of guild being absent, and neither sick nor six miles furth of the town, to pay twice as meikle ilk time as is paid be his council.

III. *Item,* The dean of guild and his council to bear the hail burden of deciding all questions of neighbourhood, and nae neighbour's work to be stayed but be him, quha shall cause the complainer consign in his hand a pledge worth the sum of twenty shillings unlaw, and the damage of the party; and the dean of guild and his council to stay the work to an day to be assigned be him to the complainer to give in his complaint, and warn the party, whilk shall be within twenty-eight hours after consignation; at the whilk day the dean of guild, and his council, or maist part of them, shall conveen upon the ground, and the complainer nocht compearand, or being found in the wrong, shall pay an unlaw of twenty shillings, with the party's damage for hindering his work, to be instantly taxed and modified be the dean of guild and his council, and paid furth of the said pledge, and the party fined; and the work not to be stayed be the dean of guild and his council, but upon consignation of the double unlaw, to be heard before the ordinary council, and if he has complained wrongously, to pay the said double unlaw.

IV. *Item,* The said dean of guild and his council to discharge and unlaw all persons unfreemen useand the liberties of an burgess, guild-brother, or freedom of crafts, as they shall find good, ay and quhile the said unfreemen be put off the town, or else made free with the town and their crafts. Sicklike, pursue before the judges competent all persons dwelland without the burgh, and usurpand the liberties and freedom thereof, obtain decreets against them, and cause the same be put to speedy execution.

V. *Item,* The dean of guild and his council to oversee and reform the mets and measures, great and small, of pint and quart, peck and firlot, of all sorts, with the elvines and with the weights of pound and stone, and to conveen and unlaw the transgressors, as they shall think expedient.

VI. *Item,* In all questions of compt and reckoning anent merchandise, whilk may happen to fall out betwixt two guild-brethren and burgesses, the party refusant to submit his cause to the dean of guild and his council to pay an unlaw of forty shillings; the cause being submitted, the party found in the wrong to pay an unlaw of twenty shillings.

VII. *Item*, Nae burgess nor guild-brother to be made, nor prentices booked, but in presence of the dean of guild and his council ; and give any bees otherwise made or booked, the same to be of nae effect to the receiver, quha shall likewise lose his money given therefor.

VIII. *Item*, That nae ships be fraughted outward, nor the same inward, but by the dean of guild and his council, at the least by the dean of guild and twa of his council, the ane to be an merchant, and the other a craftsman, with the farmerer of the wild aventures for the time, under the pain of payment of an unlaw of five pound, to be paid be them to the common clerk for receiving of the duties ; and the skipper and the merchant to be obliged to keep the town's acts, and ilk ane of them, with the acts of parliament concerning them, under the pain of an unlaw of one hundred pounds.

IX. *Item*, The said dean of guild and his council, to his power, to execute the acts of parliament, laws and statutes of this burgh, and uplift the penalties thereof, and merchants and their soverties contravening the same ; and nane to have power to sail at Leith, or within the jurisdiction of this burgh, without the ticket of the said dean of guild and his council.

X. *Item*, The dean of guild and his council to have power to raise taxations upon the guild brether, for the welfare and maintenance of their estate, and the help of their failing brether, their wives, children, and servants ; and quha refuses to pay the said tax to be unlawed in the sum of forty shillings, sua oft as they failzie, providing the same exceed not the sum of one hundred pounds at once.

XI. *Item*, The dean of guild and his council to have power, for observing of the premises, to inflict pains and unlaws thereupon, and the same to mitigate or enlarge, according to the time, place, person, and quality of the trespasser ; and further to set down heads and articles, make laws and statutes for the welfare of the town, and the provost, bailies, and council to approve the samen.

XII. *Item*, The hail unlaws mentioned in the articles before written, and contained in the laws to be set be the said dean of guild and his council, for their own half thereof, to be employed be the said dean of guild and his council, as they find maist expedient, and the other half to come into the town, except the unlaws nought exceeding the sum of five pound, whilk shall haillie pertain to the said dean of guild and his council.

XIII. *Item*, The dean of guild and his council to have power to elect ane of their own number their treasurer for inbringing of the said unlaws; and all the town-officers to assist them and their officers, in warding and poinding for the same, under the pain of twenty shillings, to be paid to the said thesaurer be the officers refusing; and the said thesaurer to make his compts sua oft as he shall be required, upon aucht days warning.

XIV. *Item*, In absence of the dean of guild, whilk shall nought be without he be sick, or six miles furth of the town, and that for an very necessary and urgent cause, to be known and tried be his council, and obtain their licence, and then to elect ane of their awn number to supply his place as his substitute.

XV. *Item*, In all the conventions of the said dean of guild and his council, that the town-thesaurer, common clerk, and collectors shall be present; and what bailies, counsellors, or deacons shall please to assist, to be welcome to give their opinion.

III.—EXTRACTS FROM DEAN OF GUILD'S ACCOUNTS.

EXPENDITURE of the money paid to the Dean of Guild of Edinburgh for the entering of non-ffreemen, and which was paid over by the Magistrates and Council in pensions, and supplies for the support and relief of the " Failet and decayet burgesses, merchants, and craftsmen, their wyfes, bairns, and auld servants, and uther poor indwellers of the town."

1st Series, from 20th July 1554 to the 2d August 1578.

2d Series, from 13th May 1601 to the 11th December 1605.

3d Series, from 4th November 1719 to the 22d August 1743,

when the Charity Workhouse was opened for the reception of paupers, and after this period the further payment of pensions ceased to be paid, and in lieu thereof, by a contract entered into between the Magistrates and Council and Kirk-Sessions and Managers of the said Charity Workhouse, £200 sterling was agreed to be paid annually by the city to the treasurer of the Charity Workhouse.

EARLY PENSIONERS OF THE CITY OF EDINBURGH.

First Series.

1554.

July 20th.—The quilk day the Provest, Baillies, Counsal, and Dykins of Craftes understandand yat Andw. Massoun, quha wes wryt to the bigging of the stallis of the queir, hes done his wark clevere and diligent, honestly and substantiously, and as ane honest reward should be pntt. to him fer his contath and reward yrof.—Thairfoir ye saidis Provest, Baillies, Counsal, and Dykins hes given and grantit, and be the tenor heirof Gives and Grantis to ye said Andw. and his assignees, ane or mae ane zeirlie pension of 20 merks vsual money of yis realm to be payit to him and yame be the Den of Gild of yes Curt. fer ye time as vse is fer the space of 20 years next harvest, beginnand ye next time's payment at Myrtimas next to cum. And gif ony small falt suld happen to be in the wark of the queir, he to remedy the samen on his expences.

Dec. 24th.—The qlk. day the Provest, Baillies, and Counsall Ordainis the Den of Gild to qntent. and pay to Alexr. Stell　　　　five lib to get him ane dublit yrwt., qlk. beand payit sall be allowit to him.

1555.

Nov. 8th.—The qlk. day the Provest, Baillies, and Counsal ordains Jas. Barron, Den of Gild, to pay to Thos. Vadle, mert., the soume of fyve pounds to support him now in his tyme of necessitie, beand sick, qlk. beand payit it sall be allowit to him.

Nov. 23d.—The qlk. day ye Provest, Baillies, and Counsal sittand in jugment ordainis the thear., Maister Archibald Graham, to deliver to Thos. Homyll als mony clayss will extend to fyve lib., and yt for and in consideration of his honestie, qlk. beand done sall be allowit.

1557.

April 9th.—The qlk. day ye Baillies and Counsal ordains the theasurer, Alex. Park, to qtent. and advance to David Wattinghame the soume of five merks of his Whitsunday time next, to be as zeirlie pension xx merks, and　　　　for doeing of ye samen sall be allowit to him.

1558.

March 3d.—A coat to Mr Kington.

April 12th.—James Majoribanks remitted one-half of his pension.

The Contracter.—Andrew Massoun the whole of his, samen day.

Sept. 27th.—Thomas Watson, pension.

1560.

Oct. 25th.—Gown to John Runciman.

Oct. 30th.—Money to Thomas Hall, jailor.

1561.

Jany. 3d.—Money to Walter Monypenny.

Feby. 7th.—Coat, hose, and dublit to Da. Foster.

1562.

Dec. 4th.—Claith to the aforesaid Dav. Foster.

1564.

July 9th.—Pension to John Roger, chaplain.

Nov. 28th.—Pension to the above Dav. Foster, who is blind.

1566.

March 5th.—To answer Da. Foster, blind, with clothes.

1569.

Sept. 7th.—Pension to widow of umql. Robt. Forrest's widow.

Nov. 23d.—Give two nobles in charity.

1570.

Jany. 24th.—Pension to Andw. Barkham.

1573.

Jany. 27th.—Act for 1st fine to Cuthbert Brown.

1574.

July 16th.—Pension to Alex. King. To John Sharp, advocate, 9th March, Andw. Sands's offences, which are great, are remitted for takeing a pirate lately on the sea, and rewarded bysides with money.

1578.

Aug. 2d.—Stephen Forrest is elected alms-gatherer for the poor, in place of drunkard John Thomson. Piracies committed by the English on Scotch merchts. from the time they sailed in ship-time, and particularly from 1554 and many years yrafter. Writings sent to the Queen of England for remedy of the town, both in capacity of Magistrats, and dealers in foraign goods pay ship expences in relief of the Scotch merchants to a great amount. Ambassadors sent. Act to uplift extent for forthsetting a ship on English pirates.

Second Series.

1601.

May 13th.—Pensions, Thomas Gibson, £30.

Oct. 21st.—Wm. Inglis's relict, £20.

Oct. 30th.—Money to Wm. Cooper, taylior, which he is to refund, one or mae events happening. Peter Ewart, for him and children, £10, samen day.

Dec. 16th.—David Clerk, £15.

Q

1602.

Feby. 17th.—Peter Hume, £46, 13s. 4d.

May 19th.—Wm. Ure, for auld services, pension of £10.

June 11th.—To the Cowgate porter for support, £10.

July 13th.—To the Master of Singing School, pension of 40 merks.

1603.

Jany. 7th.—Money to Alexr. Wilson, taylor, 250 merks.

Nov. 4th.—To give minr. of Livingston for support of his present necessity 20 merks.

1604.

July 20th.—To John Skene, clerk regr., 100 mks.

1605.

Dec. 11th.—To James Henryson yearly £40, and downwards untill 4th Nov. 1719, in record.

Third Series.

1719.*

Nov. 4th.—The same day the Counsol direct Geo. Drummond, present Town Thesr., to give to Helen Down, laul. Daughtur to Mr James Down, mercht. burges, £25 Scots quarterly, whereanent thir pnts. shall be allowand.

Nov. 18th.—Appointed the Ther. to pay to Rachil Scott, daughter of Thos. Scott, mercht. burges, fourty shillgs. sterg. for defraying her mother's funeral.

Nov. 20th.—To Margaret Piggot, relict of Mr John Goodall, Professor of Hebrew in the Colledge of this Citie, on account of her indigent condition. and to pay her husband's funeral charges, £25 sterg. as the current half-year's sallarie. To Katharine Gray, daur. lawfull to the deceast David Gray, felt maker burges, £12 Scots quarterly.

---

* *Note.*—"From this date, every Pension and Supply are here enumerated, down to the opening of C. W. House" (*Charity Work House*).

Nov. 27th.—To Isobell Lindsay, laul. daughter to the deceast Capt. John
Lindsay, mercht. burges, £10 Scots quarterly.

Dec. 11th.—To Anna Campbell, relict of Mr Joseph Foord, late preacher of the
Gospel in Skinners' Hall of this citie, for several great and
weighty reasons, £25 sterg.

Dec. 25th.—To Mr Plenderleath, one of the late Beddlis of the Old Kirk, £12
Scots quarterly.

1720.

Jany. 20th.—To Wm. Davidson and Michael Burn, late Town officers, to each
25s. sterling money quarterly.

Jany. 22d.—To Baillie John Duncan, he having long and faithfully served the
Good Town in a great variety of offices,—but being now reduced
by Providence, 100 merks Scots quy.

Feby. 3d.—To Marion Reid, relict of James Donaldson, merchant burges, £12
Scots. To Mary Wallace, spouse to Richard Howison, merchant
burges, £12 Scots. To Adam Sommervail, late Deacon of the
furriers, £15 Scots.

March 30th.—To James Murray, mercht., £20 Scots quarty. To Margt. Johnston, relict of James Ritchie, mercht. burges, £15 Scots. To
Mr Mathew M'Koll, mert. burges, £25 Scots. To Lamond
Thompson, burges, £15 Scots. To John Watson, mert. burges,
£30 Scots.

April 20th.—To James Lein, late Deacon of the hammermen, £25 Scots.

May 11th.—To John Watson, as above, in respect he was dying, £5 stg.

June 10th.—To Ann Campbell, relict of James Ramsay, of Newtown, burges,
£30 Scots. To James Allan, skinner, augment his pension from
7 to £12 Scots. To Mr Wm. Lauder, Doctor of Medicine, in
respect of the services done the Good Town by his Relations,
£50 Scots.

July 29th.—To amount of New quarterly pensions, £27 Scots (178).

Sept. 2d.—To Agnes Millar, relict of Wm. Burges, £10 Scots.

Sept. 5th.—To Issobell Wightman, relict of William Baird, late Deacon of the
bonnet makers, from 6 to £12 Scots.

Sept. 14th.—To Alex. Livingston, late Deacon of the baxters, £20 Scots. To

Janet Stewart, relict of Robt. Elliot, late Deacon of the wrights, £12 Scots,

Nov. 2d.—To Wm. Richardson, mercht. burges, £40 Scots for subsisting his ffamily.

Nov. 30th.—To James Watson, burges, augmd. from 4 to £8 Scots. To Janet Lourie, relict of Alexr. Stewart, brewer burges, £12 Scots.

1721.

Jany. 14th.—To the poor of the Episcopal clergy, £200 Scots. To Janet Dundas, relict of Robt. Hemser, brewer burges, from £15 to £24 Scots.

Jany. 22d.—To John ffairholm, from £12 to £15 Scots. To James Riddell, from £8 to £15 do.

Jany. 25th.—To Mary Wallace, spouse to Richard Howison, brewer burges, from 12 to £20 Scots.

Feby. 15th.—To Grizel Mortoun, relict Mr John Orr, late minister of the Gospell of this citie, £6 sterg. of present supply. To Alex. Muirhead, butcher burges, £30 Scots ; and to David Wright, burges, £12 Scots.

April 5th.—To John, Kaitharine, and Elizabeth Linds, grandchildren to the deceast Wm. Affleck, baxter burges, £3 stg. of supply. To Wm. Hutton, merchant Counsoller, £2, 5s. 2d. for cloaths to Gideon Murray, mercht. burges.

May 10th.—The amount of New quarterly pensions is £20 (419).

May 24th.—To Patrick Mathew, town officer, late of this citie, £10 Scots.

May 30th.—To James Murray, elder, mercht. burges, £3 stg., to buy ane suit of cloaths.

Aug. 9th.—To Deborah Howstoun, relict of James Galloway, her husband's pension of £25 Scots continued to her.

Amount of quarterly pensions is £   (Kirk Treasurer).

Aug. 23d.—To Robert Grinzan, late Deacon of the cordenirs, £15 Scots quarterly.

Sept. 8th.—To Helen Carstairs, relict of John Lothian, late Deacon of the hammermen, £15 Scots.

Nov. 8th.—To Isobell Porteous, relict of David Allan, skinner burges, £12. To James Paterson, brewer burges, £12. To Alex. Herriot, taylor burges, £12. To Doreatha Smart, relict of Wm. Adam, chirurgeon burges, £20. To Janet Ramsay, relict of John Ramsay, burges, £12,—all Scots money.

Dec. 1st.—To David Mairserton, barber burges, £15 Scots.

1722.

Feby. 4th.—To Katharine Robertson, relict of John Robertson, vintner burges, augmd. from 8 to £12. To John Maxwell, burges, do. from 10 to £14. To John Lester, mercht., do. from 10 to £18. To David Thomson, late Deacon of the masons, 12 to £16. To Charles and Rachael Smiths, from 12 to £16, payable to Mr Geo. Cunningham, chirurgeon, for their behoof. To Elizabeth Tait, relict of John Mortimer, wigmaker burges, £12,—all Scots money. To Margt. Lindsay, relict of —— Miller, from 5 to £8. To Hellen Bennie, relict of Andw. Gourlay, smith burges, 4 to £6. To Grizel Aitken, relict of Patrick Baird, bedleman, from 5 to £7. To Ann Drummond, relict of Gedeon Murray, merct., from 3 to £6. To Margt. Edward, daughr. to John Edward, tanner burges, £8. To Julian Reid, relict of Robert Caskie, fflesher burges, £6.

April 18th.—To the relict of Mr George Mair, late minister of the Gospel at Culross, £4 sterg. of supply.

May 9th.—To William Wallace, litster burges, £6. To Robert Duncan, tailer, £6. To John Moffat, £10. To Margt. Henter, relict of Wm. Lithgow, burges, £5. To Catharine Horner, grandchild to David Gillon, mercht., £6, payable to Baillie Jas. Newlands for her behoof. To Grizal ——, daur. to ——, £6. To Barbara Gray, relict of George Gray, stabler, £8. To Hellen Livingston, relict of Wm. Fulton, mason, £6. To Anna Brown, daugr. to James Brown, mert., £4. To Janet Millar, relict of Robert Porteous, mercht., £4. To Jean Ramsay, relict of Willm. Cossar, tayler, £4. To Catharine Mairten, relict of Alexr. Burges, £6. To Alison Stewart, daur. to James Stewart, currer burges, £6. To Margt. Row, daur. to John Row, printer, £5. To Elizabeth Gray, daur. to the deccast John Gray, mercht., £6. To Joan

Scott, reponed to her former pension of £6. To Betty Ramsay, relict of John Buchanan, and a child, £6.

AUGMENTATIONS.

May 9th.—Margt. Auchtermony, relict of Robert Henderson, gunsmith, from 5 to £8. Margt. Brown, relict of Thomas Liston, 4 to £6. John Scott, smith, 7 to £9. Marion Ramsay, relict of John Pringle, merct., 4 to £6. Margt. Hamilton, relict of Jas. Stewart, 4 to £6. Alex. Johnston, merct., 6 to £8. Margt. Carson, daur. to Robt. Carson, 4 to £6. Jean Muir, relict of Patrick Hunter, 6 to £8. Betsy ——, relict of Wm. Turnbull, 5 to £8.

July 25th.—To Agnes Taylor, relict of Hugh Inglis, merct. burges, £15 Scots quary.

NEW PENSIONS.

Aug. 8th.—Antonia Parson, apthy. burges, £12. Charles Hay, baxter, for the behoof of the children of Wm. Adam, chirurgeon, £14. Patrick Spence, barber burges and Gild brory., £12,—all Scots money.

Sept. 5th.—To Jean Wauchope, relict of John Padson, wryter burges, £12 Scots.

Sept. 12th.—To Andrew Nisbet, merct. burges, £12 Scots quary. To Andrew Ker, brewer burges, £3 stg. to transport his son to London.

Oct. 31st.—To Wm. Blair, student of divinitie, fourty shillings of supply.

Nov. 7th.—To Alex. Livingston, late deacon of the baxters, £15 Scots.

Dec. 2d.—To Wm. Mitchell Whyte, iron smith, £12 Scots quy. To Mr Alex. Hunter, £8 Scots quay. To John Brown, cordner, £8. To Margt. Yetts, daur. to John Yetts, wright, £6 do. To Barbara Greig, spouse to John Anderson, tayler, £4 do. To Hellen Kellie, relict of Alexr. Fergusson, wigmaker and barber, £6 do. To Isobell Buchanan, relict of Andw. Davidson, cordner burges, £4 do. To Elizabeth Inglis, relict of George Henderson, flesher, £5 do.

1723.

March 6th.—To Eupham. Bishop, daughter to Wm. Bishop, chirurgeon, £14 Scots quy.

March 20*th.*—To Jean Smealholm, daughter to the deceast George Smealholm, mercht. burges, £3 sterg. of supply.

May 1*st.*—To Peter Reid, journeyman wright, who suffered considerable damage at the town's work, 3s. stg. weekly.

May 8*th.*—To Anna Lindsay, daughter to John Lindsay, mercht., £10. To John Lauder, late deacon of the chirurgeons, £15 Scots quary., on behalf of Wm. Lauder, son to Doctor Wm. Lauder. To ditto, for —————— daughters of the above Dr Lauder, fourty shillings sterg.

May 24*th.*—To John Provan, barber burges, £10 Scots quay.

Aug. 7*th.*—To Thomas Gray, writer, £10 Scots. To Catharine Aitkenhead, daughter to the deceased James Aitkenhead, appothecary burges, £12 Scots quary.

Aug. 14*th.*—To Margt. Waste, relict of Robert Cruizean, late deacon of the cordners, £30 Scots, to enable her to pay the funeral charges of his funeral.

Oct. 23*d.*—To Mary Gray, relict of Wm. Lindsay, mercht., £20 Scots.

Nov. 1*st.*—To Robert Cristal, taylor, for behoof of James Donaldson, £16 sterg.

Nov. 13*th.*—To John Ochiltree, late deacon of the weavers, £15 Scots.

Dec. 11*th.*—To James Murray, mercht., for cloaths to him, £4 stg.

Dec. 27*th.*—To George Chiesly, son to the deceast Sir Robert Chiesley, late Lord Provest, for equipping him to go a voyage to Virginia, 2 guineas.

1724.

Jany. 29*th.*—To John Gibson, late deacon of the bonnet makers, £12 Scots.

Feby. 26*th.*—To John Hislop, mercht., £5 sterling of supply. To Catharin Telfer, relict of James Jardin, merct. burges, £25 Scots quary.

March 18*th.*—To Lillias Robertson, daughter to the deceast John Robertson, late Dean of Guild, £10 Scots qy.

April 29*th.*—To Caldie Wm. Falconer, fourty shillings sterg. for an sute of cloaths. To Wm. Somervaile, present deacon of the skinners, for Jas. Somervaile, barber burges, 25 merks Scots quy.

May 2*d.*—To Anthony Pearson, apothecary burges, £5 sterg. towards defraying the charges of transporting himself and family to London.

June 12*th.*—To the widows and orphans of the Episcopal clergy, £200 Scots.

July 15*th.*—To Robert Manderston, mercht., £38 Scots, for the use of Robert Mein, mercht.

Aug. 26*th.*—To James Hinmers, indweller burges, £12 Scots qy. To Janet Tait, daughter to the deceast John Tait, painter burges, £2 stg., to defray her expences to Ireland.

Sept. 9*th.*—To Helen Lindsay, relict of Mr Colin Lindsay, minister, £12 Scots quay.

Oct. 28*th.*—To Margt. Mack, daughter to the deceased George Mack, burges, £2 stg. supply.

Nov. 11*th.*—To Archd. Home, mercht. burges, £12. To Dorothea Somervol, relict of Mr Wm. Hadden, late maister of the High School, and for her two children, £12. To George Mathie, merchant, £12.

SUPPLYS.

Nov. 11*th.*—To —— Lauder, 25s. stg. To David Kilgour, weaver burges, £6. To John Black, vintner burges, £6. To Agnes Milne, relict of Thomas Brown, burges, £6. To Elizabeth Tallie, daughter to the deceased James Tallie, cordner burges, £4. To Janet Miekle, relict of Geo. Paterson, burges, £6. To Isobell Davidson, relict of Robert Pinkerton, trunk maker burges, £3. To Janet Balfour, relict of Robert Coupar, tayler, £3. To Christian Stirline, spouse to Geo. Stewart, £3. To Margt. Turnbull, relict of John Hadoway, mason, £6. To Betty Balingual, £18, in respect she is not to be any more troublesome to this city. To Agnes M'Aulay, £4. To William Alves, late baillie, Portsburgh, £6. To Sarah Trotter, relict of Charles Lumsden, mercht., 20s., to furnish her cloaths at the sight of Mrs Stephen.

Dec. 2*d.*—To John Campbell, mercht. burges, £40 Scots of supply. To Wm. Burnet, mercht., £12 do. To Agnes and Janet Walls, each of them £3 Scots do.

Dec. 15*th.*—To Theodore Medmus, a German minister, recommended by several persons of note, as a great object of charity, by reason of the losses he sustained by fire in his house in Germany, 4 guineas. To Peter Chaselon, furrier burges, 10s. To Willm. Keir, trades counciller, to defray Agnes Miln's funeral, 10s.

Dec. 23*d.*—To Mr Alex. Hastie, late schoolmaster, a crown, of supply. To Janet Aitkenhead, a crown, of supply.

1725.

Jany. 27*th.*—To Elizabeth Duff, a crown, of supply. To —— Lauder, son of —— Lauder, docter of medecine, £15 Scots, of supply.

Feby. 17*th.*—To William Tod, mercht., £12, of pension.

Feby. 24*th.*—To Mr John Mathison, one of the ministers of this city, £5 stg., for the use of Mr —— Woodsyde, minister of the Gospel in New England.

March 10*th.*—To Janet Cunningham, 10s. stg., of supply, to carry her to England.

March 19*th.*—To Rosina Campbell, daughter to the late Mr George Campbell, professor of divinitie in the Colledge of this city, £5 sterg.

April 28*th.*—To cadie Willm. Falconer, £2 sterling, for a sute of cloaths to him. To Anna Nisbet, relict of Colin Falconer, barber burges, £6 Scots, of supply.

May 5*th.*—To Margt. Smith and Mary Robertson, two poor women, each of them £3 Scots, of supply.

May 19*th.*—To —— Lauder, son to Mr Wm. Lauder, doctor of medicine, 25s. stg.; and to Sussana Irving, 10s. stg., both of supply.

June 2*d.*—To Agnes Angus, £3 Scots; and to the relict of Wm. Turnbull, late serjeant in the Citie Guard, £4 Scots, both of supply.

July 21*st.*—To John Campbell, son to John Campbell, mercht. burges, £2 stg. quary. for the space of two quarters. To Janet Nicolson, relict of Robert Seton, writer, 30s., to defray funeral charges.

Aug. 6*th.*—To James Somervail, barber, 15s.; and to Janet Lawson, 5s., both of supply.

NEW PENSIONS.

Aug. 18*th.*—To Agnes Angus, daugh. to James Angus, schipper, £3 Scots. To Wm. Braidwood, brewer burges, £15 Scots. To Janet Brown, relict of Alexr. Mitchell, barber, for herself and three children, £12. To Margt. Bishop, daugh. to Wm. Bishop, wright, £3. To John Callander, son to John Callander, smith, burges, for himself, wife, and child, £4. To Jean Crichton, relict of Thos. Gray, pror., for herself and 4 children, £12. To Elizabeth Duff, relict of John Gardner, £6. To Margt. Dundas, relict of David

R

Dundas, burges, for the behoof of two children. To Christian Gilchrist, relict of Alex. Johnston, mercht. burges, an old woman, £3. To Elizabeth Gray, relict of George Thorburn, taylor burges, £3. To Margt. Hackson, daur. to the deceased Wm. Hackson, burges and guild brother, for herself and seven children, £8. To Margt. John, relict of John Sinclair, mercht., for behoof of the children of John Sanders, £10. To Margt. M'Intosh, relict of John Turner, burges, for herself and child, £3. To Isobel M'Nab, relict of George Pearson, wauker burges, for herself and child, £6. To Barab. Mason, daug. to the deceased James Mason, mercht. burges, an old woman, £4. To Wm. Morrison, skinner burges, for himself, wife, and 7 children, £10. To Anna Nisbet, relict of John Falconer, barber burges, £4. To Archd. Paterson, son to the deceased Wm. Paterson, skinner, troubled with the falling sickness, £4. To John Somervill, baxter, augmd. from 8 to £10. To James Seton, mercht., for behoof of George and Elizabeth Seton, two orphans, £9. To Margt. Sime, relict of John Mackie, wright burges, £4. To Margt. Smith, relict of John Blair, litster, for herself and daur., who has a lame hand, £8. To Elizabeth Thomson, spouse to Alex. Weddell, pewtherer burges, for herself and 3 children, £6. To Elizabeth Watt, relict of David Kilgour, weaver burges, for herself and two children, £5. To Alison Wilkie, relict of Wm. Turnbull, litster, for herself and child, £6.

Aug. 25th.—To Janet Potter, daur. to the deceased Wm. Potter, wright, £3 Scots, of supply.

Sept. 8th.—To Walter Neil, smith burges, and Archd. Pringle, mercht., each of them 10s., of supply.

Oct. 13th.—To Helen Scott, relict of Thos. Waldie, burges, £10 Scots; and to Alex. Lindsay, a crown, both of supply.

Oct. 27th.—To Alison Donaldson and Dougall M'Dougall, each of them a crown, of supply.

Nov. 3d.—To John Young Baxter, baxter, late Deacon, £6 sterg. To Janet Walker, a poor woman, 10s. stg., of supply.

Dec. 1st.—To Sarah Trotter, relict of Charles Lumsdene, mercht., 20s. stg. for cloaths; and to William Aithow, glover burges, 10s., of supply.

1726.

Jany. 7th.—To Marion Inglis, daur. to the deceased Hugh Inglis, mercht. burges, £3 stg., to defray the expences of his mother's ffuneral.

Feby. 9th.—To John Tait, late Keeper of the City's Wardrope, in respect of his valitudinariness and tenderness, appoint the City Treasurer to pay him £200 Scots yearly.

Feby. 16th.—To the Widows and Orphans of the Episcopal Clergy, £200 Scots.

PENSIONS.

Feby. 16th.—Anna Chapman, relict of James Somervill, for herself and child, £8. Jean Mowbray, relict of Patrick Hallyburton, herself and 2 children, £12. John Campbell, son to John Campbell, mercht., blind, £12. Mary Park, relict of Patrick Buchanan, £12.

AUGMENTATIONS.

Feby. 16th.—To Wm. Tod, for himself and children, from 12 to £15. To Janet Horsburgh, relict of Wm. Hopkirk, belt maker, 10 to £12. To John Goodal, son to the deceased Mr John Goodal, late Professor of Hebrew in this University, £6 stg., to be applied for his behoof by Mr Wm. Wishart, Principal of the Colledge.

March 9th.—To Christian Young, relict of Willm. Burnett, writer burges, £6 Scots, of supply. To Helen Scott, relict of Thos. Waldie, mercht. burges, £6 Scotts, of supply.

March 23d.—To Anna Gairns, daur. to —— Gairns, minister, Aberdeen, £13 Scots, of supply.

April 8th.—To Edward Penman, goldsmith, 40s. stg. to defray the funeral charges of James Murray, senr., mercht.

April 15th.—To John Johnston, candlemaker burges, £16 Scots, to defray the expence of Willm. Davidson's ffuneral, late Town Officer.

April 22d.—To Bailly Archd. Wallace, mercht., £2 stg., to defray the funeral charges of —— Gray, daur. to the deceased Alex. Gray, mert.

June 8th.—To Helen Greirson, relict of Robt. Greirson, late Bailly, £30 Scots quay. To Agnes Hunter, relict of James Lein, late Deacon of the hammermen, £2 Scots.

July 20th.—To Mr Joseph Holme, ane Irish minister of the Gospel, £4 sterg. of supply. To Edwd. Muirhead, late apprentice, Mr John Weir, wigmaker burges, £20 Scots, to defray the funeral expences of Catherine Jessy, his mother, daughter to John Jessy, late Bailly of this city. To John Martin, son to the deceased John Martin, stabler burges, £3 of supply, Scots.

Aug. 12th.—To Ann Brown, daur. of the deceast Cpt. Brown, merct., fourty shillgs. sterling, to defray the funeral charges of her mother.

Aug. 17th.—To Janet, Anna, and Jean Mitchell, children to the deceast Alex. Mitchell, barber burges, to pay to Adam Mitchell, session clerk of West Church, £12 Scots quarty. To Isobel Butler, relict of John M'Intosh, one of the city's waits, £2 sterg., to defray his funeral charges.

Sept. 2d.—To Jean Bell, daug. to Mr Thos. Bell, late Professor of Humanity in the city of Edinr., a guinea of supply, to enable her to perform her journey to London.

Sept. 7th.—To Agnes Angus, a crown of supply. To Elizabeth Laing, relict of Andw. Johnston, one of the Capts. of the City Guard, 20s. stg. of supply; and 5s. relict of John Wilson, ffurrier.

Oct. 19th.—To Henry Burd, late Deacon of the weavers, 20s. stg. quay.

Nov. 11th.—To the relict of Mr John Orr, late minister of the Gospel, Edinr., £6 stg. money, of supply.

Nov. 16th.—To James Hamilton, late of Ormiston, 30s. stg., of supply.

Nov. 30th.—To Eupham. Watson, spouse to Robt. Newlands, glover burges, 30s. stg., of supply; as also to Elizabeth Tallie, daur. of James Tallie, cordiner burges, 10s. stg. To the spouse of James Murray, clerk of the weigh-house, for herself and children, £15 Scots quy.

Dec. 9th.—To Sarah Trotter, relict of Chas. Lumsdene, merct. burges, 20s. stg. for cloaths.

1727.

Jany. 4th.—To John Holmes, taylor, 10s., and to Mary Robertson, 5s., both of supply. To Mr Allan Whytfoord, merct. Counciller, 6 guineas of gold, to be remitted to David Donald, to improve himself in mathematicks in fforaign countrys.

Jany. 25th.—To Robert Smith, mercht. burges, £20 Scots quy.

Feby. 7th.—To Agnes Angus, a poor woman, 5s. To Betsy Russell, relict of Robert Smith, late Deacon of the weavers, 10s. To Janet Fulton, 5s., all of supply.

March 17th.—To John Home, late Deacon of the bonnet-makers, £15 Scots. To Janet Law, relict of Walter Purdie, burges, £3 Scots, of supply. To —— Clelland, relict of Edward Gibson, town officer, £3 Scots, of supply.

April 14th.—To Charles Hay, late Deacon of the baxters, £15 Scots, of supply. To Betty Balcanqual, daur. to the deceased Jno. Balcanqual, mercht. burges, £15 Scots.

May 3d.—To James Donaldson, poultryman burges, 10s., of supply. To James Boswall, glover burges, ane crown, of supply.

June 2d.—To Helen M'Gill, relict of John Scott, wright burges, £5 stg., in respect of damage done her property when repairing the street. To Capt. Robert Telfer, of the City Guard, £5, 19s. 1d. stg., disbursed by him on the funeral of Ensign Wm. Agnew, nephew to Mr James Alexander, who was a considerable donor to the Trinity Hospital.

June 14th.—To James Stewart, ane crown, of supply.

July 12th.—To Magdalen Harlaw, relict of James Russell, the Good Town's tenant in Canaan, 30s. stg., of supply. To Elizabeth Pollock, daur. to the deceast Wm. Pollock, baxter burges, 10s. stg., of supply. To the Widows and Orphans and the poor of the Episcopal Clergy, £200 Scots. To Janet Lothian, relict of Alex. Lindsay, mercht. burges, 40s. stg. To Janet Walker, daur. to John Walker, skinner burges, 10s. stg.; and to Mary Gray, daug. to the deceased Walter Gray, mercht. burges, 15s.

Sept. 13th.—To Willm. Polson, taylor burges, a poor man, 10s. stg. To James Keith, son to the deceased Patrick Keith, burges, 20s. stg. To Margt. Hog, relict of Wm. Barclay, late Deacon of the bonnet-makers, one crown, all of supply.

Oct. 18*th.*—To Jean Kennedy, relict of Wm. Baptie, baxter burges, 10s. To Elizabeth Pollock, baxter burges, 10s. stg., both of supply.

Oct. 25*th.*—To Agnes Angus, to enable her to go to England to her friends, £2 stg.

Dec. 13*th.*—To Sarah Trotter, relict of Chas. Lumsden, merct. burges, 20s., for cloaths.

Dec. 29*th.*—To Nicolas Porringer, relict of Jas. Hunter, burges, 10s., of supply. To —— the relict of Mr John Ord, mercht., £5 stg., of supply.

1728.

Jany. 5*th.*—To Anna Hay, daur. to the deceased James Hay, wigmaker burges, 10s. stg., of supply.

Jany. 25*th.*—To John Walker, Deacon of the skinners, 25s., to defray the funeral charges of Adam Somervail, late Deacon of the ffurriers.

Feby. 2*d.*—To Charles Hay, baxter, 10s., to defray the funeral charges of Betty Balcanquel. To John Holmes, taylor burges, £3 stg., of supply. To Isobel Lamb, relict of Henry Gladstones, 10s., of supply, mercht. burges.

March 22*d.*—To James Ker, mercht. tailor, 30s., of supply. To James Home, 5s., of supply.

April 3*d.*—To Margt. Low, relict of William Haigs, late Deacon of the Waukers, 10s., of supply.

April 7*th.*—To disbursed as the ffuneral charges of Alex. Riddle, mercht., £16 Scots. Do., at the funeral of Malcolm Walker, burges. To constable Wm. Falconer, 40s. stg., for a suit of cloaths.

April 24*th.*—To David Mitchell, Dean Conveener, £30 Scots, to provide necessaries to John Penman, goldsmith. To Margt. Watt, daur. to Jas. Watt, tailor burges, ane crown, of supply.

May 1*st.*—To George Taylor, gunsmith, and George Wightman, mercht., each of them a crown, of supply. To Jean Brown, relict of Willm. Tod, mercht. burges, £12 Scots quy. To James Ker, mercht. burges, £15 Scots qy. To John Reid, mercht. burges, 10s. To John Holmes, taylor burges, 5s. To Agnes Cleland, 5s. To Helen Stewart, 5s. To Nicolas Pottinger, relict of William Naughtie, vintner burges, 10s., all of supply.

May 24*th.*—To George Paterson, litster, 10s. stg., disbursed by him on the funeral of George Whitman, mercht.

June 12*th.*—To Agnes Lawson, relict of George Edgar, mercht. burges, 5s. sterg., of supply. To Janet Kedder, daur. of the deceased William Kedder, late Deacon of the ffleshers, 5s. stg., of supply. To Margt. Johnston, relict of John Sinclair, mercht., £20 Scots, for necessarys to Margt. Sanders, daur. of the deceased Joseph Sanders, mercht. burges, in respect she will be no more troublesome to the good town.

June 19*th.*—To John Penman, elder, goldsmith, to be paid by the City Thesr. to Edward Penman, goldsmith, £15 Scots qy. till the said John Penman be received into the Trinity Hospital.

June 21*st.*—To Isobell Dunbar, relict of John Susan, gunsmith burges, 5s. stg. of supply.

Aug. 23*d.*—To Grace Jamieson, relict of Andrew Robertson, chirurgeon, 10s., and to Isobell Lamb, relict of Henry Gladstones, mercht. burges, half-a-crown, both of supply.

Sept. 4*th.*—To the above Grace Jamieson, £12 Scots quy. To John Dunbar, late Deacon of the skinners, £3 stg., for furnishing cloaths to Wm. Cleghorn, son to John Cleghorn, late Bailie. To Mary Smith, relict of Joseph Smith, soldier in the City Guard, 10s., supply.

Sept. 11*th.*—To Margt. Hunter, daughter to the deceast Mr George Hunter, minister of the Gospel, burgis and gild brother, 5s. stg., of supply.

Nov. 13*th.*—To Jean Kennedy, relict of Willm. Baptie, burges, seven shillings and sixpence sterg., of supply.

Dec. 6*th.*—To Gilbert Clerk, mercht. 20s. stg., of supply. To Margt. Lockhart, spouse to John Learmonth, mercht. burges, £4 sterg. quay., and that towards the subsisting of her family.

1729.

Feby. 12*th.*—To Jean Fairries, daughter of Willm. Fairries, mercht. burges, ane crown, of supply.

March 21*st.*—To Willm. Gardiner, smith burges, 10s., of supply; and to Jean

Kennedy, relict of Willm. Baptie, baxter burges, ane crown, of supply.

May 23d.—To James Robertson, mercht., 25 merks Scots, towards paying the funeral expenses of Alex. Dick, mercht., being his current qur.'s pension.

1730.

May 8th.—THE SAME DAY James Nimmo, Dean of Guild, gave in an estimate of the expence of some mason work to be done to the roof of St Geil's Church, amounting to £99, 2s., which being read, the Council recommended to the Dean of Guild to cause the work to be done in the most frugal manner.

June 10th.—The Council appointed the Thesr. to give to —— Alison, relict of Hugh Graham, mercht. burges, Ten Shillings, and to Jean Scott, Ten Shillings, all of supply.

July 1st.—The Town Council appoints the Thesr. to give to Mary Draffen, relict of John Rait, mercht., Twenty Shillings sterg., of supply ;

And

Same Day Isobel Bryden, relict of John Home, late Deacon of the bonnetmakers, is enrolled a Pensioner, at £12 Scots quarterly.

July 15th.—Upon an Petition from Hugh Paterson, chirurgeon, grants to him a Pension of £6 sterg., payable quarterly, and which is made paid to Hugh Cleghorn, merchant, for the use of the said Hugh Paterson, under the express condition that he shall not reside or be seen in the town or liberties.

[*Note.*—He is said to be dead on 10th Nov. 1731.]

Aug. 5th.—Pensions continued :—Mary Reith, relict of Robt. Herdman, mercht., £12 Scots; Isobel Alison, relict of Hugh Graham, mercht., £10 Scots; Janet Warrock, relict of John Mason, burges, £10 Scots quarterly.

Aug. 5th.—Supply :—James Cowan, wright burges, £6 Scots.

Aug 5th.—Augmentations :—Elizabeth Binning, relict of James Easton, brewer burges, from £4 to £6 ; Isobel Home, relict of John Stobbo, taylor burges, from £3 to £5 ; George Mitchell, flesher burges, from £4 to £6.

The Committee observed that —— relict of James Somervile, barber burges, *alias* Castel Somever, had for herself £8 quarterly, and for her son 25 merks quarterly. Albeit he is in His Majesty's service, were of opinion her pension be continued and her son's resumed. Approved in council.

Aug. 12*th.*—To Katharine Baillie, relict of Da. Wemyss, mercht., £2, 10s. stg., of supply. To Archd. Howie, Deacon of weavers, £6 Scots, to pay expence of burying John Hutton, pensioner, who died this morning. To John Chiesley, writer, burges, £1 stg., supply.

Aug. 26*th.*—The same day the Council, upon an Petition given in for Agnes Williamson, spouse of Mr Henry Robin, late minister at Burntisland, and lawful daughter to the deceast Mr David Williamson, minister at West Kirk, appointed Mr Ja. Donaldson, City Treasr. to pay to her two guineas to enable her to send her son abroad, and to pay to her a pension of £1 sterg. quarterly.

Sept. 2*d.*—The children of James Murray, skinner, £24 Scots quarterly.

Sept. 9*th.*—Janet Buchanan, relict of Adam Cunningham, stabler burges, 20s. sterg. quarterly.

Nov. 20*th.*—Kathn. Baillie, relict of Da. Wemyss, mercht. burgess, £2, 10s. sterg., of supply.

Dec. 16*th.*—John Chiesley, writer burges, £1 sterg. Wm. Aitken, mercht., 10s. stg.; and to John Brodie, mercht., 10s.

1731.

Jany. 6*th.*—To the relict of John Holmes, taylor burges, £8 Scots towards expence of her husband's funeral.

Jany. 13*th.*—Anna Ritchie, daughter to the deceast John Ritchie, mercht., £15 Scots. Willm. Aitken, mercht. burges, £12 Scots. Isobel Law's pension augmented from £6 to £8 quarterly.

Jany. 27*th.*—Grizel Myrtoun, relict of Mr John Orr, late minr. of the Gospel, Edin., £6 sterg., of supply. The relict of James Somervile, barber, £12 Scots quarterly. Andrew Black, mercht. burges, 5s.; Jean Ferries, 5s.; Agnes Scott, daughter to the deceast Gideon Scott, mercht. burgess, 5s.

Feby. 3d.—Kathn. Baillie, relict of Da. Wemyss, mercht., £2, 10s. sterg.; and to
     James Brodie, mercht., £6 Scots, of supply.

Feby. 24th.—To Adam Young, burges, labourer at the Park, £6, supply, and to
     Robt. Dickson, weaver burges, £6 Scots, supply. Mary Dickson,
     lawful daur. of Geo. Dickson, Deacon of the taylors, her pension
     of £7 Scots quarterly continued.

March 3d.—To Baillie James Seton, which he advanced by the Co.'s order, for
     cloaths to Christian Riddel, 19s. 3d. stg.

March 17th.—To Andrew Miller, for supply, £6 Scots; John Murray, cordner,
     £3 Scots; William Cleghorn, mercht., £2 Scots, supply.

March 24th.—Augmented the pension of Margaret Todrig, daughter lawful of
     Alex. Todrig, burges, from £4 to £5 quarterly.

March 31st.—To James Bruce, 10s.; and to Christian Riddel, 5s. stg., present
     supply.

     THE COUNCIL with the EXTY. DEACONS appointed the Treasurer
     to repair the CHARITY WORKHOUSE forthwith.

     Note.—This is Paul's Work Hospital at foot of Leith Wynd, and it is
     presumed that some hundred Pounds would be expended, as it was a
     recepticle for the Poor untill the Charity Workhouse was opened in
     1744; and persons of the most respectable class were admitted.

April 7th.—The relict of Tweedie, labourer, that died in the Town's service,
     £6 Scots, of supply; and to Geo. Batherstone, feltmaker burges,
     £6 Scots, of supply. To William Stalker, mercht., £6 Scots, of
     supply; and to Agnes Angus, £12 Scots, of supply, to defray
     her expence to Hull, and rescinds her pension. Agnes Heart's
     pension augmend. from £3 to £6. She is widow of Archd.
     Baird, walker. John Simpson, mercht., £48 Scots, of pension.

April 21st.—Act. for furnishing cloaths to Thos. Spence, son to Patrick
     Spence, burges weaver, during his apprenticeship, which is for
     5 years. Adam Young, caulseylayer, £3 Scots, supply. To
     Deacon Lawson, for defraying the funeral expenses of Wm.
     Burd, weaver, £6 Scots.

May 19th.—Mrs Clark, £1 sterg., of supply; and to James Brodie, £6 Scots likewise, as supply. And Treasr. to pay to Thomas Riddell, white-iron smith, £3 sterg., to enable him to carry himself and children to London.

May 23d.—To Jean Ferries, a poor woman, of supply, 5s. stg. To Mary Simpson, a poor woman, 10s. stg., of supply.

July 28th.—James Foord, mercht., £1, 10s. sterg., supply, to defray his expence in London, but not to be paid till he is going aboard of the ship wherein he is to have his passage.

Aug. 4th.—LIST OF NEW PENSIONERS, payl. to Lammas 1731, viz.,—Jean Robertson, relict of John M'Rabie, for her two children, one 10 years and the other 4 years old, £8. Agnes Hog, relict of Mathew M'Ewan, beddel, £10. Helen Trotter, relict of John Smith, stabler, £6. Thomas Thomson, founder burges, £6. Mary St Clair, relict of George Baldeston, burges, £3. Mary Smith, relict of John Brown, mercht., £5. Janet Tait, relict of Alexr. Murehead, baxter, £6. Janet Beal, relict of Robert Bruce, for her two children, the one 7 and the other 5 years, £6. Bethea Finlay, relict of James Ball, cooper, £4. Elizabeth Harlaw, relict of Robert Dickson, weaver, £3. Mary M'Kinnon, relict of Jas. Brown, taylor, £4. Alison Douglas, daur. of Stephen Douglas, mercht. burges, £6. Jean Hadden, for herself and daughter, at present being infirm, £3. Isobel Bell, daur. of Andrew Bell, wheelwright, £3. Barbary Hay, relict of James Swan, candlemaker, £3. Barbara Gray, relict of George Ker, stabler, £6—in all, £82 Scots.

Aug. 6th.—Janet Tait, relict of Alex. Muirhead, her pension augmented (as established by the last day's minutes) to £10 quarterly.

Aug. 11th.—Mary Hamilton, spouse to Alex. White, wigmaker, £10 Scots, of supply, to defray her expence to carry her from this place, and stops further payment of any more pension to her, and to be intimated. To Helen Scott, daur. of Wm. Scott, mercht. burges, £3 Scots, of supply. John Mossman, son of the deceased George Mossman, stationer burges, £12 Scots of pension quarterly.

Aug. 18th.—Katharin Edward, daur. of the deceased Alex. Edward, taylor, £12

Scots of pension quarterly. Archd. Heron, sometime Deacon of the cordiners, £15 Scots qrterly.

Aug. 25th.—Margt. Letstere, relict of Robt. Robertson, baxter burges, augments her pension of £4 quarterly to £8.

SEPTEMBER SUPPLIES.

To Isobel Johnston, £6 Scots; and to Alison Walker, £3 Scots. To Janet Hall, in behalf of James Leishman's four children, £6 Scots; and to Mary Moubray, £6 Scots, as supply.

Oct. 13th.—John Anderson, 10s. stg., as supply.

Oct. 27th.—Jean Lockhart, relict of Papelhall, 10s. sterg., of supply, to carry her to London.

Nov. 3d.—William Smith, coachman, £6 Scots, as supply.

Nov. 10th.—Treasurer allowed to take credit for £1, 10s., as a quarter's pension due at Marts. next to Hugh Paterson, deceased. And for £5 sterg. paid to Mrs Wemyss, as half a year's pension and at preceding Lammas last. But discharges payment of her pension hereafter, while she resides in the Abbey.

Nov. 17th.—Ann Hamilton, relict of John Murray of Arthurston, late one of the Captains of Town Guard, £25 Scots quarterly. Rachel Rutherford, relict of James Campbell, taylor, £3 Scots, supply.

Nov. 24th.—Mary Hamilton, spouse to Alex. White, wigmaker, £12 Scots, to defray her expences to London, but the same to stop.

Dec. 1st.—Grizel Myrton, relict of Mr John Orr, late minister of the Gospel of this city, £5 sterg., of supply, in respect of the present distress of her family. Ann Paterson, relict of Alex. Edgar, chyrurgeon burges, £1 sterg. quarterly during pleasure.

Dec. 29th.—James Hamilton of Orbiston, B. & G. B., £2 sterg., of supply.

1732.

Jany. 5th.—Helen Scott, daur. of William Scott, mercht. burges, 10s. sterg., of supply, to carry her to Dumfries.

Jany. 12th.—Thomas Whitelaw, sadler, £10 sterg., of supply; and to Janet Adam, his servant, 20s. sterg., in consideration of the loss they sustained at the late fire, West Bowhead, on 4th Jany. inst. Robt. Anderson, burges, £3 Scots, of supply. And to Sarah Cuningham, £3 Scots, supply, to help to carry her to Dumfries.

Jany. 19th.—James Henderson, mercht. B., 5s. sterg.

Feby. 2d.—John Grant, elder, mercht. B., £12 Scots.

SUPPLIES.

Feby. 2d.—Adam Grindly, smith, 5s. stg. Marion Paterson, relict of James Lawrie, baxter burges, 5s. stg.; and James Stewart, carrier burges, 5s. stg.

Feby. 9th.—Katharin Baillie, relict of David Wemyss, mercht. B., £30 Scots, of pension. John Blair, mercht., master of John's Coffee House, £1 stg., for providing cloaths to Elizth. Chrystie, daur. to the deceast Robt. Chrystie, mercht. B. Mrs Jean Menzies, relict of Wm. Hamilton, £1 stg., to enable her to return to England.

Feby. 16th.—James Wallace, B., £1 stg. qrtly.

March 1st.—Wm. Clerk, Deacon of the taylors, £15 Scots quarterly, for the use of Christian Lawson, daur. to John Lawson, taylor B., disordered in her mind, during pleasure. Robt. Mitchell, smith, and spouse, 15s. sterg. Elizabeth Gillespie, relict of Pat. Fyffe, bower burges, £6 quarterly.

March 8th.—Henry Wilson, late Dn. of masons, £18 Scots quarterly.

March 15th.—Christian Elder, relict of John Ray, silk weaver, 15s. sterg., supply.

March 22d.—The pension given to Wm. Braidwood, brewer, to be paid to Geo. Livingston, one of the under clerks of session, for behoof of said Wm. and family. David Alison, cordner, 10s. stg., supply. John Crawfurd, skinner B., £8 Scots quartly.

April 12th.—John Dalgliesh, D. of hammermen, 10s. stg., to help to defray the expences of Margt. Watson, daur. of the deceast Jo. Watson, pewtherer B., for burial; and to John Chiesly, writer to the Signet, £1 stg., of supply.

April 19th.—Agnes Scott, grandchild to James Angus, skipper B., 10s. stg., of supply.

May 3d.—Mary Duncan, spouse to Patrick Muirhead, mercht. burges, £3 Scots supply.

May 24th.—Elizabeth Seton, *alias* Morton, relict of James Seton, late Janitor of College, £15 Scots quarterly.

PENSIONS AUGMENTED.

Janet M'Intosh, relict of Robt. Smellie, from 3 to 6—£3. Marion Kello, relict of Robt. Kello, from 4 to 6—2. Margt. Paterson, relict of James Laurie, from 4 to 6—2. Marion Cockburn, relict of Wm. Reid, baxter, from 4 to 6—2. Thos. Brown, smith, from 8 to 10—2. Mary Bruce, relict of Henry Spittle, bookbinder, for behoof of her son, from 6 to 7—1. Grizel Stenhouse, relict of Pat. Thornton, hatter, from 4 to 5—1. James Glen, wright burges, from 3 to 5—(*sic*) 1.

PENSIONS RESCINDED.

Agnes Robertson, relict of John Gibson, late Dn. of bonnet-makers, had £6 quartly, but rescinded in respect she is married. Katharin Edward, six pounds rescinded, because preferred to the Hospital.

SUPPLYS.

Christian Watson, an old gentleman, £6. Janet Mitchell, £3. Mrs Ramage, £3. Elizabeth Veitch, £3.

May 31st.—Ann Campbell, relict of Alex. Somervill, writer, £15 Scots, being the quarter's aliment due by the deceast James Seatón, late Janitor to College. Christian Patullo, relict of Wm. Young, baxter B., 10s. stg. To Jean Weir, widow of James Abell, taylor B., and Janet Weir, daur. to Alex. Weir, taylor B., £12 Scots each quarterly.

June 21st.—Baillie Seaton, for the use of Wm. Dick, mercht., £1, 10s. ster., supply.

July 19th.—Robt. Yule, mercht., 5s. stg., of supply; and to Jean Lockhart, a poor woman, and two children, to carry them to Innerlochy. Grizel Morton, relict of Mr John Orr, sometime minister of the Gospel in this city, £5 stg., supply.

Aug. 30th.—Wm. Braidwood, brewer, £12 Scots, of supply; and Christian Riddel, daur. of Alex. Riddel, mercht. B., £3 Scots.

Sept. 20th.—Janet Tait, relict of Thomas Shoarswood, taylor B., £10 Scots quarty.

Oct. 11th.—Henry Waterston, sometime Deacon of the weavers, and his spouse, two old people, £15 Scots quarterly pension.

Nov. 8th.—To Marjory Young, £12 Scots, to enable her to pay her debt, that she may not be distressed for the same in Trinity Hospital.

Nov. 15th.—Thomas Brown, smith, £12. Isobel Low, relict of Wm. Haigs, hatter, £12.

PENSIONS AUGMENTED.

Barbara Gray, relict of George Ker, mercht., from 6 to £8. Bessie Dempster, relict of Wm. Turnbull, baxter, from 6 to £8. Agnes Fleming, from 5 to £7. Robert Simpson, from 6 to £8. Marion Ferguson, relict of Ninian Anderson, cordner, from 6 to £7. Margaret Hogg, relict of Wm. Barclay, late Deacon of baxters, from 6 to £10. Robt. Anderson, from 6 to £10. Elizabeth Clerk, from 5 to £6. Janet Swan, from 6 to £8.

SUPPLIES.

Jane Torie, daur. of Robt. Torie, taylor, £12, payl. to Ja. Nimmo, late Dn. of taylors, for her behoof. Adam Rae, son to Colonel Rae, £1, 10s. stg. Edward Wallace, writer, £12 Scots. Alison Baptie, relict of Hugh Cook, burges, 10s. stg.; and James Pewtherer, taylor burges, £12 Scots.

Nov. 22d.—BAILLIE ROBERT LINDSEY reported from the Committee on Public Works, that they having inspected the several tradesmen's accompts relative to the reparations made by George Miller, merchant in Edinburgh, expended by him in repairing the Charity Workhouse, in the New Greyfriars Yard, in consequence of a Contract betwixt the Good Town and the said Geo. Miller, dated the 1st of September 1731 years; and they having also inspected the said reparations themselves: ffand that the said George Miller has expended more than the sum of Forty Pounds sterg. upon the said reparations; and that the reparations made are profitably and most usefully done, and laid out by him, and that he ought to be lawfully exonered by the Council of the forty pounds stg. allowed to him by the foresaid contract; and to which sum the Committee were of opinion the said reparations should be restricted—As the Report bears: WHICH having been considered by the Council, they with the Extra-Deacons approved thereof; and do hereby restrict the above reparations to the sum of Forty Pounds sterg., and Exoners and Discharges the said George Miller, his heirs, executors, or assignees, of the said sum and reparations above mentioned—prestable on him by the said contract. And thir presents are declared to be an sufficient warrant.

Nov. 29th.—The Council allows Mr Maitland, old treasurer, to take credit in his general Accompts for six guineas depursed (*sic*) by him, by the concurrence and consent of the Lord Provost and Magistrates, upon a stranger who was found in very lamentable and extraordinary circumstances. To the children of the deceast James Seton, Janitor of the College, £40 Scots.

Dec. 13th.—To John Johnston, burges, 5s. stg.; and to Agnes Waldie, relict of Magnus Black, vintner burges, 5s., of supply. To Elizabeth Tarras, relict of John Kello, mercht. burges, £12 Scots quarterly.

1733.

Jany. 10th.—Deacon Howie, £4 Scots.

Jany. 17th.—The Council, upon an Petition from Rachel Currie, daughter to the deceast James Currie, sometime Provost of Edinburgh, appointed Thomas Dick, present Dean of Guild, and his successors in office, to pay to her during the Council's pleasure Fifty merks Scots quarterly, beginning the first quarter's payment thereof at the term of Candlemas next, whereanent these presents shall be a warrant.

Feby. 7*th.*—Janet Hall, relict of James Wallace, baxter burges, twenty shillings stg., of supply.

Feby. 14*th.*—James Hamilton, writer, twenty shillings sterg., of supply.

PENSIONS.

Mr John Anderson, merchant, twelve pounds. Isobel Johnston, daughter to —— Johnston, shoarmaster in Leith, £12.

AUGMENTATIONS.

Elizabeth Harlaw, relict of Robt. Dickson, sometime Deacon of the weavers, from £3 to £6. Janet Blacklaw, relict of David Pinkerton, stabler burges, from £4 to £5. Janet Carmichael, daughter of James Carmichael, merchant burges, from £3 to £5. William Fleming, taylor burges, from £4 to £6. Marion Sinclair, relict of George Batherston, feltmaker, from £3 to £6. Isobel Dunbar, relict of William Wright, weaver, from £3 to £6. Andrew Young, merchant, from £7 to £10. John Anderson, cordner, from £8 to £10.

Feby. 28*th.*—Christian Riddle, £6 Scots, of supply.

March 7*th.*—Helen Anderson, relict of Robert Middleton, merchant, £8 Scots, of supply.

March 14*th.*—Catharin Dallas, a poor woman, £3 Scots, as supply.

April 4*th.*—To widow Mitchelson, £3; and to Mary Ramsay, £6 Scots, both as supply.

May 2*d.*—John Chiesly, writer, £1 stg.

May 30*th.*—Elizabeth Taylor, relict of Geo. Bell, stationer burges, £12. Jean Maitland, relict of James Hay, merchant burges, £12. Mary Macpherson, £12, of supply. To William Chrystie, to enable him to carry away himself and children to England.

June 6*th.*—Charles Telfer, late Baillie, £5 sterling quarterly. Mr Duncan Willison, £12 Scots, of quarterly pension. Jean Mitchell, relict of Nicol Mason, merchant in Leith, £3 Scots, supply.

June 13*th.*—Captain James Ker, taylor, £18 Scots quarterly.

July 18*th.*—To Robert Ross, writer, for John Seton, merchant, £2 Scots, of supply.

T

Aug. 8th.—Marion Bogle, relict of Alex. Pearson, stabler, £7. Isoble Allan, daughter to Andrew Allan, skinner, £6. Anna Logie, relict of John Young, brewer, £6. John Chalmers, merchant, £10. Janet Petrie, relict of Francis Park, £5. Jean Davidson, relict of Alex. Graham, taylor, £7. Marion Morrison, relict of Wm. Brown, wright, £7. Isoble Scott, relict of James Johnston, £6. Thos. Clerk, wigmaker, £6. Bethia Gibson, relict of Thomas Riddle, £6. Andrew Ker, son to the deceased Wm. Ker, merchant burges, £12 Scots; and rescinds his pension of eight pounds, payable by the Kirk Treasurer. Janet Thomson, relict of Wm. Henderson, from five to £7. Helen Thomson, relict of Wm. Scott, from £6 to £8. Janet Ramsay, relict of John Ramsay, from six to eight pounds.

Aug. 15th.—Elizabeth Currie, relict of Robert Smith, merchant burges, £15 Scots qarty.

Sept. 12th.—Christian Morison, spouse to James Carmichael, barber, two guineas, of supply, to carry her to London to her husband ; and to pay to John Din, of supply, for the use of Mary Ramsay, two guineas.

Sept. 24th.—Elizabeth Hope, £12 Scots, of supply.

Sept. 26th.—To George Miller, merchant in Edinr., £40 sterg., to enable him to make alterations and reparations in the Charity Workhouse, conform to contract. To Bailie Archd. Wallace, £3 sterg., to be by him applied for the behoof of Janet Henry, spouse to John Laing, mercht. burges, and her three small children ; as also to give to Bailie Crockat, ten shillings sterg., for behoof of Rachel Scott, daughter to Thos. Scott, merchant burges.

Nov. 21st.—Christian Riddle, daughr. to Alex. Riddle, mercht. burges, £3 sterg. Marion Wright, relict of Wm. Davidson, barber burges, one pound sterg., of supply ; and to John Seton, wigmaker burges, £1, 1s., of supply, with this certification, as he is able and capable to yearn his bread, that he is to be no further burdensome to this city.

Nov. 28th.—Robert Stewart, writer burges, is provided with cloathing to his two children, not exceeding two pounds 10s. sterg., to enable them to go to Georgia.

Dec. 19th.—To James Ker, mercht., £1, 10s. stg., supply, as also to give to Grizel Napier, relict of Robt. Bruce, skinner and burges, twenty shillings stg., of supply ; and to James M'Kenzie, 10s. stg., for the above purpose. Treasurer Blackwood is authorised to cause provide cloaths to James Campbell, son to John Campbell, mercht., to the extent of fourty shillings sterg., and appointed the like sum once in the two years to be applied by the City Treasurer for the time being, for cloaths to the said James during the Council's pleasure.

1734.

Jany. 2d.—To James Forrest, coachman, £3 sterg., of charity, in respect of his indigent condition, and that he is to be no more troublesome to the City.

Feby. 13th.—On report from the committee for the poor, pensions to the following persons, viz.:—Marjory Buchanan, relict of Cornl. Miln, wright, eight   Scots, to enable her to pay the funeral charges of Euphem. Buchanan, relict of James Clerk, wright burges, her sister.

PENSIONS AUGMENTED.

Laurance Kyll, weaver, from 6 to £9. Elizabeth Tallie, daughr. to James Taillie, cordner burges, from 4 to £6. Christian Reoch, relict of George Inch, burges, from 6 to £8. Christian Spittle, relict of Wm. Young, baxter, from £4 to £6. Christian Blair, daugh. of John Blair, clothier, from £3 to £6. Robert Simpson, burges, from £8 to £9. Margt. Moodie, relict of John Young, locksmith, from £4 to £6. Isoble Spence, relict of James Reid, stabler burges, from 4 to £5.

March 4th.—David Alison, son to James Alison, white iron smith, £8 Scots, supply.

March 27th.—Wm. Chrystie, £1 stg., supply.

April 10th.—Alex. Baillie, son to the deceased Alex. Baillie, burges of this city, a pension of £5 sterg. yearly, for a term of four years, to enable him to attend on his education.

April 24th.—Marion Heart, relict of Thos. Herron, wright burges, £4; and to James Wood, merchant burges, £4 sterg. each yearly.

May 1st.—Thomas Rutherford, carter burges, fourty shillgs. sterg., of supply; and to pay to James Robertson, fourty shillgs. sterg., as above.

May 22d.—Margt. Scott, relict of James Keir, mercht. burges, £12 Scots. Christian Minniman, relict of Alex. M'Gill, mercht. burges, £12 Scots. Willm. Crooks, for his son David Crooks, £3 stg., to furnish him with cloaths, and to pay him eighteen pound Scots, of 'quarterly pension. Upon considering a petition for John Seton, barber and wigmaker burges, appointed Alex. Blackwood, city treasurer, to pay six guineas to Baillie James Seton, for the use of the said John Seton, to be applied to enable him to follow furth his trade, the said John Seton being to be no farther burdensome to this city. In respect that the Dean of Guild has gone to London, and that the old Dean of Guild is valitudenera, appointed Robert Montgomery Guild Counciller to preside in the Guild Court in absence of the Dean of Guild; and

May 31st.—Thomas Young, old Treasurer, £5 sterg., to be given by him to Christian Sandilands, relict of Thos. Temple, merchant, to enable her to earn her bread without being farther burdensome to the town; and to give to James Littlejohn, stabler, £1, of supply.

June 12th.—Wm. Hawthorn, forty shillings sterg., of supply. The Council appointed the Dean of Guild, and his council, to admit and receive John Hume, coachmaker, to be burges and Guild brother of this city, by right of Alex. Home, writer, his ffather, burges and Guild brother thereof, dispensing with the dues for good services.

July 10th.—Robert Smith Skinner, £2, 10s. sterg., of supply, in respect of his distressed condition.

Aug. 2d.—James Hamilton, late of Orbiston, writer in this city, £1 sterg., of supply. James Littlejohn, stabler burges, £5 Scots.

AUGMENTATIONS.

Thomas Clewchs, pension augmented to 18 tet. Margt. Gouderd, daugh. of Peter Gouderd, feltmaker burges, £12 Scots, of supply.

Sept. 4th.—Elizabeth Ker, relict of the deceased Mr Wm. Abercrombie, late minister of the Gospel in this city, forty shillings sterg. quarterly, for support. Thomas Wallace, baxter burges, 10s. sterg., supply.

Sept. 11th.—Wm. Braidwood, brewer burges, 10s., of supply, sterg.

Oct. 23d.—George Marr, late keeper of the city bells, £15 Scots quarterly, until he be otherwise provided for. George Grant, late precenter of the New Kirk, £3 stg., of supply.

PENSIONS AUGMENTED.

Nov. 13th.—Jane Tait, relict of Thos. Shoarswood, taylor burges, from £10 to £12 Scots. Margt. Litster, relict of Robt. Robertson, baxter burges, from £8 to £12. Grizel Napier, relict of Robert Bruce, glover, from £8 to £12. Grizel Myrton, relict of Mr John Orr, late Minister of the Gospel in Edinr., £5 sterg., of supply. As also to give to Mr Samuel Arnot, printer, £6 Scots, as aforesaid.

Nov. 20th.—Katherine Wymess, relict of Robt. Kay, baxter, £5 Scots, of supply. Mary Turnbull, 10s. sterling, of supply; and to Jane Lockhart, 10s. stg., of supply, to defray her expence to Innerlochy. To Adam Robertson, baxter, 10s. stg.; and to Thos. Rutherford, baxter, 20s. stg., as above. Isobel Elias, relict of the deceased Wm. Braidwood, brewer burges, £1 stg., of pension, quarty. Andrew M'Alwraith and Wm. M'Vye, soldiers in the City Guard, each of them 10s. sterg., in respect they got several hurts and bruizes in a mob.

Dec. 13th.—Isoble Stewart, relict of Charles Cash, bookbinder burges, £9 Scots, of supply. Patrick Mathie, officer to the new gift, because of his age and valdisposition, being devested of that office, obtains £3 stg., for buying of cloaths to him, and £21 Scots of quary. pension.

1735.

Jany. 8th.—Wm. Crooks, mercht., forty shillings sterg., of supply, and to Andw. M'Alfreer, 10s. sterg., as above.

Jany. 15th.—Sussanah Carfrae, relict of Alex. Inglis, mercht., £1 stg., supply. . James Lamb, mercht. burges, £1, 10s. stg., supply.

New Pensions.

Feby. 14th.—Wm. Crooks, mercht., £25 Scots. Thos. Rutherford, baxter, £18 Scots. Mary Turnbull, daugh. of Robert Turnbull, mercht. burges, augmented from £10 to £15 Scots.

Supplies.

John Millar, taylor burges, £6 Scots. Margt. Arnot, daug. of Mr Sam. Arnot, burges, £6 Scots. David Leslie, mason burges, £9 Scots. James Ainslie, hatter burges, £6 Scots.

Feby. 28th.—Charles Hunter, merchant, £2 stg., supply. James Lothian, mercht., £1 stg., do., and James Bruce, white-iron smith burges, 10s., do.

April 16th.—Margt. Baptie, a poor woman, £1 stg., supply.

April 30th.—Margt. Jackson, relict of Nathl. Walker, town officer, 10s. stg. ; and to Margt. Watt, daugh. to James Watt, taylor burges, 10s., supply. . Janet Chatto, relict of Jno. Scott, burges and Guild brether, £12 Scots pension.

Augmentations.

May 21st.—Wm. Crooks, mercht., from £25 to £30 Scots.

Supplies.

The children of Jno. Reid, mercht. burges, 40s. ster. John Burns, upholsterer, and family, 20s. stg. James Robertson, baxter, £9 Scots, of supply ; and to James Lothian, stabler burgess, £12 Scots, do. Andw. Black, mercht., £12 Scots, do.

June 4th.—Margt. Todrig, 10s. stg. ; and to Agnes Livingston, relict of Alex. Livingston, grave maker, 15s. stg., both supply.

June 11th.—John Constable, wigmaker burgess, £2 stg., supply.

June 18th.—Margt. Wallace, 10s. stg., as the rent of her house, for her services

in cleaning the Council house. Christian Craw, widow of
Charles Duncan, goldsmith, £2, 10s., supply; and to Cathn.
Campbell, widow of Mr Alex. Buchan, Minister at St Kilda, a
guinea, as supply.

July 9th.—Thomas Anderson, lawful son to the deceased, Alex. Anderson,
mercht. and late baillie of this city, £4 stg. yearly, to be bestowed
for cloaths to him—he being much disordered in his senses, and
that the same shall be paid into some proper hand who shall see
it faithfully bestowed for above purpose.

July 16th.—Robert Anderson, burges, £12 Scots, supply; and to Elizabeth
Frew, relict of James Marr, mill wright, £1, 10s. stg., supply, to
enable her to travel to London.

Aug. 6th.—Mrs Kyll, to enable her to go to her husband at York, £3, 3s.; and
to   Ewing, daugh. to Wm. Ewing, taylor, 15s. sterg., supply.

PENSIONS AUGMENTED.

Aug. 29th.—Janet Henry, spouse to John Laing, mercht., for herself and children,
from £9 to £12. Marion Wright, relict of Wm. Davidson, barber,
from £9 to £12.

SUPPLIES.

Elizabeth Neil, relict of William Fedes, £6 Scots. James Lamb,
mercht., £12, 12s. Scots. Margt. Preston, relict of John M'Phail,
£12, Scots. Rosana White, relict of John Mowbray, wright, £12
Scots, payable to James Syme, senior, for her behoof.

NEW PENSIONS.

James White, fflesher burgess, £6 Scots. James Ainslie, hatter
burges, £6 Scots. Bessy Arbuckles, daugh. to John Arbuckles,
skinner burgess, £4 Scots. Elizabeth Calderwood, relict of John
Greig, merchant burgess, £4 Scots. Christian Holmes, relict of
John Constable, barber burges, £6 Scots. Agnes Livingstone,
relict of Alex. Livingston, baxter burges, for herself and two
children, £6 Scots. Helen Handyside, relict of Leonard Thin,
mercht., £6 Scots. Magdn. Graham, relict of Robert Nimmo,

burges, for her children's behoof, £8 Scots. Mary Paterson, daughter to Andw. Paterson, candlemaker burges, £4 Scots. Wm. Cunningham, skinner burges, £8. Margt. Carmichael, relict of James Brown, white iron smith, £5 Scots. Margt. Baptie, daughter to Wm. Baptie, baxter, £6. Sarah Hogg, relict of Wm. Baillie, writer burges, £6. Agnes Hodge, relict of James Boyd, fflesher, £4 Scots. James Hamilton of Orbiston, £1 sterg., supply; and to James Smith, shoemaker, £1, ditto. The Relict of John Robertson, burges, 10s. stg. James Lind, burges, 15s. sterg. Wm. Currie, wright burges, 10s. do. Margt. Pringle, 10s. do. Agnes Halliburton, relict of Wm. Montgomery, burges, 20s. do., and Margt. Paterson, 20s. do., to be paid to Baillie Heriot for her behoof.

Sept. 10th.—Christian Craw, relict of Charles Duncan, goldsmith, to pay her during the Council's pleasure, annually £6 stg., and £4 stg. for Duncan her son; the pension to her son to endure only for a term of 5 years. John M'Vicar, late soldier in the City Guard, a quarterly pension of £12 Scots, being granted only in respect of his service for thirty-seven years. Mrs Campbell, for the use of John Campbell, printer, £1 stg., of supply.

Sept. 24th.—Robert Paterson, skinner, 15s. sterg., of supply.

Oct. 15th.—Ann Smith, relict of James Smith, mason, £30 Scots, of quarterly pension. Isoble Sharp, relict of George Fletcher, cook burgess, 10s. sterling, of supply. Agnes Bowie, relict of John Reid, printer burges, 10s. sterg.; and to Colin Rind, mason, 20s. sterg., both of supply.

Nov. 12th.—Margt. Falconer, £1 stg., of supply. Willm. Hawthorn, mercht., £1 sterg., supply; and to Jane Clerk, Spouse of John Seton, mercht., £2 sterg., of supply, to enable her to cloath her son, and put him to an apprenticeship.

NEW PENSIONS.

Nov. 19th.—Charles Hunter, mercht. burges, £12 Scots. Christian Campbell, relict of Archd. Campbell, and daughter to Thos. Campbell, sometime Deacon of the ffleshers, £15. Katharin Denoon, relict of Robert Finlay, minister of the Gospel at Rosemarkins, burges and Gild brother, £12.

PENSIONS AUGMENTED.

Katharine Ramsay, relict of James Yorgston, goldsmith, from 6 to £12 Scots. Janet M'Intosh relict of Robert Smelie, taylor, 10 to £12. Margt. Campbell, relict of Wm. Tock, barber burges, from 8 to £12. Mary Stewart, relict of Mr Thos. Buchanan, writer burges, from £6 to £12.

SUPPLIES.

William How, glover, for the behoof of the children of John Reid, mercht., £12. John Hunter, cooper, £12. Ann Mitchell, relict of James Witherspoon, brewer burges, £9. Relict of John Mowbray, wright, and her three children, £12 payable to James Syme, Jun., for their behalf. Marion Lauder, daur. to Wm. Lauder, Doctor of Medicine, £6. James Aikenhead, son to Davd. Aikenhead, burges and Gild brother, £3. Janet Ker, relict of Alexr. Armstrong, barber, £6. Helen Thomson, relict of Alexr. Moffat, £9. Katharin Walker, daughter to John Walker, mercht. burges, £6. Alex. Brown, skinner, for his children, £9.

AUGMENTATION.

Isoble Elliss, relict of Wm. Braidwood, brewer burges, from 12 to £15 Scots. On account of the demission of John Duncan, Sen., mercht., from the office of Session Clerk of this City, authorise the Dean of Gild to pay him a pension of 400 mks. By an Act of Council, dated 24th May 1727—John Duncans, Senr. and Jun., late Clerks to the Kirk Sessions, were burdened with a pension of £200 Scots to Mary Purdie, relict of John Lenox, glover, and considering that the aforsaid Act is now rescinded, whereby the said pension is determined, and that said Mary Purdie's circumstances are such that she may want some relief from this City,

U

Therefore do appoint Thomas Young, City Treasurer, and his successors in office, to pay to the said Mary Purdie during the Council's pleasure, £10 stg. quarterly, and thir presents, with her receipt, shall be a Warrant.

Dec. 10th.—Upon Petition from Marion Finnie, Relict of John Young, baxter burges, appoint the City Treasurer to pay her quarterly sa pension of £60 Scots. To Alison Stewart, 5s. sterg., of supply; and to Rachel Rutherfoord, Relict of James Campbell, burges, 5s. sterg., of supply.

Dec. 17th.—To Grizel Myrton, Relict of Mr John Orr, late minister of the Gospel in this city, £5 sterg., of supply. To Andrew Buchan, mercht., £9 Scots, of supply. To David Hutton, taylor burges, £15 Scots, of supply; as also to Janet Bull, relict of Geo. Brown, mercht. burges, £9 Scots, of supply.

Dec. 26th.—To Wm. Ross and Andw. Black, each of them £1 sterg., of supply.

1736.

Jany. 7th.—Allowed the City Treasurer to take credit in his general accompts for £35, 2s. Scots, disbursed by Archd. Blair in the Council Chamber, to poor people, by order of the Magistrats. Allowed the City Treasurer to pay to Mary Purdie, relict of John Lenox, glover, £2, 10s., being one quarter of her pension in advance.

Jany. 14th.—Appointed the Treasurer to give to John Campbell, £1 sterg., and to Patrick Gibson, mercht., £1 sterg., both of supply.

Jany. 21st.—To James M'Naught, stocking weaver, £6 Scots, of supply.

Jany. 28th.—Upon considering a petition from Wm. Hopkin, belt maker, appoint Treasurer Young to pay to David Hodge, Deacon of the Hammermen, £5 sterg., to be given by him to the said William Hopkin, to enable him to follow furth proper processes for recovery of an Estate to him belonging, that the City may be relieved of a pension of £4 sterl., granted to the said Wm. Hopkin's spouse. To the Archbishop of Nicosia, 4 guineas, of charity, and to John Rattray, £1 stg., of supply, and to pay towards defraying the burial of Jane Tait, a late pensioner, £6 Scots.

PENSIONS PAYABLE BY THE CITY TREASURER.

Feb. 13*th.*—Margt. Chiesly, relict of Mr Samuel Gray, pror. fiscal of this City, £15 Scots. David Hutton, taylor burges, £16 Scots. Barbara Gray, relict of Geo. Ker, burges, augmented from 8 to £12 do. James Campbell, son to John Campbell, mercht., from 12 to £15 do. Margt. Primrose, Relict of John Parker, stabler, from 14 to £16 do.

SUPPLYS.

James Hamilton of Orbiston, 10s. to be given to Baillie Hamilton for his behoof. Janet Bull, £6 Scots. James Smith, cordner, £6 Scots. William Wilson, cordner, £6 Scots. Jane Campbell, daugh. to John Campbell, burges, £6, payable to William Armstrong, coppersmith, for her behoof. Elizabeth Walker, daughter to John Walker, coppersmith burges, £3 Scots. Considering that Andrew Key has granted a demission of his office of one of the Conjunct Keepers of the Parliament House, in order to provyde a Burges that otherwise would have wanted some relief from this City, and that Magdalen Fleeming, spouse to the said Andrew Key, is daughter to the deceast Sir James Fleming, late Lord Provost of this City, and as such is well entituled to some Relief from this City proportionable in some measure to her condition and circumstances, therefore did, and hereby do appoint, Thomas Young, City Treasurer, and his successors in office, to pay to the said Magdalen Fleeming, dureing her life, £10 sterg., annually by equally quarterly portions, beginning at Whitsunday next. Appointed City Treasurer to pay to the Rev. Mr Mathew Wood, Minister, £12 sterg., to be by him applyed to the relief of Wm. Hutcheson's spouse and children. To pay to Margt. Savage, spouse to Wm. Graham, mercht., during the Council's pleasure, £15 Scots, of quarterly pension. To Robert Douglas, mercht. £12 Scots, as above. To James Simpson, late Dean of Gild, £18 Scots, for the behoof of Thos. Scott, late a waiter at the ports. To Mary Campbell, spouse to John Campbell, poultryman burges,

£12 Scots. To William Hawthorn, mercht., £2 sterling; and to Catharin Crokat, relict of Robert Wilson, mercht. burges, 30s. sterling, all of supply.

Feb. 18*th.*—To Isobel Strachen, £12 Scots, of supply.

Feb. 25*th.*—To David Ffairly, baxter, £5 sterg., of supply.

March 3*d.*—To Wencherlaus Radozze, Polish Bursar in Brown's Mortification, two guineas, to carry him to Holland. To Willm. Moffat, son to John Moffat, hat maker, £9 Scots, of supply. To Margt. Belshes, widow of James Ronaldson, bedle, £6 Scots, of supply.

March 10*th.*—To Janet Walker, spouse to John Haddin, skinner burges, £1 stg., of supply.

March 31*st.*—To Magdalen le Mercies, widow of the deceast Mr Wm. Scott, Professor of Moral Philosophy in the Colledge of this City, £10 stg., of supply.

April 7*th.*—To Agnes Clow, relict of John M'Claren, mercht. burges, £1 sterg., of supply. To Alex. Hay, Ringer of the Tron Kirk bells, 30s. sterg., of supply.

April 21*st.*—To James Robertson, baxter, £1 sterg., of supply.

May 12*th.*—To Robert Simpson, skinner burges, £12 Scots, of supply.

May 28*th.*—The Committee appointed by the Council and Kirk Sessions of this City to audite the accounts of John Grant, late Kirk Treasurer. There was found a balance due to him of £442, 13s. 5¼d., as super expended, which sum ought to be paid to him by the City Treasurer.

PENSIONS.

To John Kilpatrick, mercht. burges, and his spouse, £2 sterg. Mary Campbell, relict of Robert Lightbody, mercht., £1 sterg.

SUPPLYS.

To Mary Piggot, relict of John Laurie, barber burges, in respect she is to leave the place, and her pension of £3 Scots to be rescinded after this quarter, £1 sterg., of supply, to help to transport herself to Greenock. Janet Ker, relict of Alex. Armstrong, wigmaker burges, £1 sterg., of supply. Janet Heriot, daur. to George

Heriot, taylor burges, 10s. sterg., do.   Helen Johngston, daughter to Major Johngston, £1 sterg., of supply.   To Margaret Peggot, relict of Mr John Goodall, Professor of Hebrew in the Colledge of this City, £12 Scots, to enable her to pay a year's rent of her house.   To William Hawthorn, mercht., £12 Scots, of supply.

June 2d.—To John Bell, mercht., £14 sterling, in full of the damage sustained by him in takeing down part of his property which was a great incroachment on the High Street.

June 9th.—To Janet Bull, Relict of William Brown, mercht. burgess, 15s. sterg., and to Agnes Mergton, daughter to Thos. Mergton, 15s. sterg., both of supply.

June 16th.—To David Wallace (wounded at Andrew Wilson's execution), seven shillings.   To John Niven, wounded, 10s. 6d.   To James Philip, 5s., all of supply.   To Margt. Airth, 5s., do., and paid charges of burying James Pinkerton, a boy drowned, and for taking a precognition, and apprehending the mother, suspected of wickedly drowning her said child, £1, 11s. sterling.   To paid charges of burying a child found drowned in a well in the Cowgate, 2s. 7d. stg.   To David Wallace, 10s. sterling, of supply.   To paid for necessarys to Jean Scott, wounded, till cured, £1, 17s. 3d. stg.

June 23d.—To Lillias Cunningham, relict of Alex. Polson, stabler, £1 sterg., of supply.   To John Campbell, late corrector in Mrs Anderson's printing-house, £1 stg., do.   To George Johngston, mercht., £1 sterling, do.   Appointed Thomas Young, City Treasurer, to give to Schach Sibiat, of Berytus in Asia, £7, 9s. stg., of charity.

June 30th.—To expence of Charles Stewart's funeral, 17s. stg.

July 14th.—To Helen Drummond, relict of Chas. Hunter, burges, £1 sterg., of supply ; also to pay to Deacon Hodge, £6 Scots, towards defraying the funeral expence of the deceast Andrew Waddel, Beddal in the Colledge Kirk.

July 28th.—To David Wallace, who was wounded, of supply, 10s. stg.   To Margaret   , who was wounded, fyve shillings—18. Appointed Robert Montgomerie to provide a suit of cloaths, and some shirts, to Alex. Polson, son to the deceast Alex. Polson, stabler-burges, in order to equip him for the sea, that thereby the City may be disburdened of further expence concerning him.

Aug. 4th.—Appointed Thesr. to pay to John Petrie, Servant to Thos. Morison, plaisterer, £1, 10s. sterg., of supply, he having received a dangerous wound in his arm in assisting the City Guard to apprehend ane offender.

Aug. 11th.—To Mary Ronaldson, relict of Jas. Thomson, mercht. burges, from 8 to £12 Scots, supplies, payable by the City Treasurer. John Anderson, fflesher, £6 Scots. Anna Mossman, relict of Wm. Hardie, mercht., £9 do. Mary Armstrong, relict of John Campbell, burges, £24 do. Alex. Guthrie, burges, £6 do. Andrew Buchanan, mercht., payable to his wife for the use of her children, £9 do. Margaret Joysie, daur. to the deceast Alexr. Joysie, burges, £6. Margaret Preston, relict of John M'Phell, taylor burges, £1 sterg., of supply. To Wm. Bruce to see John Anstruther, who was wounded apprehending Christopr. Ffaundie, £1 sterg., of supply.

Sept. 1st.—Allowed Treasurer Young to be creditor in his general accounts for the sum of £45, 3s. 8d., paid by him to the surgeons for cureing the persons wounded in the Grass Mercat, 14th of April last, at the Execution of Andrew Wilson. The Council appoint the Thesr. Young to pay to Wm. Hawthorn, mercht., £1 sterline. To Marion Lauder, 10s. sterg. To Elizabeth Chalmers, relict of Andw. Waddell, beadle, 10s. stg., and to George Johngston, mercht., 10s. sterg., all of supply.

Sept. 8th.—Appointed the City Treasurer to pay to the Treasurer of the West Kirk ten guineas, towards building of a Manse for the Revd. Mr Thomas Pitcairn, one of the Ministers of the said Kirk. Appointed Treasurer Thos. Young, to pay to Robert Inglis, ffiscal in the Council Chamber, £5, 5s. sterg., for his trouble and pains in the precognition anent Robertson's escape, etc.

Sept. 10th.—Allowed Treasurer Young to take credit in his accompts, £10, 13s. sterling, paid by him to the Magistrates as disbursements by them in the Council Chamber.

Sept. 15th.—Also to take credit for £2, 3s. 6d. sterg., of charity money, disbursed as above.

Sept. 22d.—To John Crawford, who was wounded, 5s. sterg. To David Wallace, do., 10s. stg., of supply. To Margt. Airth, of supply, to enable her to go to the North, £1 sterg. To David Wallace, more of supply, he being obliged to stay in the country for his health. To John Shaw, indweller, of supply, £18 Scots.

Oct. 27th.—To Lorentze Detlofsen, commander of the ship "Anna Christiana" of Flensbourgh in Norway, who was shipwrecked upon the Coast of Ireland, 4 guineas, to carry him to his own country; and to Isobell. Arthur, 10s. sterg., of supply.

Nov. 10th.—To Anna Edmonston, relict of George Stewart, bookseller, £18 Scots. To George Paterson, ingraver, pension augmented from 6 to £12 Scots.

SUPPLYS.

To James Smith, burges, £6 Scots. Alex. Chain, burges, £6 do. Alison Stewart, daur. to James Stewart, currier, £6 Scots. Margt. Tod, daur. to Wm. Tod, £3 Scots. Elpeth Robertson, relict of James Crichton, burges, £3 Scots; and to Marion Lauder, daur. of the deceased Doctor Lauder, £1 stg. Marion Inglis, £6 Scots. Elizabeth Chalmers, £6 Scots, all of supply.

Nov. 24th.—Appointed Robert Montgomerie, City Treasurer, to pay to Alex. Davidson, Bookseller, £5, 5s. sterg., to transport himself and family to Georgia, that the City may hereafter be relieved of being furder burdened with them, and also to pay to Michael Anderson, £2, 2s. sterling to carry him abroad, so as that he shall not hereafter be more burdensome, and to be paid only when the Treasurer shall be satisfied that he is to transport himself somewhere abroad.

Dec. 1st.—To Alex. Hay, smith, £9 Scots, and Janet Ker, relict of Alex. Armstrong, burges, £12 Scots, both of supply.

Dec. 8th.—Anne Bell, relict of Wm. Snodgrass, wright burges, £1 sterg., of supply. Mary Mowbray, daughter to the deceased Robert Mowbray, silkweaver burges, 15s. stg., of supply.

Dec. 22d.—The Treasurer to take credit for £3, 5s. stg., disbursed in charity, by George Lindsay, conjunct depute Clerk, by order of the Magistrats. To William Thomson, wright burges, £15 Scots. Alexr. Cowan, schoolmaster, £12 Scots. Janet Bull, relict of Geo. Brown, mercht. burges, £6 Scots. Capt. Clelland, £12 Scots, to be applyed by him for buying cloaths to the children of Roderick Brown, late Turnkey of the Tolbooth.

1737.

Jany. 5th.—Andw. Lawson, barber and wigmaker, £2 stg., of supply.

Jany. 19th.—James Smith, cordner burges, 10s. sterling, of supply.

Jany. 26th.—William Thomson, poultryman, 18s. sterling. Jean Pennicuick, spouse to James Square, flesher, £20 Scots, both of supply.

Feb. 9th.—David Lesly, mason burges, 10s. stg., do.

NEW PENSIONS.

Sarah Cockburn, daughter to the deceast James Cockburn, goldsmith, being blind for forty years past, augmented from 10 to £12 Scots, per quarter. Agnes Smith, relict of John Penman, goldsmith, augmented from 10 to £12 Scots. James Littlejohn, stabler, £12 Scots, for this quarter and no more. Peter Stewart, wigmaker, and his wife, from 9 to £12 Scots. Anna Edmonston, relict of Mr Geo. Stewart, bookseller, an old infirm woman with 3 children, from £18 per quarter to £24 Scots. Janet Stark, relict of John Rannie, mercht., from £9 to £12 Scots.

SUPPLIES.

George Bell, burges, £4 Scots. William Pilmoir, burges, £12 do. John Ross, son to Leonard Ross, glover, £12 Scots. Robert Cuming, mercht., £12 Scots. James Maxwell, cordner burges, £12 Scots.

Feb. 23d.—James M'Naught, stocken weaver, £1 sterg., of supply.

March 11th.—Margaret Hope and her child, 12s. stg. John Campbell, printer, £1 stg. Margt. Lauder, £1 stg., all of supply.

March 23d.—Mrs Rattray, £1 sterg., of supply. Isobel Polson, spouse to William Cuming, fflesher, one guinea, of supply, when the Treasurer shall be satisfied she is to transport herself to London.

April 6th.—Alison Stewart, 10s. stg., of supply. Elizabeth Chalmers, relict of Andw. Waddel, beadle, 10s. stg., do.

April 20th.—Mrs Polson, 15s. sterg., to be by her applied towards buying of cloths for her son, who was lately shipwreckt.

May 12th.—The City Treasurer to take credit in his accompts for the sum of £3, 16s. stg., for charity disbursed in the Council Chamber, by order of the Magistrats.

May 25th.—Appointed Treasurer Montgomery to pay to Wm. Hawthorn, mercht., £1, 18s. sterg., of supply ; and to Jane Brown, relict of Deacon Watterston, weaver, 20s. sterg., of supply.

June 1st.—Janet Thomson, relict of John Knox, mercht., 15s. sterling, and Anna Preston, relict of David Hutton, taylor, 20s. sterg., both of supply. By Act of Council, dated 1st June 1737, proceeding upon a report from the Committee appointed by the Council and Kirk Session of the City to audite the accounts of John English, late Kirk Treasurer, there was found a balance due to him of £671, 1s. 6½½d. sterling, which he had paid to pensioners of the same class as those paid by the City Treasurer. This arose by reason of the decrease of the collections and other poors-funds, and increase of the pensions and supports, &c., and the different Sessions retaining the collections made at their respective kirk doors, &c., whereby the foresaid large balance has arisen due to the said John English. The Council therefore appointed Mr Montgomerie, City Treasurer, to pay to the said Mr English the foresaid balance of £671, 1s. 6½½d. sterling, with interest, from 1st Jany. last till payment.

June 8th.—Anna Hallyburton, relict of Wm. Montgomerie, writer burges, 10s. sterg., of supply.

June 15th.—Mary Burns, widow of John Robertson, poultryman burges, 10s. sterg., of supply.

June 22d.—Catherin Forbes, relict of ——— Durie, £2 sterg., of supply, in such

X

a manner as he shall think proper ; and to John Campbell, printer, £1 sterg., of supply.

Aug. 12th.—Reported by Treasurer Montgomerie that he has paid to John English, late Kirk Treasurer, £671, 1s. 6½½d. stg., with £14, 0s. 10½d. stg., of interest, for which he is allowed to take credit in his general accounts, conform to Act of Council in that behalf, the first of June last.

Aug. 17th.—Appointed Treasurer Montgomerie to pay to George Lindsay, depute clerk, £3, 6s. sterlg., of charity, disbursed by him in the Council Chamber, conform to accompt attested by the Magistrates.

Aug. 19th.—Baillie Stewart delivered in a list of quarterly pensions, to be paid by the City Treasurer, with the Committee's report thereon, whereof the tenor follows :—Margt. Anderson, relict of James Purdie, skinner, £0, 16s. 8d. Isobel Alison, relict of Hugh Graham, £0, 16s. 8d. William Aitken, burges, his three children, 15s. Catherin Baillie, relict of David Wemyss, mercht., £2. Thomas Brown, smith, £1. Thomas Cleugh, mercht., 13s. 4d. Sarach Cockburn, daughter to James Cockburn, mercht., 16s. 8d. Ann Chapman, barber's widow, 20s. James Campbell, a blind lad, 10s. Elizabeth Cowie, relict of Robert Smith, mercht., 20s. William Crooks, mercht., £2, 10s. Christian Craw, relict of Charles Duncan, goldsmith, £1, 10s. Do. for Alexr. Duncan, her son, 20s. Margt. Campbell, relict of William Toack, 15s. Christian Campbell, daughter to Deacon Campbell, flesher, 25s. Margt. Chiesly, relict of Mr Saml. Gray, 20s. Do. for Samuel Gray, her son, 20s. Mary Campbell, relict of Robert Lightbody, mercht., 20s. Janet Chatto, relict of John Scott, mercht., 20s. Janet Dundas, relict of Wm. Dickie, stationer, 20s. Catherine Denoon, relict of Mr Robt. Finlay, minister, 15s. Robert Douglas, payable to Alex. Boswall, 15s. Isoble Ellies, payable to George Livingston, under clerk of session, 20s. Ann Edmonston, relict of George Stewart, bookbinder, 30s. Magdn. Fleeming, daughter to Provost Fleeming, £2, 10s. Margaret Gibson, relict of Wm. M'Millan, flesher, 20s. Barbara Gray, relict of George Ker stabler, 10s. Isoble Gordon, relict of Capt. John Porteous, £3. Magdalen Graham, relict of Robert Nimmo, burges, 20s. Doreatha Houston, relict of James Galloway, 20s. Janet Horsburgh, relict of William Hopkins, 20s. Archd. Herion, cordiner, and late deacon, 25s. Margaret Home, relict of William Mitchell, stabler, £2. Marion Heart, relict of Thomas Herion, 20s. Jane Heriot, relict of John Reid, 20s. Janet Henry, spouse to John Laing, mercht., 20s. Isobella Johnstoun, daughter to ——— Johnstoun, 20s. Andrew Ker, son to the deceased Wm. Ker, mercht., 15s. Elizabeth Ker, relict of Mr William Abercrombie, £1, 10s. John Kilpatrick and his spouse, £1, 10s. Janet Lourie, relict of Alex. Stewart, mercht., 15s. Ann Lindsay, daughter to John Lindsay, mercht., 16s. 8d. John Leslie, mercht. taylor in Edinburgh, 20s. Isobella Low, relict of Wm. Haigs, hatter, 20s. Margaret Litster, relict of Robert Robertson, baxter, 20s. William Mitchell, white-iron smith burges, 10s. Elizabeth Moston, relict of James Seton, college janitor, 20s. Christian Miniman, relict of Alex. M'Gill, 16s. 8d. George Marr, late keeper of the city bells, 20s. Janet M'Intosh, relict of Robert Smellie, taylor, 15s. Grace Napier, relict of Robert Bruce, skinner, and three children, 20s. John Ochiltree, weaver, 25s. Margaret Pringle, relict of John Parker, burges, 16s. 8d. Mary Park, relict of Patrick Buchanan, 10s. Mary Purdie, relict of John Lennox, glover, £2. George Paterson, engraver, 15s. Lilias Robertson, daughter to D: G. Robertson, £1, 15s. Ann Ritchie, daughter to the deceased James Ritchie, 20s. Catharine Ramsay, relict of James Yourston, goldsmith, 20s. Mary Ronaldson, relict of James Thomson, mercht., 15s. Sarah Raith, relict of Robert Steidman, mercht., 20s. Patrick Spence, barber, 10s. Mary Sinclair, spouse to Robert Cameron, bookbinder, 13s. 4d. John Simpson, mercht., 20s. Margaret Scott, relict of James Ker, mercht. taylor, 20s. Isobella Stewart, relict of Charles Cash, bookbinder, 20s. Mary Stewart, relict of Thomas Buchanan, 20s. Ann Smith, relict of Mr James Smith, mason, £1, 13s. 4d. Janet Stark, relict of John Rannie, mercht., 20s. Peter Stewart and his spouse, 20s. Agnes Smith, relict of John Penman, goldsmith, 20s. Dorothea Sommervail, relict of Mr Wm. Haldane, schoolmaster, 20s. Jean Todrig, relict of William Smith, mercht., 16s. 8d. Elizabeth Tait, relict of John Mortimer, barber, 15s. Charles Telfer, late Baillie of Edinburgh, £5. Mary Turnbull, daughter to Robert Turnbull, mercht., £1. Henry Wilson, mason in Edinburgh, £1, 10s. Jean Weir, relict of James Abel, taylor, 20s. Janet Weir, daughter to Alex. Weir, taylor, 20s. Duncan Willison, merchant, £1. Martin Wright, relict of William Davidson, barber, 15s. Mary Finlay, relict of John Young, barber,—amounting in all to ninety-one pounds, one shilling, eightpence sterling.

Edinburgh, August 17th, 1737.—We, the Committee appointed to examine the circumstances and the titles of the quarterly pensions upon the City Treasurer, have, upon a distinct and accurate enquiry, reduced the foresaid number of eighty-two persons to the respective sums opposite to their names, amounting quarterly to the sum of ninety-one pounds, one shilling, eightpence sterling, and we are of oppinion that the city's revenue cannot affoord more, and therefore such as are not contained in this establishment are struck off as not deserving or not compearing; and we are further of oppinion that none are entituled to the city's charity but such as are resideing in the town. (Signed) James Stewart, Baillie; Thomas Heriot, D.G.; Robert Montgomery, James Colhoun, Pat. Ffairly, John Newbiggan—as the said Report bears—which having been considered by the Councill, they, with the Extraordinary Deacons, approved of the said Report, and appointed Robert Montgomery, City Treasurer, and his successors in office, to pay dureing the Councill's pleasure to the fornamed persons the forsaid sums annexed to their respective names, per advance quarterly, begining the first term's payment immediately ffor the quarter commenceing at Lammas last; and ordered that an extract of the forsaid list be delivered to the said City Treasurer, and that he conform himself thereto; and that hereafter no quarterly pensions shall be paid by the City Treasurer, or by his successors, but such as shall be continued in a List or Establishment entered upon Record, and under the subscription of the clerk ; and Resolved and Agreed that hereafter no quarterly pensions shall be continued or granted to any person whose constant residence is not within the royalty. Ordered Treasurer Montgomery to pay an guinea and a half to any skipper who shall transport to London Isoble Polson, spouse to Wm. Cuming, flesher, with her child, on a certificate of said transportation by the skipper after his return. Mr Robert Blackwood, late a Baillie of Edin., was chosen into the office of collector of both cess and watch money. He was short time in office, but had great commendation from the Councill for his great labour and attention in the exercise of that important trust ; and his books for both collections were made up to the day of his death, so that he had the labour without reaping the benifit of his salary for that current year. It was therefore resolved and agreed by the Councill that the salary and emoulements for the service of that current year should belong to Margt. Halliburton, his widow, for her own and her children's use, who are ten in number, very young ; and that the sum of fifty pounds sterling shall be paid to her for her own and children's behoof while she is in life, and after her decease to the said children till they are educated and attained to such age as they may be capable to do for themselves, and this is made a burden upon the person who is to be elected into that office.

Aug. 26*th.*—Appointed Treasurer Montgomery to pay to Margt. Savage, spouse to Willm. Graham, £1, 5s. ; and to Elizabeth Tarras, relict of John Kello, mercht., £1 stg. ; also to Anna Prestoun, relict of David Hutton, taylor, £1, all of supply.

Aug. 31*st.*—To James Campbell, a blind boy, 10s. sterg. John Campbell, printer, £1 ; and to widow Watterston, relict of Deacon Watterston, weaver, 10s., all of supply.

Sept. 7*th.*—To Elizabeth Tayleor, relict of George Bell, bookbinder, 10s. sterg. ;

and to Janet Warroch, relict of John Mason, burges, 10s., of supply.

Sept. 14*th.*—Appointed Treasurer Montgomery and his successors in office to pay to Margaret Learmonth, spouse to James Wood, keeper of the Westport, Potterrow, and Bristo Ports, £12 sterg. yearly, payable quarterly from Martinmas last, dureing the Councill's pleasure, and the said James Wood contineing in the office of keeper of the said ports. Appointed Treasurer Montgomery to pay to Margt. Learmonth, spouse to James Wood, keeper of the West Port, £2 stg., of supply; and to Barbara Preston, relict of Jno. M'Phell, £1; also to Margt. Lauder, relict of —— Tayler, £1, supply.

Oct. 12*th.*—To Robert Bull, mercht. councilor, one guinea and a half, to be by him paid to any shipmaster who shall carry Wm. Coutts, tayleor burges, to London, upon a certificate of his being arrived there.

Nov. 9*th.*—To Christian Hopkirk, daughter to the deceased William Hopkirk, mercht., £1 stg., of supply, to enable her to pay her ffather's funeral charges; and to Andw. Buchan, mercht. burges, 10s.; and to John Chiesley, writer, 10s., all of supply.

Nov. 18*th.*—Amount of quarterly pensions from lammas to Hallowmass is ninety-five pounds, seven shillings, sixpence sterling. To Anne Ker, relict of James Simpson, bookbinder, £6 Scots, to pay the expence of her husband's funeral.

Nov. 23*d.*—To David Mitchell, late Deacon of the goldsmiths, £6 Scots, to defray the expence of Mrs Buchanan's funeral.

Dec. 7*th.*—To John Campbell, printer, £1 stg.; and to   , widow of Jas. Morrison, town officer, 10s., to defray the funeral expence of her husband. To Alex. Learmonth, mercht., £5 stg., of supply, for the use of Mr Livingston, late conveener.

1738.

Sums ariseing from fines for fornication being exhausted, the City Thsr. is ordered to pay to K. Thesr £200 out of city's revenue.

SUPPLIES.

Jany. 4th.—To Janet Warroch, daugh. to Wm. Warroch, mercht., £1 stg.   Elizabeth Mason, widow of James Service, wright, £6 Scots.

AUGMENTATION.

To Mary Cameron, spouse to Alex. Hay, ringer of the bells in the Tron Church, did augment her pension from £8 to £100 Scots, payable to her by the Dean of Guild.

Feby. 15th.—Amount of quarterly pensions at Candlemass and supplies is ninety-seven pounds, eighteen shillings, twopence ⅓ sterg.

March 1st.—To James Stewart, late baillie, £3, 8s. 6d. stg., of supplies, paid out at different times by the said James Stewart.

March 22d.—To John Johnstoun, 20s. sterling, of supply, to carry him to London.

April 5th.—Ordered Robert Montgomery, city treasurer, to pay to David Ferguson, mercht., £18 Scots, for transporting several whores from the correction house ; and to John Campbell, printer, £12 Scots, of supply.

April 21st.—Did appoint the City Treasurer to pay to Geo. Lindsay, conjunct depute clerk, £3, 6s. 6d. stg., of charity, disbursed by him in the Council Chamber by order from the Magistrates.   To Grizel Myrten, widow of Mr John Orr, late minister of this city, £5 sterg., of supply.

May 17th.—Amount of quarterly pensions and supplies from Whitsunday to Lammas next is ninety-eight pounds, fifteen shillings, one penny sterg.

June 7th.—The Treasurer to repay to the Lord Provost, ten shillgs. sterg., of supply, advanced by him to —— M'Kenzie, a poor woman.

July 19th.—Allowed Treasurer Montgomery to take credit in his general accounts for the sum of £120 stg., advanced to John Bowie, kirk treasurer, conform to receipt, dated 5th April last, and for one hundred pounds sterling, also advanced to the said John Bowie, conform to another receipt, dated 2d June last.

Aug. 11th.—Amount of quarterly pensions and supplies, from Lammas last to

Martinmas next, is one hundred one pounds, thirteen shillings, fourpence sterling.

Aug. 30th.—Allowed the City Treasurer, to take credit in his accompts for £4, 8s. sterg., of charity, disbursed by Geo. Lindsay, clerk depute in the Council Chamber, by order of the Magistrates. Do., three pounds one shilling stg., disbursed by James Stewart, old baillie.

Sept. 1st.—Do. to George Thomason, cheif of the Maronlls in Syria, 3 guineas.

Nov. 15th.—Amount of quarterly pensions, from Martinmas last to Candlemas next, is ninety-eight pound, three shillings, fourpence sterg.

1739.

Jany. 24th.—To Robert Comb, wright, one of the fireman who had his leg broke at the late fire in Leith, 20s. sterg., of supply.

Feby. 7th.—Amount of quarterly pensions and supplies, from Candlemas last to Whitsunday next, is ninety-seven pounds, fifteen shillings, eightpence sterg. Allowed Treasurer Shairp to take credit in his general accompts for £4, 18s. stg., paid by him to George Lindsay, depute clerk, for charity, disbursed by order of the Magistrates.

May 16th.—Amount of quarterly pensions and supplies, from Whitsunday to Lammas currt., is ninety-two pounds, two shillings, and twopence sterg.

June 20th.—Appointed Treasurer Shairp to pay the expence of the funeral of John Duncan, late Dean of Gild, amounting to £3, 5s. stg., in respect the pension he had from the city has determined at his death, and that his children are not able to affoord the said expence.

Aug. 8th.—Amount of quarterly pensions and supplies, from Lammas last to Martinmas next, is ninety-one pounds, twelve shillings, and tenpence sterg.

Sept. 28th.—Allowed Treasurer Shairp to take credit for £4, 12s. 6d. sterg., of charity, laid out by Geo. Lindsay in the Council Chamber, by order of the Magistrates, since the 4th June last.

Nov. 14th.—Amount of quarterly pensions and supplies, from Martinmas last to Candlemas next 1740, is eighty-nine pounds, seven shillings, and tenpence sterling. The Lord Provost, Magistrates, Councillours, and Deacons of Crafts, ordinary and extraordinary, being in Council assembled, and takeing their consideration that by the articles or proposals which are prefixed to the subscriptions for the building and indowing an hospital or workhouse within this city for the more regular mentaining and imploying the whole poor thereof, there is to be paid out of this city's revenue the sum of two hundred pounds sterling annually towards the indowing the said hospital or workhouse in manner herein after mentioned: Therefore the said Lord Provost, Magistrates, Councillors, and Deacons of Crafts did, and hereby doe, order and appoint Alex. Shairp, the said City's Treasurer, and his successors in office, to pay to David Brown, present Kirk Treasurer, and his successors in office, out of the revenue of the said city, the sum of two hundred pounds sterling annually, at Whitsunday and Martinmas, by equal portions, beginning the first term's payment thereof at the first term of Whitsunday or Martinmas which shall happen immediately after that the said hospital or workhouse shall be built and fitted up, so as to be capable for the reception of the poor of the said city, and thereafter to be due and payable for ever yearly at the foresaid terms, which is to be applicable only towards the mentinance and imployment of the poor of the said city within the said hospital or workhouse, and to be under the management and direction of the persons chosen or to be chosen directors and managers of the said hospital or workhouse, in manner mentioned in the minutes of a meeting of the contributors to the said building and indowment, which was held within the city on the 24th day of July last.—Whereanent thir presents are declared to be a sufficient warrant. The Lord Provost, Magistrats, and Deacons of Crafts, ordinary and extraordinary, in Council assembled, haveing had under their serious consideration, that it was communed and agreed betwixt them and the reverend ministers, elders, and deacons of the several parishes within the said city, that a large hospital or workhouse

Y

should be built for the more regular mentinance and employment
of the whole poor of the said city, and for taking care of orphants
and ffoundlings, to be under the management herein after mentioned, and to be endowed with the particular funds herein after
specified, as is at large mentioned in the minutes of a meeting of
the said Magistrats, Council, Deacons of Crafts, ministers, elders,
deacons of the church, and other persons contributing to the
aforsaid building and indowment, held in the said city on the
24th day of July last, and that in implement of the aforsaid
communing and agreement, the said Magistrates, Councillors, and
Deacons of Crafts, for themselves and as representing the said
whole body and community of the said city, should, in conjunction with the said reverend ministers and other members of
the said Kirk Sessions of the said city, assign, dispone, convoy,
and make over the severall funds herein before and after mentioned in manner herein after exprest : Therefore the said Lord
Provost, Magistrats, Councillors, and Deacons of Crafts did, and
hereby unanimously doe, authorise and empower James Colhoun,
Esqr., Lord Provost ; Charles Hope, John Rochead, Robert
Montgomery, and John Brown, Baillies ; George Halliburton,
Dean of Gild ; Alexander Shairp, Treasurer ; and George Cunningham, Deacon, Convener of the Trades of the said city, or
any four of them, in conjunction with the said reverend
ministers and other members of the several Kirk Sessions
within the said city, or their commissioners thereto, to be appointed and authorised to assign, dispone, convoy, and make
over in the most habile manner to and in favours of David
Brown, present Kirk Treasurer of the city of Edinburgh, and
his successors in office, for the uses and purposes herein after
specified, and no otherwise, and under the direction and man-
adgement hereafter sett down, all and whole the funds and sums
of money that shall arise and grow, due annually from the
particular subjects before and after mentioned for the subsistance
and imployment of the poor of the said city who shall be ad-

mitted and received into the said intended hospital or workhouse from time to time, and for granting supplys to out-pensioners, not exceeding two hundred pounds sterling annually, as mentioned in the minutes of the forsaid meeting, dated said 24th day of July last, and articles therein referred to, vizt., the whole money that shall arise dayly, weekly, and yearly from collections at the church doors and at episcopal meeting houses, dues for marriages not solemnized in churches, one-third of the dues of the dead or passing bell, dues for burial warrands green turfs, charity collected in the poor's box at the Grayfriars gate, annual rents of sums of money and rents of houses, shops mortified for the use of the poor of the said city, annuity of two per cent. of poor's rate established by Act of Parliament, fines for fornication, all sums that hereafter shall be bequeathed or left by any person or persons to the use of the said poor, with the sum of two hundred pounds sterling to be payed annually out of the revenue of the said city by the City Treasurer and his successors in office, in manner mentioned in an Act of Council in that behalf, made of the date hereof, and from and after the term of

immediately after the said intended hospital or workhouse shall be built and finished, and so fitted up as it may be capable for the reception of the said poor, and thereafter in all time comeing the interim administration of the foresaid funds being to continue and remain in the said Lord Provost, Magistrats, Councillors, and Deacons of Crafts, and members of the said Kirk Sessions, as it now is, till the said hospital and workhouse be built and made fitt for the reception, entertaining, and imploying of the said poor, and no longer; the same thereafter for ever being to devolve upon the directors and managers of the said hospital and workhouse and their successors, as in manner settled in the inpart above recited minutes of the said Magistrats, Councillors, and Deacons of Crafts, and members of the said Kirk Sessions, and other contributors to the said building and indowing, dated the said 24th day of July last: Provideing and declareing that the said David Brown, present Kirk Treasurer, and his successors in office, from and after the commencement of the administration of the said funds in the said directors and managers of the said hospital or workhouse, as is herein before exprest, shall account for, reocken, and pay to the said directors and managers, or to their committee or committees thereto by them duly authorised, all and every sum of money which the said Kirk Treasurer and his successors in office shall intromett with out of all and every of the funds herein before specified, and that annually or oftener if desired by the said directors and managers, or their said committees, and that receipts and discharges to be granted by the said directors and managers, or their said committees, after that the said administration shall devolve on them, as aforsaid, shall be a sufficient exoneration to the said Kirk Treasurer and his successors in office; and the said Lord Provost, Magistrats, Councillors, and Deacons of Crafts do hereby promise to hold firm and stable whatever shall be done by their said commissioners touching the premisses: Declareing thir presents to be a sufficient warrant for the same.

1740.

Jany. 18*th.*—Whereas the sum of £87, 15s. 7d. sterg., the amount of charity gathered at the church doors on the 9th Jany. inst., and distributed by the several Kirk Sessions, has not been sufficient to relieve all the poor from their present distress, by the severity of the weather, namely, poor householders having pensions from the city—being either burgeses or widows or children of burgeses, and who had no share of the aforsaid charity,—therefore the Lord Provost and Council have given the orders necessary to purchase 80 bolls of oatmeal and 80 deals of coals, to be distributed to the above poor burgeses, &c.

Jany. 23*d.*—Reported by Baillie Chas. Hope that the above 80 bolls of meal and 80 deals of coals were purchased and given to the poor.

Feby. 6*th.*—Amount of quarterly pensions, from Candlemas last to Whitsunday next, is seventy-nine pounds, one shilling, eightpence sterling.

Feby. 13*th.*—Further reported by Treasurer Shairp, that he has imprest into the hands of Wm. Sands, Kirk Treasurer, £120 stg., towards payment of pensioners for this current quarter, for which Treasurer Shairp is to take credit in his general accompts.

March 19th.—Considering that usually there is given in charity by this city to the indigent Episcopal Clergy £200 Scots, every two years, and the severity of last winter makes it necessary to vary said custom, therefore ordered Treasurer Sharp to pay Mr Alex. Hunter, and Mr James M'Kenzie, Collectors of the Charity for the Episcopal Clergy, 200 merks for this year, declaring that it shall not be made a precedent for hereafter. By Act of Council, dated the 16 of April 1740, proceeding upon a report from the Committee appointed by the Council and Kirk Sessions of this city to audite the accounts of David Brown, mercht., and late Kirk Treasurer, there was found a balance due to him of £215, 6s. 3½⅔d. sterg., as super expended, therefore they were of opinion the above balance should be paid to the said David Brown by Alex. Shairp, City Treasurer, and for his doing so thir presints with a discharge will be a sufficient warrant.

May 21*st.*—Amount of quarterly pensions from Whitsunday last to Lammas next is seventy-nine pounds, sixteen shillings, and tenpence sterling. Allowed Treasurer Shairp to take credit in his general accompt for £5, 15s. 6d. stg., of charity, laid out by George Lindsay, by order of the Magistrats.

June 23*d.*—*Edinburgh, 23d June* 1740.—The Committee subscribing having examined the account of donations by different Noblemen and Gentlemen of money and coals for the poor during the time of the (the late) storm of frost, do find that the City Treasurer, Alex. Shairp, has super expended on account of the city the sum of £53, 12s. 6d., and that he should take credit in his general accompts for the above balance.

July 16*th.*—Treasurer Shairp reported that he had bought of Alex. Arbuthnot & Co., 220 bolls, 3 firlots of oatmeal at £8, 10s. Scots per boll, is £156, 7s. 8½d. sterling, which was ordered to be sold out of the city's granary by Jas. Moir, at 10d. sterling per peck, to the poor of this city, under the regulations of 25 June last, the current price of oatmeal being from 13¼d. to 15d. per peck.

July 30*th.*—Considering that John Fergusson, late Baillie of this city, by sickness and infirmity, is disabled from executing the office, and doing the duty proper to a Lieutennant of this city's company of Fusiliers, and that the said John Fergusson has held and discharged the said office of Lieutennant while he was able to doe the duty, and the office of one of the Magistrats of this city, and several other public inferiour offices therein, with approbation of the whole community, and that his circumstances in the world are such that he cannot subsist himself, wife, and family, without some aid by the city which has been usually given to persons of like circumstances with him; therefore the Lord Provost, Magistrates and Council, with the Deacons of Crafts, did, and hereby do give and grant to the said John Fergusson, dureing all the days of his lifetime, an aliment of £25 stg. yearly, for the subsistance of him, his wife, and children only during his lifetime as aforsaid, to be payable by Alex. Shairp, City Treasurer, and his successors in office per advance at Lammas, Martinmas, Candlemas, and Whitsunday, by equal portions, whereanent these presents are hereby declared to be a sufficient warrant, first quarter's payment to commence at Lammas next, and so furth.

Aug. 8*th.*—Amount of quarterly pensions from Lammas last to Martinmas next, is eighty-six pounds, twelve shillings, and tenpence sterling.

Sept. 24*th.*—Allowed Treasurer Shairp to take credit for £4, 15s. sterg., of charity, disbursed in the Council Chamber by Geo. Lindsay, depute clerk, conform to an accompt attested by the Magistrates.

Nov. 12*th.*—To Jean Fisher, spouse of John Cunningham, glover, 10s. sterg., to defray her expence with her children to Newcastle. Amount of quarterly pensions from Martinmas last to Candlemas next, is eighty-five pounds, seventeen shillings, and tenpence sterling.

SUPPLIES.

Nov. 19*th.*—To Margt. Dickson, spouse to Wm. Ogilvie, taylor, £6 Scots. To

Rachel Gemmels, relict of Thomas Cockburn, 6 Scots. To Isobel Thomson, relict of Adam Ainslie, hatter, 6 Scots. To Elizabeth Taylor, relict of George Bell, bookbinder, 3 Scots. To Janet Neish, widow of David Hodge, Deacon of the Hammermen, £3 Scots. To George Brotherston, mercht., £3 Scots. To Margt. Laing, relict of James Laing, late Baillie, of supply, £2 sterg.

1741.

Jany. 7th.—Allowed David Inglis, City Treasurer, to take credit in his general accounts for £4, 10s. stg., as charity, payed by Geo. Lindsay, depute clerk, by order of the Magistrats.

Feby. 6th.—Amount of quarterly pensions from Candlemas last to Whitsunday next, is eighty-three pounds, thirteen shillings, and fourpence sterg.

SUPPLIES.

The Committee on the poor did appoint David Inglis, City Treasurer, to pay the following supplys, viz., Mary Dickson, spouse to Wm. Ogilvie, taylor, £4 Scots. Rachel Gemmells, relict of Thomas Cockburn, £4 Scots. Isobel Thomson, relict of William Ainslie, hatter, £4 Scots. Janet Neish, or the Widow Hodge, £3 do. George Batherstone, merchant, £3 do. Arthur Straiton, mercht. burges, £4 do. Robert Hutton, mercht. burges, £3 do. Elizabeth, Scott, relict of David Allan, burges, £3 do. Patrick Stewart, hatter burges, £6 do. Marion Telfer, daughter to James Telfer, taylor, £3 do. John Hunter, cowper burges, £3 do. John Waldie, mercht. burges, £3 do. Janet Daes, £3 do., in all forty-six pounds Scots.

April 1st.—Upon a petition by Robert Nuccol, mason, appointed David Inglis, City Treasurer, to pay to Robert Clerk, writer, two pounds sterling, towards defraying the expence of burying Mr Thomas Anderson, son to the deceast Baillie Alexander Anderson, whereanent thir presents shall be a warrant.

April 8th.—By Act of Council, dated 8 April 1741, proceeding upon a report from the Committee appointed by the Council and Kirk Sessions of this city to audite the accounts of William Sands, Kirk Treasurer, there was found a balance due to him of £156, 0s. 6¼¼d. sterling, as super expended, therefore they were of opinion the above balc. should be paid to the said Wm. Sands by David Inglis, City Treasurer, and for his doing so thir presents shall be a warrant. Ordered David Inglis, City Treasurer, to pay to Alex. Knox, late Deacon of the Skinners, fourty shillings sterg., and to Robert Aiton, late Town Officer, 10s. sterling, both of supply.

May 6th.—Upon a petition from Robert Hodge, barber, appointed David Inglis, City Treasurer, to pay to Baillie George Millar, £1, 5s. sterling, to be by him given to the said Robert Hodge, to enable him to transport himself and family to Newcastle, that hereafter they may be no more burdensome on the city. To Wm. Cleghorn, son to the deceased John Cleghorn, 10s. stg., of supply.

Edinr., *19th May* 1741.—Baillie John Dewar, from the Committee on the Poor, produced a list of pensions to be paid by David Inglis, City Treasurer, for the current quarter from Whitsunday to Lambas next, with the Committee's report subjoined thereto, whereof the tenor follows :—

	£	s.	d.
Elizabeth Baillie, relict of Alex. Simpson, brewer, and late baillie,	£1	0	0
Catharin Baillie, relict of David Wemys, mercht.,	1	13	0
Thomas Brown, smith,	0	16	6
Robert Brown, wigmaker,	0	16	6
Alison Brown, daughter of John Brown, mercht.,	1	10	0
Janet Bull, relict of George Brown, mercht.,	0	12	6
Barbara Baptie, daughter of —— Baptie, baxter,	0	8	0
Thomas Cleugh, merchant,	1	0	0
Ann Chapman, relict of Jas. Sommerville, wigmaker,	1	0	0
Sarah Cockburn, daur. of James Cockburn, goldsmith,	0	13	6
Willm. Crooks, mercht.,	1	13	0

Christian Caw, relict of Chas. Duncan, goldsmith,	£1	0	0
Ditto, for Alex. Duncan, her son,	1	0	0
Margt. Campbell, relict of Wm. Took, barber,	0	12	6
Christian Campbell, daughter of Thos. Campbell, flesher,	1	0	0
Margt. Chiesly, relict of Mr Saml. Gray, pror. fiscal,	0	15	0
Ditto, for Samuel Gray, her son,	0	15	0
Mary Campbell, relict of Robt. Lightbody, mert,	0	16	6
Robert Cumming, mercht.,	0	16	6
John Cunningham, coppersmith,	1	5	0
Alex. Clark, glazier,	0	15	0
Janet Clarkson, relict of John Scott, overseer of the city's works,	1	10	0
John Clark, painter,	0	15	0
Alex. Cowan, schoolmaster,	0	13	6
Rachel Currie, daughter of Provost Currie,	2	15	0
Janet Dundas, relict of Wm. Dickie,	0	16	0
Margaret Denham, relict of Archd. Colhoun, glover,	0	10	0
Catharin Denoon, relict of Robert Finlay, minister,	0	12	6
Robert Douglas, payable to Alex. Boswall, painter,	0	12	6
Elizabeth Drummond, relict of Wm. Howlylover, for behoof of Isobel Reid and Isobel Braid, her grandchildren,	0	10	0
Isobel Ellies, relict of —— Braidwood, payl. to Geo. Livingston, clerk of session,	0	16	6
Ann Edmonston, relict of Geo. Stewart, stationer,	1	5	0
John Fergusson, one of the chaplains of the City Guard, and one of the baillies of this city, per Act of Council, 30th July 1740, during life £25 per ann.,	6	5	0
Magdelen Fleming, daughter of Provost Fleming, by Act of Council, 13th February 1736, £10 sterl. during her life,	2	10	0
Chas. Fisher, brewer,	1	0	0
Marion Finnie, relict of John Young, baxter,	0	16	0
Archd. Herron, cordiner, and late deacon,	1	0	0
Marion Hart, relict of Thos. Herron, wright,	0	13	4
Jean Heriot, relict of John Reid, writer burges,	0	13	6
Janet Henry, spouse of John Laing, mercht.,	0	17	0

z

Isobel Johnston, daur. of Andw. Johnston, shoarmaster, . .	£1	0	0
Andw. Ker, son to the deceased Wm. Kerr, mercht., . .	0	12	0
Elizabeth Ker, relict of Wm. Abercrombie, chaplain to the Tolbooth, ...	1	0	0
Andw. Lawson, merchant, ...	1	5	0
Isobel Lon, relict of Wm. Haigs, hatter, ...	0	16	6
Margt. Litster, relict of Robt. Robertson, baxter, . .	0	16	6
Sybilla Lyon, relict of Chas. Dickson, goldsmith, . .	0	11	0
Elizabeth Morton, relict of James Seton, College janitor, .	0	15	0
George Marr, late keeper of the city's bells, . .	0	15	0
Isobel Murray, relict of James Bonnas, skinner, . . .	1	0	0
Betty Nimmo, daur. of Robt. Nimmo, ...	0	15	0
John Ochiltree, weaver, and late deacon, . . .	1	0	0
Margt. Pringle, relict of John Barker, stabler, . .	0	13	0
Mary Purdie, relict of John Lennox, glover, . .	1	15	0
Agnes Potter, relict of Robt. Paterson, clothier, . .	1	5	0
Lillias Robertson, daur. of Dean of Guild Robertson, .	1	0	0
Ann Ritchie, daur. of the deceased Jas. Ritchie, mercht., .	0	15	0
Catharin Ramsay, relict of the deceased Jas. Yorston, goldsmith,	0	12	6
John Simpson, mercht., ...	0	16	0
Margaret Scott, relict of Jas. Ker, mercht., taylor, .	0	16	0
Patrick Stewart, hatter, and late deacon, . .	1	0	0
Isobel Stewart, relict of Chas. Cost, bookbinder, . .	0	16	0
Mary Stewart, relict of Thos. Buchanan, writer, . .	0	16	0
Ann Smith, relict of James Smith, mason, . .	1	10	0
Peter Stewart, wigmaker, ...	0	16	0
Dorothea Sommervile, relict of Mr Wm. Haldane, one of the masters of the High School, ...	1	0	0
Margaret Savage, daughter of John Savage, brewer, .	0	15	0
Janet Shairp, relict of Duncan Willison, mercht., .	0	13	0
Charles Telfer, mercht., and late baillie, . . .	4	0	0
Mary Montgomery, spouse to Capt. Telfer, . .	1	0	0
Mary Turnbull, daur. of Robt. Turnbull, mert., . .	0	15	0
Elizabeth Terras, relict of John Kello, mercht., . .	0	12	6

Willm. Thomson, wright, .	.	.	.	.	.	£1	0	0
Janet Warrock, relict of John Mason, wright,	.	.	.	0	15	0
Mary Williamson, relict of George Andw., mert.,	.	.	1	0	0
Henry Wilson, mason, and late deacon, .	.	.	.	1	0	0
Jean Weir, relict of James Abel, taylor, .	.	.	.	0	12	0
Janet Weir, daur. of Alex. Weir, taylor, .	.	.	.	0	12	0
Margaret Weir, daughter of Thomas Weir, surgeon,	.	.	0	12	0
Marion Wright, relict of William Davidson, barber,	.	.	0	12	0

$$£83 \quad 0 \quad 10$$

The Committee having considered and revised the establishment of pensions paid by the City Treasurer at Candlemas last, and likewise the petitions of those who have at this time applied for pensions, were of opinion the preceding list shall be the establishment for pensions for the current quarter till Lambas next, and that David Inglis, City Treasurer, should be ordered to pay the same per advance to the forenamed persons, amounting to eighty-three pounds and tenpence sterling, as the report, signed by the Committee, bears : Which having been considered by the Magistrates and Council, with the Deacons of Crafts, ordinary and extraordinary, they approved of the said report, and ordered David Inglis, City Treasurer, to pay to the several persons in the foresaid list the sums annexed to their names, as their pensions for the current quarter to Lambas next, amounting to eighty-three pounds 10d. sterl., whereanent thir presents, with their receipts, shall be a warrant.

QUARTERLY PENSIONS—*Continued.*

Quarter from Lambas to Hallamass (Marts.) 1741 is £83, 3s. 10d. Ditto from Hallamass to Candlemas 1742 is £75, 18s. 10d. Ditto from Candlemas to Whitsunday 1742 is £77, 15s. 4d. Ditto from Whitsunday to Lambas 1742 is £78, 14s. 4d. Ditto from Lambas to Martinmas 1742 is £79, 0s. 10d.

Edinburgh, 15th September 1742.—The Council authorised David Inglis, city treasurer, to pay to John Inglis, merchant, twenty shillings sterl. towards defraying the funeral of Isobel Johnston, late one of the city's pensioners.

Amount of pensions from Martinmas 1742 to Candlemas 1743, £77, 15s. 4d.

12th November 1742.—Upon report of Baillie Dundas and the Committee on the Poor, the Council did appoint John Forrest, City Treasurer, to pay the following supplies, viz.:—To Janet Daes, spouse to Andrew Martin, £3. To —— Veitch, spouse to Alex. Oliver, dyer, £3. To Isobel Innes's children, £4. To Deacon Knox, £6. To Margaret Pringle, daughter of Robert Pringle, flesher, £3. To Elizabeth Johnston, widow of David Ross, £4. To Bethia Ramsay, £3. To Mrs Forsyth, £4. To Margaret Wallace, £3. To the widow of Deacon Kirkpatrick, taylor, for her two children, £6. To Jean Johnston, £3. To Esther Craig, £3—in all, £45 Scots.

Edinburgh, 24*th August* 1743.—Baillie Robert Dundas, from the Committee on the Poor, gave in an additional establishment of pensions to be paid by Mr Forrest, City Treasurer, for the current quarter from Lambas to Martinmas next, with the Committee's report thereto subjoined, whereof the tenor follows :—

Ann Chapman, relict of James Sommerville, wigmaker, . . £0	15	0
Alex. Cowan, schoolmaster, ... 0	13	6
Wm. Craig, merchant, ... 1	0	0
Alex. Clerk, glazier, ... 0	15	0
Christian Campbell, daughter of Thomas Campbell, flesher, . 0	10	0
Isobel Stuart, relict of Patrick Cosh, bookbinder, . 0	16	0
Mary Stewart, relict of Thos. Buchanan, writer, . . 0	16	0
Marion Wright, relict of William Davidson, barber, . 0	10	0
Mary Turnbull, daughter of Robert Turnbull, merchant, . 0	15	0

Edinburgh, 22*d August* 1743.—The Committee subscribing, appointed to revise and consider the petitions of such of the pensioners as by their last Report were either struck off or reduced, having accordingly considered the same, and enquired into their several situations, are of opinion that the persons contained in the above additional establishment, should be payed the sums severally annexed to them for the current quarter, from Lambas to Martinmas next, amounting to six pounds, ten shillings, and sixpence sterling. (Signed) Robert Dundas, Baillie; Tho. Trotter, M.C.; George Langlands, D.C.; Tho. Clelland, T.C.; Edward Lothian, Andrew Good, D. Which having been considered by the Magistrates and Council, they, with the extraordinary Deacons, approved of the said Report, and authorised John Forrest, City Treasurer, to make payment to the said persons before named of the several pensions annexed to their names for the current quarter to Martinmas next, amounting in all to six pounds, ten shillings, and sixpence sterg., whereanent thir presents shall be a warrant.

By the foresaid Contract or Agreement between the Lord Provost, Magistrates, and Town Council, and the Ministers and Kirk Session of the City of Edinburgh, for building and endowing the Charity Workhouse, dated 23d Feby. 1740, it is provided and declared among other things, that £200 sterling annually shall be paid out of the Revenue of the City of Edinburgh towards the mainteinence of the Establishment, the first payment whereof was in June 1744, about one year after the opening of the house for reception of paupers. And it is of the following tenor :—

"*Edinburgh, 13th June* 1744.
" The Magistrates and Council authorized Mr Forrest, City Treasurer, to pay " to James Stirling, Merchant, Treasurer to the Poor's House, the sum of two " hundred pounds sterling, as the annual sum engaged to be paid by the " City for the support of the Workhouse, being the first year's allowance, and " that from the 15th of June 1743, to the 15th day of June 1744 years."

Consequently the further payments of pensions ceased, the above sum having been granted in lieu and place thereof.

But here it is proper to remark, that over and above the foresaid fixed annual sum, there are charities disbursed in the Council Chamber, by order of the sitting Magistrate, to a very considerable amount yearly, not less than £234 on an average, the greatest part being given to those of the first description of citizens, who previous to the opening of the Charity Workhouse obtained pensions.

It is here proper to note,—That the great sums paid to the Kirk Treasurers by the City Treasurers happened on account of the deficiencies which unavoidably arose from maintaining and cloathing illegitimate children and orphans, the expences of legal prosecutions against the alleged parents, and other causes. These payments ceased at opening the Charity Workhouse in 1743.—*See Proceedings of Council, 14 Novemb. 1739.**

* Nota.—This is the original Scroll, from the Search,—a clean copy having been made, and sent by W. F. to Kincaid Mackenzie, Esquire, late Lord Provost, with a letter accompanying the same.

IV.

BY ORDER OF THE
LORD DEAN OF GUILD OF EDINBURGH.

WEIGHTS AND MEASURES.

DEAN OF GUILD'S OFFICE, PARLIAMENT SQUARE, SEPTEMBER 16, 1801.

AS it is intended that a survey of all WEIGHTS, DRY and LIQUID MEASURES, in use within this City and Liberties, shall shortly take place—NOTICE is hereby given to all concerned, that they may have their Weights and Measures stamped, by applying to the Dean of Guild Officer, between and the 15th day of October next.

It being the Dean of Guild's intention to have all Weights and Measures in future stamped at THIS OFFICE ONLY, all Tradesmen and others are prohibited and discharged from using his Stamps for that purpose; and if any Weights or Measures are found in the possession of any Dealer, or other Person making use of the same, after the said 15th day of October next, they will not only be forfeited, but every such person severely fined, or otherwise punished.

The above reprinted from the *Edinburgh Advertiser*, No. 3937, from Friday, September 18, to Tuesday, September 22, 1801. Printed for JAMES DONALDSON, and sold at the Printing Office, Castle Hill, Edinburgh, etc.

V.—EXTRACTS from BURGH RECORDS of ABERDEEN, as Furnished to the Committee of the House of Commons, in regard to the Constitution of the Royal Burghs in 1793, with relative Translations in English.

1399.

LIBER communitatis burgi de Aberdene. Est iste qui incipit die Lune proximo post festum Beati Michaelis Archangeli, anno Domini millesimo trecentesimo nonagesimo nono. Quo die electus fuit Adam de Benyn cum consensu et assensu totius communitatis dicti burgi in officium aldermani. Et Willmus Blyndule, Simon de Benyn, Joh. Wormot, et Johes filius Thome, electi sunt in officium ballivorum, et Mauricius filius Roberti, Donaldus Ka, Fergusius filius Ade, et Johes de Lucris, electi sunt in officium serjandorum. Eodem die electi sunt in communes consiliarios dicti burgi Willmus de Camera pater, Lawrencius de Leth, Willmus de Camera filius, Alexander Bannerman, Thomas Spryng, Willmus Andro, Johes Andro, Johes de Ledale, David de Scrogs, Johes Scherar, Robertus filius David, Johes Loccon, Hugo Arbuthnot, Johes Ruthirfuird, Willmus de Gray, Simon Lamb, Ricardus de Lownan, Willmus Borthwick, Johes Strang, et Ricardus Fichet.

THE Book of the Community of the Burgh of Aberdeen. This is that which beginneth on the next Monday after the Feast of St Michael the Archangel, in the year of the Lord 1399, on which day, Adam de Benyn was chosen to the Office of Provost, with assent and consent of the whole Community of the said Burgh, and William Blydule, Simon de Benyn, Joh. Wormot, and Joh. the son of Thom, were chosen into the office of Bailies, and Maurice son of Robert, Donald Ka, Fergus son of Adam, and Joh. de Lucris were chosen into the office of Serjeants. The same day were chosen Common Councellors of the said Burgh, William de Camera, Father or Senior, &c.

1408.

LIBER communitatis burgi de Abirdene incipiens die Lune proximo post festum Beati Michaelis Archangeli de anno Domini millesimo quadringentesimo octavo. Quo die Robertus filius David electus fuit in officium aldermanni; Andreas Giffard, Richardus Fitchet, Johes filius Henrici, et Willmus Jacson, electi fuerunt in officium ballivorum; Johannes Trayle, Fergusius Ade, Johes Lucris, et Johannes Sellar, electi fuerunt in officium serjandorum.

Commune consilium—Willmus de Camera pater, Lawrencius de Leith, Willmus de Camera filius, Thomas Spryng, Johes Fitchet, Johes Wormot, Thomas Lamb, Willmus Kyntor, Duncanus de Marr, Willmus Blyndsele, Adam Thome, Johes Jacobi, Ricardus de Lownan, Johes filius Alani, Johes Scherar.

THE Book of the Community of the Burgh of Aberdeen, beginning the Monday next after the Feast of St Michael the Archangel, 1408: Which day Robert Davidson was chosen into the office of Provost, Andrew Giffard, &c., were chosen into the office of Bailies, John Trail, &c., were chosen into the office of Serjeants. *Common Council*—William de Camera, the Father or Senior, &c.

1435.

DIE Lune tertio die mensis Octobris, Ann. Dom. millesimo quadringentismo trecesimo quinto (viz.) die Juridico post festum Beati Michael. Anni per dicti electus fuit per commune consilium et confratres gilde, Johannes de Scroggs in officium præpositi hujus burgi de Abdene, Alex. de Camera, filius et heres, Thome de Camera, Johannes de Marr, junior, Matheus Fitchet, et Johannes Vokel filius in officia ballivorum. Willelmus Atkynson, Matheus dic. Duer, Johannes . . . totam communitatem burgi sm. leges ejusdem in officio beddellorum five serjandorum; qui omnes officiarii, in pntia totius communitatis, ad servand. leges, et consuetudines laudabiles ac statuta utilia hujus burgi fact. et faciend. juxta consilium communis consilii, vel majoris et sanioris partis ejusdem, corporalia juramenta prestituerunt.

Subscripti personæ electi fuerunt et jurati ad com. consilium burgi (viz.) Thomas de Camera, Johannes de Vaus, Gilbertus Meignes, Ricardus de Rutherford, Johannes de Fyfe, Andreas Aynecroft, Johannes Vokel, Pat-Willelmus de Kyntor, Andreas de Culane, Symon Blakra, Stephanus de Balrong, Thomas de Stone, Johannes Gray, Angusius Ade, Thomas de Crauford, Alex. de Kyntor,

Andreas Branche, Robertus Will, Johannes Blyndzele, Robertus Blyndzele Willelmus Sherar, Thomas Blyndzele, Adam de Hill, Johannes Burnell, Willelmus de Fodringham, Duncanus de Clatt et Patricius de Badynach, ac Johannes Fichett, et Th. Umfrason, Willmus Giffard, et Johannes de Culane.

MONDAY, 3d October 1435, being the fifth lawful day after the Feast of St Michael: There were chosen by the Common Council and the Guild Brethren, John Scroggs into the office of Provost of this Burgh of Aberdeen, Alex. Cameron, &c., into the office of Bailies. William Alkinson, &c., by the whole community, according to the laws of the same, into the office of Beadles, or Serjeants, all which Officers, in presence of the whole Community, took their Corporeal Oath to observe the laws, laudable customs, and useful statutes of this Burgh, such as are already made, or may afterwards be made, after the advice of the Common Council, or the greater or most intelligent part thereof.

The underwritten persons were chosen and sworn in to the Common Council of the said Burgh, viz., Thomas Cameron, &c., &c.

1439.

CURIA Gilde burgi de Abdene tent, coram Gilberto Megnes præposito nono die mensis Octobris, Anno Domini XXXIX. · Quo die, sectis vocatis, et curia affirmata, absentes patent in rotulo sectarum et amerciamentarum.

Electi ad commune consilium.

JOANNES DE VAUS,
JOANNES DE FIFE,
RICHARDUS DE RUTHERFURD,
JOHES VOKEL, Pater,
JOHNES GRAY,
STEPHANUS DE BALRONY,
ROBERTUS WILLIAMSON,
ANDR. MENZIES,
ROGERUS WILLIAMSON.
THOMAS BLYNDSEIL,
THOMAS DE CRAWFURD,
DUNCANUS PATERSON,
THOMAS DE ROLLAND,

JOHANNES DE SCROGGS,
JOHES DE MARR,
ANDREAS AYNCROFT,
DUNCANUS DE CLAT,
ANDREAS BRANCHE,
PATRICIUS DE BADENACH,
ANDREAS DE CULANE,
MATHEAS FICHET,
ROBERTUS BLYNDSEIL,
JOHES HARRISON CULANE,
JOHES VOKEL, Filius,
WALLERUS GIFFARD.

AT a Guild Court of the Burgh of Aberdeen, holden before Gilbert Menzies
Provost, 9th October A.D. 39 (*i.e.* 1439), which day the divisions being
called, the Court fenced, the absentees marked in the roll of divisions
and of fines:

There were chosen to be a Common Council, John Vass, &c., &c.

1474.

CURIA capitalis burgi de Abirdene, tenta in pretorio ejusdem per ballivos X.
tertio die Octobris Anno Domini millesimo quadringentesimo septuagesimo quarto, quo die sectis vocatis, et curia affirmata, absentes
patent in rotulo sectarum.

Eodem die Alexander de Camera electus fuit in officium prepositure pro
anno sequente, et ad deserviend. fideliter in dicto officio juramentum prestitit
corporale.

Johannes de Vaus, David Meignies, David Symson, et Gilbertus de Camera
electi fuerunt in officia ballivorum, prestitis per eosdem solitis juramentis.

Johannes Lawrie, sen. Alex. de Camera, Alex. Andree, et Duncanus de
Straloch, eodem die continuati fuerunt in officio serjandorum pro anno futuro.

Curia gilde burgi de Abirdene, tenta per prepositum et fratres gilde, quinto
die mensis Novembris, anno millesimo quadringentesimo septuagentesi-
mo quarto.

Quo die subscripti electi fuerunt in communes consiliarios hujus burgi pro
anno sequente.

Commune consilium.

ANDREAS ALANSON,
ALEX. MEIGNIES,
JOHES DE MARR,
RICARDUS DE KYNTOR,
JOHES DE KNOLLIS,
ROBERTUS CULANE,
DAVID COLYSON,
ALEX. BLYNDSCHEL,

THOMAS DE CAMERA,
GILBERTUS VAUS,
THOMAS DE CULANE,
WILLMUS VOKEL,
EDWARDUS LOWSON,
WILLMUS RETTIE,
JOHES GLEMALVYN.

AT a Head Court of the Burgh of Aberdeen, held in the Hall of the same,
by the ten Bailies, 3d October 1474, which day the divisions being

called, the Court fenced, and the absentees marked in the roll of the divisions :

The same day Alexander Cameron was chosen into the office of Provost for the following year, and for his serving faithfully in said office, he took his Corporal Oath.

John Vass, &c., were chosen into the office of Bailies, they having taken the usual Oaths.

John Lawrie, &c., were the same day continued in the office of Serjeants for the year to come.

At a Guild Court of the Burgh of Aberdeen, held by the Provost and Guild Brethren, 5th November 1474.

Which day the Underwritten were chosen to be Common Councillors of this Burgh for the year ensuing :

Common Council—Andrew Allanson, &c.

1475.

CURIA capitalis burgi de Abirdene, tentain pretorio per ballivos ejusdem, die secunda mensis Octobris, Ann. Domini millesimo quadringentesimo septuagesimo quinto ; quo die, sectis vocatis, et curia affirmata, absentes patent in rotulo sectarum.

Quo die Alexander Meignies electus fuit in foticium prepositure pro anno sequente, et ad deserviend. fideliter in dicto officio juramentum prestitit corporale.

Item, eodem die, David Leslie, Thomas de Fyfe, Robertus Blyndsell, et Jacobus Cumyng electi fuerunt in officio ballivorum, et ad deserviend. in dicto officio fideliter pro commune commodo juramenta prestiterunt corporalia.

Item, Johannes de Vaus, Alex. Chaumir, Alex. Androson, et Duncanus de Straloch, continuati fuerunt in officio serjandorum pro anno sequente.

Subscripti electi sunt, et jurati in communi consilio hujus burgi pro anno sequente.

ALEX. CHAUMIR DE MUIRTHILL,
ANDREAS SCHERAR,
JOHES DE MARR,
MATHEUS FICHEL,
JOHES DE KNOLLIS,
DAVID COLYSON,
JOHES WODE,
ALEX. HOWISONE,

JOHES DE KYNTOR,
ALEX. REDE,
DAVID MATHOUSON,
ADA DE CRAWFUIRD,
WILLMUS MALLYSON,
JOHES WORMOT,
ALEX. DE MARR.

AT a Head Court of the Burgh of Aberdeen, held in the Hall by the Bailies of the same, on the 2d October 1475, which day the divisions being called, the Court fenced, the absentees were marked in the roll of the divisions, which day, Alexander Menzies was chosen into the office of Provost for the ensuing year, and took his Corporal Oath for his faithful serving in the said office.

Also, the same day David Leslie, &c., were chosen into the office of Bailies, and took their Corporal Oaths for faithfully serving in said office for the common advantage.

Also, John Vass, &c., were continued in the office of Serjeants for the ensuing year.

The Underwritten were chosen into the Common Council of this Burgh for the ensuing year, viz., Alexander Chalmers of Murtle, &c.

1477.

CURIA capitalis burgi de Aberdene, tenta in pretorio per ballivos ejusdem die sexta mensis Octobris, Anno Dom. mo. CCCC.LXXVII. Quo die, sectis vocatis et curia affirmata absen. patent in rotulo sect.

Eodem die Alexander de Camera electus fuit in officium prepositure pro anno sequente, et ad deserviend. fideliter in dicto officio juramentum prestitit corporale.

After the Election of the four Bailies and the Town Serjeants, with the verdict of an inquest, on a brieve, in favour of Isabel Barclay, there is recorded as follows (viz.) :—

It. Eodem die subscripti electi fuerunt, et jurati in communes consiliarios hujus burgi pro anno instanti.

ANDREAS SHERAR,	PETRUS KYNIOR,
ALEX. MENGZIES,	ALEX. HOWISONE,
JOHES DE MARR,	ANDREAS REEDE DE BADSOTHEL,
JOHES DE KNOLLIS,	ALEX. REIDE,
DAVID COLLISON,	JOHNES DE KYNTOR,
JOHES WODE,	DAVID STMPSONE,
THOMAS DE FIFE,	EDMUNDUS LOWSONE,
THOMAS DE CAMERA,	GILBERTUS DE CAMERA,
GILBERTUS VAUS,	ADAM DE CRAWFURD,
DAVID MATHOSONE,	JOHES STEVINSON,
ALEX. DE MARR,	ALEX. HAY,
THOMAS PRATT,	DAVID DE KYNTOR.

AT a Head Court of the Burgh of Aberdeen, held in the Hall by the Bailies of the same, 6th October 1477, which day the divisions being called, the Court was fenced, the absentees were marked in the roll of divisions.

The same day Alexander Cameron was chosen into the office of Provost for the ensuing year, and took his Corporal Oath for his faithful serving in the said office.

Also, the same day, the Underwritten were chosen Common Councillors of this Burgh, and sworn in to that office for the ensuing year:—Andrew Shearer, &c.

1494.

Curia capitalis burgi de Aberdene, tenta in pretorio ejusdem, sexta die mensis Octobris, Ann. Domini millesimo quadringentesimo nonogesimo quarto : quo die, sectis vocatis, et curia affirmata, absentes patent in rotulo sectarum.

Eodem die David Menzies electus in officium prepositure pro anno instante, prestito, solito juramento.

Eodem die Johannes Menzies, Gilbertus Menzies, Andreas Branche, et Jacobus Collisone, electi fuerunt in officium ballivorum, prestitis solitis juramentis, pro anno instante.

Eodem die Philippus Dumbreck, Andreas Nauchly, Thomas Jamesone, et Henricus Owyne, electi fuerunt in officium serjandorum pro anno instante, prestitis solitis juramentis.

Curia ballivorum legalis de Aberdene, tenta in pretorio ejusdem, decimo die Octobris, annoque supra.

There are several amerciaments and convictions by the court, and an assize ;—then follows

Consilium.

Alex. Rede, Alex. Chamir the fader, Sir John Ruthirfuird, Alex. Menzies. Robert Bliedsell, John of Cullane.

John Colisone, Thos. Prat, Alex. Chamir the sone.

Andrew Murray elder, David Matheson.

Andro' Culane the younger, Andrew Culane elder.

Wm. Fitchet, Robert Graye.

Alexr. Marr, David Marr, William Bluidsell.

At a Head Court of the Burgh of Aberdeen, held in the Hall of the same, 6th October 1494, which day the divisions being called, the Court fenced, the absentees were marked in the roll of divisions. The same day David Menzies was chosen into the office of Provost for the year now commencing, he having taken the usual Oath.

Same day, John Menzies, &c., were chosen into the office of Bailies for the year now commencing, they have taken the usual Oaths.

Same day, Philip Dumbreck, &c., were chosen into the office of Serjeants for the year now commencing, they having taken the usual Oaths.

At a Bailie Court legally held at Aberdeen, in the Hall, 10th October, above year :

Council—Alexander Reid, &c.

1502.

Curia capitalis ballivorum de Aberdene, tenta in pretorio ejusdem, quarto die mensis Octobris, anno Domini millesimo quingentesimo secundo : quo die, sectis vocatis, et curia affirmata, absentes patent, &c.

Eo die Alexander Menzies electus fuit in officium propositure pro anno instante, prestito solito juramento.

Eodem die Thomas Lesly, Jacobus Collyson, Johannes Marr et David Marr, electi fuerunt in officium ballivorum pro anno instante, prestitis solitis juramentis.

Eodem die Willmus Scrimgeoure, Andreas Nauchtie, Gilbertus Prestone, et Johannes Cuik, electi fuerunt in officium serjandorum pro anno instante, prestitis solitis juramentis.

Curia Gilde, tenta in pretorio burgi de Abirdene, septimo die mensis Octobris, annoque supra.

Eodem die Gilbertus Menzies et Andreas Cullane electi fuerunt decani gilde pro anno instanti, prestitis solitis juramentis.

Eodem die Robertus Bluidsell, Johannes Cullane, Alexr. Reid, Johannes Wormit, Andreas Murray, Willmus Fitchet, et Alexr. Gray, electi fuerunt auditores computorum decanorum gilde anno elapso.

Consilium.

Johannes Leslie de Wardes, Dominus Johannes Ruthirfuird miles, Robertus Bluidsell, David Menzies, Johannes Culane, Alexr. Chaumir, Alexr. Rede, John Knollis, Johannes Collyson, Alexr. Marr, Johannes Wormet, Willmus Chaumir, Andreas Murray, Thos. Wauss, Willmus Fitchet, Alexr. Gray, Willmus Bluidsell, Matheas Branche, Willmus Murray, Johannes Blak, W. Gray, David Stewart, Duncanus Collison, Patricius Rede, Johannes Greg.

AT a Head Court of the Bailies of Aberdeen, held in the Hall of the same, 4th October 1502, which day the divisions being called, the Court fenced, absents marked, &c.

The same day Alexander Menzies was chosen into the office of Provost for the ensuing year, he having taken the usual Oath.

The same day, Thomas Leslie, &c., were elected Bailies for the ensuing year, they having taken the usual Oaths.

The same day, William Scrimgeour, &c., were chosen into the office of Serjeants for the ensuing year, having taken the usual Oaths.

At a Guild Court, held in the Hall of the Burgh of Aberdeen, 7th October, in the above year.

The same day, Gilbert Menzies and Andrew Cullen were chosen Deans of Guild for the ensuing year, having taken the usual Oaths.

The same day, Robert Bluisdale, &c., were chosen Auditors of Accounts of the Dean of Guild for the past year.

Council—John Leslie of Wardes, &c.

1509.

CURIA capitalis ballivorum de Abirdene, tenta in pretorio ejusdem, primo die mensis Octobris, anno Domini millesimo quingentesimo nono : quo die, sectis vocatis, et curia affirmata, absentes patent.

ANDREAS WATSON,	SYMON MITCHELL,
THOMAS DAVYSON,	DAVID HAY,
DUNCANUS ANDERSONE,	GEORGIUS JOHNSTONE,
ROBERTUS DAVISONE,	JOHES WATSONE in Garnenly.
WILLMUS RICHARDSONE,	ANDREAS GORDONE,
THOMAS LAISK at Newbyth,	WILLMUS VYNE,
ANGUS WAT at Mony Cabok,	JOHES HENRISON,
ANDREAS BAXTER at Newburgh,	ALEXR. TULIDIF,
RICHARDUS WATSONE,	ROBERTUS FRASER,
THOMAS WATSON in Gowllis,	ALEXR. NEISTER.
THOMAS WIDMAN,	PATRICIUS RAMSAY,
ANDREAS WATSON in Cullan,	DAVID BANNERMAN, Jun.
WILLMUS BLAKHALL, dead.	

Electio Prepositi.

Eodem die Gilbertus Menzies electus fuit in officium prepositure pro anno instante, prestito solito juramento.

Electio Ballivorum.

Eodem die Johannes Colisone, Johannes Mar, Patricius Leslie, et Alexr. Menzies, electi fuerunt in officium ballivorum pro anno instanti, prestitis solitis juramentis.

Electio Serjeandorum.

Eodem die Willhelmus Scrimgeoure, Normandus Leslie, Andreas Naughtie, et Johannes Cuik, electi fuerint in officium serjeandorum pro anno instante, prestito solito juramento.

Curia Gilde burgi de Abirdene, tenta in pretorio ejusdem, quinto die mensis Octobris, anno Domini millesimo quingentesimo nono.

Consilium.

JOHANNES LESLEY of Wardes,
Sir JOHN RUTHIRFUIRD,
JOHNE OF CULANE,
ANDREW CULLANE,
JAMES COLLYSONE,
THOMAS CHAUMIR,
ALEXANDER GRAY,
ROBERT GRAY,
DUNCAN COLLYSONE,
DAVID MAR,
WILLZEAM PORTAR,
GEORGE BISSET,
ALEXANDER MALLYSONE,

WILLZEAM FITCHET,
WILLZEAM WORMET,
JOHN ANDERSONE,
DAVID STEWART,
PATRY REED,
WILLZEAM MURRAY,
THOMAS WAUS,
THOMAS WODE,
MATHEW BRANCHE,
CHARLES STEVINSON,
DAVID FYNIE,
ANDREW LOWSON.

Decani Gilde.

Eodem die Thomas Chaumir et Duncanus Colisone electi fuerunt decani gilde pro anno instanti, cum adjutorio præpositi, prestitis solitis juramentis.

Magistri Fabris Ecclesie.

Eodem die Patricius Leslie et Georgius Bisset, electi fuerunt magistri fabris ecclesie pro anno instante, prestitis solitis juramentis.

Auditores computorem Magistrorum Fabris Ecclesie et Decanorum Gilde.

Eodem die Gilbertus Menzies prepositus, Johes Leslie de Wardes, Johannes Cullane, Andreas Cullane, Patricius Leslie, Thomas Waus, Thos. Wode et David Mar, electi fuerunt auditores computorum magistri fabris ecclesie, et decanorum gilde, prestitis solitis juramentis.

AT the Head Court of the Bailies of Aberdeen, held in the Hall of the same, 1st October 1509, which day the divisions being called, the Court fenced, absentees marked.

Andrew Watson, &c.

Election of the Provost.—The same day, Gilbert Menzies was chosen into the office of Provost for the ensuing year, having taken the usual Oath.

Election of Bailies.—The same day, John Collison, &c., were chosen into the office of Bailies for the ensuing year, having taken the usual Oaths.

Election of Serjeants.—The same day, William Scrimgeour, &c., were chosen into the office of Serjeants for the ensuing year, having taken the usual Oaths.

At a Guild Court of the Burgh of Aberdeen, held in the Hall of the same, 5th October 1509:

Council—John Leslie of Wardes, &c.

Deans of Guild.—The same day, Thomas Chalmers and Duncan Collison were chosen Deans of Guild for the ensuing year, with the assistance of the Provost, they having taken the usual Oaths.

Masters of Kirk Works.—The same day, Patrick Leslie and George Bissat were chosen Masters of Kirk Works for the ensuing year, having taken the usual Oaths.

Auditors of Accounts of the Masters of Kirk Works and Deans of Guild.—The same day, Gilbert Menzies, Provost, &c., were chosen Auditors of Accounts of the Master of Kirk Work, and of the Deans of Guild, they having taken the usual Oaths.

1523.
Curia Gilde.

CURIA Gilde Burgi de Abirdene, tenta in pretorio, ejusdem die Veneris, nono Octobris, anno Domini millesimo quingentesimo vigesimo tertio.

Eodem die Jacobus Collisone et David Anderson re-electi fuere in officium decanorum gilde et magistrorum, fabricie ecclesie divi Nicholai nostri gloriosissimi patri, prestito solito juramento.

Nomina Consulum et Linieatorum.

Sir JOHN RUTHIRFUIRD,	ROBERT MOYSES,
ANDREW CULLANE,	WALTER CALLUM,
JOHN COLLISONE,	PATRICK LESLIE,
JOHN MARR,	JOHN MURRAY,
DUNCAN COLLISONE,	AL. RUTHERFORD,
AL. GRAY,	GEORGE BISSET,
JOHN ANDERSON,	JOHN BLACK.
GAWAN MURRAY,	

Nomina Auditorum Computorum.

Sir JOHN RUTHIRFUIRD,	ALEXANDER GRAY,
ANDREW CULLANE,	JAMES COLLISON,
JOHN COLLISONE,	WILLIAM ROLLAND,
JOHN MARR,	PATRY LESLIE.
THOMAS MENZIES,	

GUILD COURT.—At a Guild Court of the Burgh of Aberdeen, held in the Hall of the same, Friday, 9th October 1523.

The same day, James Collison and David Anderson were re-elected into the office of Deans of Guild and Masters of Kirk Work of our most glorious father Saint Nicholas, having taken the usual Oath.

Names of Councillors and Measurers.—Sir John Rutherford, &c.

Names of Auditors of Accounts.—Sir John Rutherford, &c.

1526.

CURIA capitalis ballivorum burgi de Abirdene, tenta in pretorio ejusdem, primo die mensis Octobris, Anno Dom. millesimo quintengesimo vige-simo sexto ; quo die, sectis vocatis, curia affirmata, absentes patent, &c.

Eo die honorabilis et circumspectus vir Gilbertus Menzies de Findone electus fuit in officium prepositure burgi de Abirdine, de commune omnium burgensium consensu, pro anno instante, et prestito solito juramento.

Eo die honorabiles viri Willmus Rolland, David Andersone, Duncanus Mar, et Patricius Forbes, electi fuerunt in officium ballivorum dicti burgi, de communi omnium burgensium consensu, pro anno instante, prestito solito juramento.

Eo die Normannus Leslie, Thos. Blair, David Herroun et Walterus Sauray, electi fuerunt in officium serjeandorum dicti burgi, de communi omnium burgensium consensu, pro anno instante, prestito solito juramento.

Curia ballivorum burgi de Abirdine, tenta in pretorio ejusdem, quinto Octobris, Anno Domini millesimo quingentesimo vigesimo sexto.

Nomina Consulum et Lineatorum terrarum in burgo.

THOMAS MENZIES of Petfoddellis,
Schir JOHNNE RUTHIRFUIRD, Knyght,
ANDREW CULLANE,
ALEXANDER GRAY,
THOMAS CHALMER,
DUNCAN COLLYSONE,
ALEXANDER RUTHIRFUIRD,
THOMAS RUTHIRFUIRD,
Maister ANDROW TULLIDEFF,
PATRICK LESLIE,

ROBERT MOYSES,
THOMAS MURRAY, Elder,
GEORGE BESSAT,
WALTER CULLANE,
JOHNE BLACK,
RICHARD WAUS,
MATHOW BRANCHE,
JOHNE ARTHUR,
WILLIAM GRAY.

Deynis of Gild and Masters of Kirkwark.

The said day David Andersone, George Bissat, and Robert Moyses, was chosen to be the awyss of the Provost, Bailies, and Counsall above written, Deynis of Gild, and Maisters of Kirkwark for this instant zeir, the gryt ayth be thame beand sworne to wiss the said offices for the common weil as wss is.

Auditores Computorum.

THOMAS MENZIES,
Dominus JOHANNES RUTHIRFUIRD,
ANDREAS CULLAN,
ALEXANDER GRAY,

WILLUS ROLLAND,
GEORGIUS BISSAT,
ROBERTUS MOYSES.

AT a Head Court of the Bailies of the Burgh of Aberdeen, held in the Hall of the same, 1st October 1526, which day the divisions being called, the Court fenced, absentees marked, &c. :

The same day, that prudent and honourable Gentleman, Gilbert Menzies of Findon, was chosen into the office of Provost of the Burgh of Aberdeen, with the common consent of all the Burgesses, for the ensuing year, he having taken the usual Oath.

The same day, these gentlemen, William Rolland, &c., were chosen into the office of Bailies of the said Burgh, with the common consent of all the Burgesses, for the ensuing year, they having taken the usual Oath.

The same day, Norman Leslie, &c., were chosen into the office of Serjeants of the said Burgh, with the common consent of all the Burgesses, they having taken the usual Oath, for the ensuing year.

At a Bailie Court of the Burgh of Aberdeen, held in the Hall of the same, 5th October 1526.

Names of the Council and Measurers of Lands in the Burgh.—Thomas Menzies of Pitfoddles, &c.

Auditors of Accounts.—Thomas Menzies, &c.

VI.—

VI.—CHAPTER ON THE GOVERNMENT OF ROYAL BURGHS.

By Lord KAMES.

By a royal borough is, in Scotland, understood, an incorporation that hold their lands of the crown, and are governed by magistrates of their own naming. The administration of the annual revenues of a royal borough, termed the *common good*, is trusted to the magistrates; but not without control. It was originally subjected to the review of the Great Chamberlain; and accordingly the chap. 39, sec. 45 of the *Iter Camerarii* contains the following articles, recommended to the Chamberlain, to be inquired into:—" Giff there be an good assedation and uptaking of the common good of the burgh, and giff faithful compt be made thereof to the community of the burgh; and giff no compt is made, he whom and in quhaes hands it is come, and how it passes by the community." In pursuance of these instructions, the chamberlain's precepts for holding the ayr, or circuit, is directed to the provost and bailies, enjoining them " to call all those who have received any of the town's revenues, or used any office within the burgh, since the last chamberlain-ayr, to answer such things as shall be laid to their charge." *Iter Camer. cap.* 1. And in the third chapter, which contains the forms of the chamberlain-ayr, the first thing to be done, after fencing the court, is, to call the bailies and serjeants to be challenged and accused from the time of the last ayr.

This office, dangerous by excess of power, being suppressed, the royal boroughs were left in a state of anarchy. There being now no check or control, the magistracy was coveted by noblemen and gentlemen in the neighbourhood, who, under the name of office-bearers, laid their hands on the revenues of the borough, and converted all to their own profit. This corruption was heavily complained of in the reign of James V.; and a remedy was provided by Act 26, Parl. 1535, enacting, 1st, That none be qualified to be provost, bailie, or alderman but an indwelling burges. 2dly, " That no inhabitant purchase lordship out of burgh, to the terror of his comburgesses. And, 3dly, That all provosts, bailies, and aldermen of boroughs bring yearly to the chequer, at a day certain, the compt-books of their common good, to be seen and considered by the Lords auditors, giff the same be spended for the common well of the burgh, or not, under the penalty of losing their freedom. And that the saids provosts, bailies, and aldermen warn yearly, fifteen days before their coming to the chequer, all those who are willing to come for examining the said accounts, that they may impugn the same, in order that all murmur may cease in that behalf." And to enforce these regulations, a brieve was issued from the chancery, commanding the magistrates to present their accounts to the exchequer, and summoning the burgesses to appear and object to the same.

A defect in this statute made it less effectual than it was intended to be. Magistrates, to avoid the penalty, brought the count-books of their common good to the exchequer; but they brought no rental of the common good to found a charge against them. This defect was remedied by Act 28, Parl. 1693, containing the following preamble:—" That the royal boroughs, by the mal-administration of their magistrates, have fallen under great debts and burdens, to the diminution of their dignity, and the disabling of them to serve the crown and government as they ought; and that the care, oversight, and controul of the common good of boroughs belong to their majesties by virtue of their prerogative royal; therefore, for preventing the like abuses and misapplications in all time thereafter, their majesties statute and ordain, That every burgh-royal shall, betwixt and the first day of November next, bring to the Lords of Treasury and Exchequer an exact account of charge and discharge, subscribed by the magistrates and town-clerk, of their whole public-good and revenues, and of the whole debts and incumbrances that affect the same." This completed the remedy, by putting means into the hands of the barons of exchequer to control the accounts enjoined by the former statute to be yearly given in.

The foregoing regulations are kept in observance. Every year a precept issues from the exchequer, signed by one of the barons, addressed to the director of the chancery, requiring him to make out a brieve for every royal borough. The brieve is accordingly made out, returned to the exchequer, and sent to the several sheriffs, to be served in all the royal boroughs within their bounds, as directed by the statute. These brieves are accordingly so served by the sheriffs; and particularly it is a constant form in most of the royal boroughs to issue a proclamation, fifteen days before the day named for appearance in exchequer, warning the inhabitants to repair there, in order to object to the public accounts of the town; and further, in order to give them opportunity to frame objections, the book and counts are laid open for these fifteen days, to be inspected by all the inhabitants.

We learn from the records of exchequer that, from the year 1660 to the year 1683, accounts were regularly given in to exchequer, in obedience to the statute. The town of Edinburgh only having failed for some short time, Captain Thomas Hamilton, merchant there, by an action in exchequer, compelled the magistrates to produce upon oath their treasurer's accounts, which were accordingly audited. And we also learn that, from the restoration down to the Union, a clerk to the borough-roll was appointed by the Crown, whose proper business it was to examine and audit the accounts of the boroughs.

Notwithstanding the foregoing salutary regulations, and the form constantly practised to make them effectual, the boroughs of late years have forborn to present their accounts in exchequer, hoping that they would be overlooked by the English Court of Exchequer, established in Scotland after the Union, which accordingly happened. This neglect in the Court of Exchequer is greatly to be regretted, because it reduces the royal boroughs, by the mal-administration of their magistrates, to the same miserable condition that is so loudly complained of in the statutes above mentioned. It is undoubtedly in the power of the barons to restore good government to the boroughs, by compelling the magistrates to account yearly in the Court of Exchequer, according to the foregoing regulations; no more is necessary, but to signify publicly that they are resolved to put these regulations in execution.

. How beneficial that step would be to this country in general, and to the royal boroughs in particular, will appear from considering, first, the unhappy consequences that result from suffering magistrates to dispose of the town's revenues without any check or control; and next, the good effects that must result from a regular and careful management, under the inspection of the king's judges.

The unhappy consequences of leaving magistrates without any check or control are too visible to be disguised. The revenues of a royal borough are seldom laid out for the good of the town, but in making friends to the party who are in possession of the magistracy, and in rioting and drunkenness, for which every pretext is laid hold of, particularly that of hospitality to strangers. Such mismanagement tends to idleness and corruption of manners, which accordingly are remarkable in most royal boroughs. Nor is the contagion confined within the town; it commonly spreads all around.

Another consequence no less fatal, of leaving magistrates to act without control, is a strong desire in every licentious burgess of stepping into the magistracy, for his own sake, and for that of his friends. Hence the factions and animosities that prevail in almost all the royal boroughs, which are violently and indecently pursued, without the least regard to the good of the community.

The greatest evil of all, respects the choice of their representatives in Parliament. A habit of riot and intemperance makes them fit subjects to be corrupted by every adventurer who is willing to lay out money for purchasing a seat in Parliament. Hence the infamous practice of bribery at elections, which tends not only to corrupt the whole mass of the people, but, which is still more dreadful, tends to fill the House of Commons with men of dissolute manners, void of probity and honour.

But, turning from scenes so dismal, let us view the beautiful effects that result from an administration regularly carried on, as directed by the statutes above mentioned. The revenues of the royal boroughs are supposed to be above £40,000 yearly. And were this sum, or the half of it, prudently expended for promoting arts and industry among the numerous inhabitants of royal boroughs, the benefit, in a country so narrow and poor as Scotland, would be immense; it would tend to population, it would greatly increase industry, manufactures, and commerce, beside augmenting the public revenue. In the next place, as there would be no temptation for designing men to convert the burden of magistracy into a benefit, faction and discord would vanish, and there would be no less solicitude to shun the burden than at present is seen to obtain it. None would submit to the burden but the truly patriotic—men who would cheerfully bestow their time, and perhaps their money, upon the public, and whose ambition it would be to acquire a character by promoting industry, temperance, and honesty among their fellow-citizens.

And when the government of the royal boroughs comes to be in so good hands, bribery, which corrupts the very vitals of our constitution, will be banished, of course. And considering the proper constitutional dependence of the royal boroughs upon the king's judges, we may have reasonable assurance that few representatives will be chosen but who are friends to their country and to their sovereign.—KAMES' *Sketches of the History of Man,* vol. iii. pp. 464-71.

VII.—NAMES of GENTLEMEN who have filled the Office of DEAN OF GUILD from 1583 to the Present Time.

1583.	James Adamson.	1631.	Joseph Majoribanks.	1677.	John Boyd.
1584.	Nicholl Edward.	1632.	Nicholl Edward.	1678.	James Dick.
1585.	Do.	1633.	William Dick.	1679.	James Fleeming.
1586.	Michael Chisholme.	1634.	John Sinclair.	1680.	Do.
1587.	Do.	1635.	Do.	1681.	Archibald Hamilton.
1588.	Do.	1636.	Sir John Sinclair.	1682.	Do.
1589.	Alexander Edward.	1637.	Do.	1683.	Charles Murray.
1590.	Do.	1638.	James Cochran.	1684.	Do.
1591.	Do.	1639.	Do.	1685.	Magnus Prince.
1592.	Do.	1640.	Peter Cockburn.	1686.	Do.
1593.	James Nicholl.	1641.	Archibald Todd.	1687.	James Nicholson.
1594.	Alexander Edward.	1642.	Do.	1688.	Do.
1595.	Do.	1643.	George Swittie.	1689.	Thomas Crawford.
1596.	Thomas Aikenhead.	1644.	Do.	1689.	James M'Lurgg.
1597.	Do.	1645.	Do.	1690.	Do.
1598.	David Williamson.	1646.	Do.	1691.	Michael Allan.
1599.	Do.	1647.	Do.	1692.	Do.
1600.	John Robertson.	1648.	Do.	1693.	Hugh Blair.
1601.	Do.	1649.	Do.	1694.	Do.
1602.	William Auld.	1650.		1695.	John Robertson.
1603.	Do.	1651.		1696.	Do.
1604.	John Robertson.	1652.	James Rochhead.	1697.	Patrick Hallyburton.
1605.	Do.	1653.	George Swittie.	1698.	Patrick Hamilton.
1606.	Roger M'Naught.	1654.	Do.	1699.	James M'Lurgg.
1607.	John Robertson.	1655.	David Wilkie.	1700.	Sir James M'Lurgg.
1608.	Do.	1656.	Do.	1701.	Adam Brown.
1609.	Roger M'Naught.	1657.	Do.	1702.	Do.
1610.	Richard Dobie.	1658.	Do.	1703.	Robert Blackwood.
1611.	Do.	1659.	Robert Murray.	1704.	Sir Robert Blackwood.
1612.	David Aikenhead.	1660.	Edward Edgar.	1705.	Sir Samuel M'Clellan.
1613.	Do.	1661.	Do.	1706.	William Neilson.
1614.	Do.	1662.	Robert Sandilands.	1707.	Do.
1615.	Do.	1663.	Do.	1708.	George Warrender.
1616.	Do.	1664.	Do.	1709.	Do.
1617.	Do.	1665.	Francis Kinloch.	1710.	John Duncan.
1618.	Do.	1666.	Do.	1711.	Do.
1619.	John Byres.	1667.	Do.	1712.	William Hutchison.
1620.	Do.	1668.	Do.	1713.	Do.
1621.	Do.	1669.	Do.	1714.	Robert Craig.
1622.	Do.	1670.	Do.	1715.	Do.
1623.	Do.	1671.	Do.	1716.	John Wightman.
1624.	Do.	1672.	Walter Borthwick.	1717.	Do.
1625.	Thomas Inglis.	1673.	Thomas Calderwood.	1718.	James Cleland.
1626.	John M'Naught.	1673.	Robert Baird.	1719.	Do.
1627.	Do.	1674.	Do.	1720.	Robert Wightman.
1628.	Do.	1675.	Do.	1721.	Do.
1629.	Joseph Majoribanks.	1675.	Francis Kinloch.	1722.	George Drummond.
1630.	Do.	1676.	Do.	1723.	Do.

1724.	Archibald Macauley.	1779.	John Grieve.	1834.	John Macfie.
1725.	Do.	1780.	John Wordie.	1835.	Peter Lamont.
1726.	Patrick Lindsay.	1781.	Thomas Cleghorn.	1836.	Do.
1727.	Do.	1782.	Do.	1837.	James Thomson.
1728.	James Nimmo.	1783.	Arch. Macdowall.	1838.	Do.
1729.	Do.	1784.	Do.	1839.	Samuel Aitken.
1730.	John Osburn.	1785.	William Galloway.	1840.	Do.
1731.	Thomas Dick.	1786.	Do.	1841.	John Ramsay.
1732.	Do.	1787.	James Gordon.	1842.	Do.
1733.	James Simpson.	1788.	Do.	1843.	William Dick.
1734.	Do.	1789.	Donald Smith.	1844.	Do.
1735.	Thomas Heriot.	1790.	Do.	1845.	David Jugurtha Thomson.
1736.	Do.	1791.	William Gillespie.		
1737.	James Colquhoun.	1792.	Do.	1846.	Do.
1738.	George Haliburton.	1793.	John Gloag.	1847.	Do.
1739.	Do.	1794.	Do.	1848.	George Wilson.
1740.	Thomas Crokat.	1795.	Neil Macvicar.	1849.	Do.
1741.	Do.	1796.	Do.	1850.	John Duncan.
1742.	Hugh Hawthorn.	1797.	Charles Kerr.	1851.	Do.
1743.	Do.	1798.	Do.	1852.	James Blackadder.
1744.	Thomas Allan.	1799.	James Jackson.	1853.	Do.
1745.		1800.	Do.	1854.	Peter Scott Fraser.
1746.	Do.	1801.	Thomas Henderson.	1855.	Andrew Wemyss.
1747.	Do.	1802.	Do.	1856.	Do.
1748.	Robert Montgomery.	1803.	John Muir.	1857.	Duncan Mackinlay.
1749.	Do.	1804.	Do.	1858.	Do.
1750.	James Stewart.	1805.	William Coulter.	1859.	Adam Mossman.
1751.	Do.	1806.	Do.	1860.	Do.
1752.	David Flint.	1807.	William Calder.	1861.	Charles MacGibbon.
1753.	Do.	1808.	Do.	1862.	Do.
1754.	James Grant.	1809.	William Tennant.	1863.	Do.
1755.	Do.	1810.	Do.	1864.	George Lorimer.
1756.	James Rocheid.	1811.	Kincaid Mackenzie.	1865.	John Shennan.
1757.	Do.	1812.	Do.	1866.	Do.
1758.	John Carmichael.	1813.	John Walker.	1867.	William Law.
1759.	Do.	1814.	Do.	1868.	Do.
1760.	Gilbert Laurie.	1815.	Robert Johnston.	1869.	John Russel.
1761.	Do.	1816.	Do.	1870.	Do.
1762.	Patrick Lindsay.	1817.	Alex. Henderson.	1871.	Do.
1763.	Do.	1818.	Do.	1872.	Do.
1764.	John Nisbet.	1819.	Alexander Smellie.	1873.	James Craig.
1765.	Do.	1820.	Do.	1874.	Do.
1766.	John Learmonth.	1821.	John Turnbull.	1875.	Do.
1767.	Do.	1822.	Robert Anderson.	1876.	John Smith.
1768.	William Ramsay.	1823.	John Waugh.	1877.	Do.
1769.	Do.	1824.	Do.	1878.	Do.
1770.	James Stoddart.	1825.	Robert Wright.	1879.	Do.
1771.	Do.	1826.	Do.	1880.	Robert Hutchison.
1772.	Charles Wright.	1827.	James Hill.	1881.	Do.
1773.	Do.	1828.	Do.	1882.	Do.
1774.	John Kidd.	1829.	William Child.	1883.	Do.
1775.	Do.	1830.	Do.	1884.	Do.
1776.	Charles Innes.	1831.	John Smith.	1885.	James Gowans.
1777.	Do.	1832.	Do.	1886.	Sir James Gowans.
1778.	John Grieve.	1833.	John Macfie.		

VIII.—LIST OF MEMBERS OF THE DEAN OF GUILD COURT OF EDINBURGH, from 1833 to the Present Time.

1833.

John Macfie, Dean of Guild.
Councillor James Smith, Old Dean of Guild.
John Anderson, Junior, }
John Lauder, } Merchants.
Robert Dobson, Builder.
John Clark, Slater.
Charles MacGibbon, Wright.

1834.

John Macfie, D.G.
Councillor James Smith, O.D.G.
John Anderson, Junior, }
Maurice Lothian, } Merchants.
Alexander Jamieson, }
Robert Dobson, }
James Ritchie, } Builders.

1835.

Peter Lamond, D.G.
John Robertson, O.D.G.
John Anderson, Junior, }
Alexander Jamieson, } Merchants.
Thomas Caldwell, }
John Nicol, } Masons.
David Paton, Wright.

1836.

Péter Lamond, D.G.
John Robertson, O.D.G.
Alexander Jamieson, }
James Thomson, } Merchants.
Thomas Caldwell, }
John Nicol, } Builders.
David Paton, Wright.

1837.

James Thomson, D.G.
Councillor Robert Dobson, O.D.G.
Alexander Jamieson, }
John Ramsay, } Merchants.
Thomas Caldwell, }
John Nicol, } Builders.
David Paton, Wright.

1838.

James Thomson, D.G.
Councillor Robert Dobson, O.D.G.
Alexander Jamieson, }
William Duncan, } Merchants.
Thomas Caldwell, }
John Nicol, } Builders.
David Paton, Wright.

1839.

Samuel Aitken, D.G.
Councillor Robert Dobson, O.D.G.
Alexander Jamieson, }
William Duncan, } Merchants.
Thomas Caldwell, }
John Nicol, } Builders.
David Paton, Wright.

1840.

Same as 1839.

1841.

John Ramsay, D.G.
Councillor Robert Dobson, O.D.G.
Alexander Jamieson, }
Thomas Heriot, } Merchants.
David Paton, }
John Nicol, } Builders.
William Beattie.

1842.

Same as 1841.

1843.

William Dick, D.G.
Councillor Robert Dobson, O.D.G.
Alexander Jamieson, }
Joseph Hood Stott, } Merchants.
David Paton, }
William Beattie, } Builders.
William Stark,

1844.

William Dick, D.G.
Councillor William Wilson, O.D.G.
Alexander Jamieson, } Merchants.
Joseph Hood Stott,
William Beattie,
William Stark, } Tradesmen.
George Drummond,

1845.

David Jugurtha Thomson, D.G.
Councillor William Wilson, O.D.G.
Alexander Jamieson, } Merchants.
Joseph Hood Stott,
William Beattie,
William Stark, } Tradesmen.
George Drummond,

1846.

David Jugurtha Thomson, D.G.
Councillor James Burgess, O.D.G.
Alexander Jamieson, } Merchants.
Joseph Hood Stott,
William Beattie,
William Stark, } Tradesmen.
George Drummond,

1847.

David Jugurtha Thomson, D.G.
Councillor James Burgess, O.D.G.
Alexander Jamieson, } Merchants.
William Wilson,
William Beattie,
William Stark, } Tradesmen.
George Drummond,

1848.

George Wilson, D.G.
Councillor George Drummond, O.D.G.
Alexander Jamieson, } Merchants.
John Duncan,
William Beattie,
William Stark, } Tradesmen.
Robert Smith,

1849.

George Wilson, D.G.
Councillor George Drummond, O.D.G.
John Duncan, } Merchants.
James Martin,
William Beattie,
William Stark, } Tradesmen.
Robert Smith,

1850.

John Duncan, D.G.
Councillor George Drummond, O.D.G.
James Martin, } Merchants.
Alexander Sclanders,
William Beattie,
William Stark, } Tradesmen.
Robert Smith,

1851.

John Duncan, D.G.
John Kay, O.D.G.
James Martin, } Merchants.
Alexander Sclanders,
William Beattie,
Robert Smith, } Tradesmen.
George Drummond,

1852.

James Blackadder, D.G.
Councillor Alexander Sclanders, O.D. .
James Martin, } Merchants.
Thomas Sibbald,
William Beattie,
Robert Smith, } Tradesmen.
George Drummond,

1853.

Same as 1852.

1854.

Peter Scott Fraser, D.G.
Councillor Robert Symington Grieve, O.D.G.
Thomas Sibbald, } Merchants.
James Martin,
Robert Smith,
George Paterson, } Tradesmen.
George Lorimer,

1855.

Andrew Wemyss, D.G.
Councillor Andrew Tait, O.D.G.
Thomas Sibbald, } Merchants.
Wm. Whitehead,
Robert Smith,
George Lorimer, } Tradesmen
George Beattie,

1856.

Andrew Wemyss, D.G.
Councillor Duncan Mackinlay, O.D.G.
Thomas Sibbald,
William Whitehead, } Merchants.
Robert Smith,
George Lorimer, } Tradesmen.
George Beattie,

1857.

Duncan Mackinlay, D.G.
Councillor Alexander Hay, O.D.G.
Thomas Sibbald,
William Whitehead, } Merchants.
George Lorimer,
George Beattie, } Tradesmen.
John Shennan,

1858.

Duncan Mackinlay, D.G.
Councillor Alexander Hay, O.D.G.
Thomas Sibbald,
William Whitehead, } Merchants.
George Beattie,
John Shennan, } Tradesmen.
Charles MacGibbon,

1859.

Adam Mossman, D.G.
Councillor William White, O.D.G.
Councillor Alexander Hay, } Merchants.
Robert Marshall,
John Shennan,
Charles MacGibbon, } Tradesmen.
George Lorimer,

1860.

Adam Mossman, D.G.
Councillor William White, O.D.G.
Councillor Alexander Hay, } Merchants.
Robert Marshall,
James Paterson,
John Shennan, } Tradesmen.
Charles MacGibbon,

1861.

Charles MacGibbon, D.G.
Councillor William White, O.D.G.
Councillor Alexander Hay, } Merchants.
Robert Marshall,
John Shennan,
James Paterson, } Tradesmen.
Adam Beattie,

1862.

Charles MacGibbon, D.G.
Councillor William White, O.D.G.
Councillor Alexander Hay, } Merchants.
Robert Marshall,
J. R. Swann,
James Paterson, } Tradesmen.
Adam Beattie,

1863.

Charles MacGibbon, D.G.
Councillor Alexander Hay, O.D.G.
Councillor Robert Marshall, } Merchants.
Councillor James Ritchie,
Convener Beattie.
J. R. Swan.
John Shennan.

1864.

George Lorimer, D.G.
Councillor Alexander Hay, O.D.G.
Councillor Robert Marshall, } Merchants.
Councillor James Ritchie,
John Russell Swann,
John Shennan, } Tradesmen.
John Smith,

1865.

John Shennan, D.G.
Councillor Thomas Scott, O.D.G.
Councillor Robert Marshall, } Merchants.
James Ritchie,
John Smith,
David Rae, } Tradesmen.
William Raffin,

1866.

John Shennan, D.G.
Councillor James Lewis, O.D.G.
Robert Marshall,
William Whitehead, } Merchants.
David Rae,
William Raffin, } Tradesmen.
William Beattie,

1867.

William Law, D.G.
Councillor James Lewis, O.D.G.
Robert Marshall,
John Weir, } Merchants.
David Rae,
William Beattie, } Tradesmen.
George Roberts,

1868.

William Law, D.G.
Councillor John Russell, O.D.G.
John Weir,
Councillor David Lewis, } Merchants.
George Roberts,
Adam Beattie, } Tradesmen.
John Smith,

1869.

John Russel, D.G.
Councillor John Tawse, O.D.G.
John Weir,
George Harrison, } Merchants.
George Roberts,
Adam Beattie, } Tradesmen.
John Smith,

1870.

John Russel, D.G.
Councillor John Tawse, O.D.G.
John Weir,
George Harrison, } Merchants.
Adam Beattie,
John Smith, } Tradesmen.
David Rae,

1871.

John Russel, D.G.
Bailie John Tawse, O.D.G.
George Harrison,
Alexander Aitken, } Merchants.
John Smith,
George Roberts, } Tradesmen.
James Watherston,

1872.

John Russel, D.G.
Bailie John Tawse, O.D.G.
George Harrison,
Alexander Aitken, } Merchants.
George Roberts,
James Watherston, } Tradesmen.
Adam Beattie,

1873.

James Craig, D.G.
Councillor George Roberts, O.D.G.
Alexander Aitken,
John Clapperton, } Merchants.
James Watherston,
Adam Beattie, } Tradesmen.
William Raffin,

1874.

James Craig, D.G.
Councillor George Roberts, O.D.G.
Alexander Aitken,
John Clapperton, } Merchants.
Adam Beattie,
John Smith, } Tradesmen.
William Watherston,

1875.

James Craig, D.G.
Councillor George Roberts, O.D.G.
John Clapperton,
Josiah Livingston, } Merchants.
John Smith,
William Watherston, } Tradesmen.
Adam Beattie,

1876.

John Smith, D.G.
Councillor George Roberts, O.D.G.
Councillor John Clapperton,
Josiah Livingston, } Merchants.
William Watherston,
William Beattie, } Tradesmen.
Robert Hutchison,

1877.

John Smith, D.G.
Bailie George Roberts, O.D.G.
Councillor John Clapperton,
James Roy, } Merchants.
William Beattie,
Robert Hutchison, } Tradesmen.
Alexander Kemp,

1878.

John Smith, D.G.
Bailie George Roberts, O.D.G.
Councillor John Clapperton,
James Roy, } Mercha ts.
William Beattie,
Robert Hutchison, } Tradesmen.
William Outerson,

1879.

John Smith, D.G.
Councillor Thomas Sloan.
    „   John White.
    „   Archibald Sutter.
    „   Thomas Hall, and
    „   James Steel, ; and
Mr Adam Beattie.
  „ Robert Bryson.
  „ Robert Hutchison.
  „ James Roy, and William Watherston.

1880.

Robert Hutchison, D.G.
Councillor John White.
  „   Archibald Sutter.
  „   Thomas Sloan.
  „   James Alexander Russell.
Convener John Smith.
Mr Robert Bryson.
  „ James Roy.
  „ William Watherston.
  „ William Beattie.
  „ John Muirhead.

1881.

Robert Hutchison, D.G.
Councillor John White.
  „   Archibald Sutter.
  „   James Alexander Russell.
  „   Thomas Tait.
  „   Alexander Reid.
Mr William Watherston.
  „ William Beattie.
  „ John Muirhead.
  „ Robert Bryson.
  „ James Gowans.

1882.

Robert Hutchison, D.G.
Councillor John White.
  „   Archibald Sutter.
  „   James Alexander Russell.
  „   Thomas Tait.
  „   William Gilmour.
Mr William Watherston.
  „ John Muirhead.
  „ John Wilson.
  „ George James Beattie.
  „ Alexander Hay.

1883.

Robert Hutchison, D.G.
Councillor White.
  „   Sutter.
  „   Russell.
  „   Tait.
  „   Miller.
Mr William Watherston.
  „ John Muirhead.
  „ George James Beattie.
  „ Alexander Hay.
  „ Robert Shillinglaw.

1884.

Same as 1883.

1885.

James Gowans, D.G.
Bailie Russell.
Convener John White.
Councillor Thos. Tait.
  „   Robert Miller.
  „   John Charles Dunlop.
Mr William Watherston.
  „ John Muirhead.
  „ George James Beattie.
  „ Robert Shillinglaw.
  „ James Crichton.

1886.

Same as 1885.

Sir James Gowans, D.G.

Clerks to the Guildry,
with Date of Election.

1833. John F. M'Farlane.
1833. Thomas Ireland, junior.
1835. James Ritchie.
1841. James Wilson.
1847. Robert S. Grieve.
1850. Joseph Robertson.
1852. David Dickson.
1885. Thomas G. Stevenson.

Treasurers to the Guildry,
with Date of Election.

1833. John Ramsay.
1840. James Burgess.
1848. D. Young.
1850. James Grant.
1855. James Wilson.
1883. Andrew M'Donald.

COLSTON AND COMPANY, PRINTERS, EDINBURGH.